# ABOVE
# THE BATTLE

# ABOVE THE BATTLE

## WAR-MAKING IN AMERICA FROM APPOMATTOX TO VERSAILLES

THOMAS C. LEONARD

NEW YORK
**OXFORD UNIVERSITY PRESS**
1978

Copyright © 1978 by Oxford University Press

Library of Congress Cataloging in Publication Data

Leonard, Thomas C   1944–
    Above the battle.

    Bibliography: p.
    Includes index.
    1.  United   States—History,  Military.    2.  War—Public  opin-
ion.     3.   Public    opinion—United   States.    4.  War   in   literature.    I.   Title.
E181.L5      973       76-57287
ISBN 0-19-502239-4

A different version of Chapter 5, "Keepers of the Peace," appeared in *American Quarterly*, May 1973.

Printed in the United States of America

TO CAROL AND PETER

# CONTENTS

# ABOVE
# THE BATTLE

# INTRODUCTION

Everyone who has gazed upon the monuments to our soldiers in American parks senses the enigma of the nation's first modern wars. One may be amused, at first, at the chiseled-stone beard of the Civil War soldier, the winged victories that mark the defeat of Spain, the careful step of the doughboy as he avoids the bronze barbed wire. But these statues are not laughed at. They compel respect. Despite pigeon droppings and graffiti, they have kept their dignity.

The statues are earnest pleas for remembrance—but of what? Surely of more than a victory or peace treaty. These stone men force us to think of how the soldiers faced death and what the bloodshed meant to the Americans who survived it. The stern faces, the lists of the dead and battle sites, the laconic notes of courage—all try to express this meaning, but they can never say enough.

Students of war have dispelled some of this mystery. Their meticulous studies of the logistics, tactics, and strategy have become as imposing as the military campaigns themselves. This vast literature suggests that every moment and emotion of combat has been explored, but much of this scholarship has had an opposite effect: the piling up of layer on layer of detail has systematically obscured something deeper. Much of what has been written about America's wars has itself become a monument, hiding secrets.

Some important questions have rarely been asked. How did fighting men see themselves—and their enemy? What was attractive, and alarming, about the power of weapons? How did soldiers choose to understand—and then remember—the violence they endured? And how were enemies, weapons, and violence perceived by the political leaders who defined the issues, by the inventors who created the new arsenal, and by the most articulate Americans who argued about what war meant? This is my subject.

I have cast a wide net, taking in both civilians and the professional military, battle veterans as well as students of war who knew only what they had read in books. I might have selected out only those Americans who were always well-informed and ready for war. (Consider Nelson A. Miles, a colonel during the Civil War, the conqueror of Chief Joseph and Geronimo in the West, the leader of the invasion of Puerto Rico in 1898 . . . and finally a volunteer for World War I and prophet of air power.) This book does not deal only with such remarkable veterans, because wars are not waged by people who know this much. Crisis and accident brought most Americans to talk about war and their attention waned when the emergency passed. The nation built an army and an arsenal as if from rubber— taking in a whole generation and most of the industrial capacity in the 1860's, shrinking back to a skeleton force in the next decades, briefly puffing up at the turn of the century, before the final spasms of expansion and contraction after 1917. American conceptions of warfare, like American preparedness, were improvised in a mood of crisis. Yet Americans initiated into wars shared many of the same thoughts and feelings with the veterans of battle.

To put together the patterns of these responses we need study nothing more than what Americans tried to tell us. We need not put words in the mouths of Americans at war, treat their actions purely as symbols, or hunt for lost manuscripts (as useful as those approaches may be). What the Americans who faced modern wars believed and felt they put on paper and, more often than not, published. In the six decades I cover there was effective censorship of military or civilian discussion only between 1917 and 1918. Talk about war was quickly set in type. Every word spoken at the meetings of peace societies can be found in richly bound sets. Before American intervention in World War I, more than 300 visitors to the Western Front rushed into print. Again, the bulk of these written monuments to war has obscured the message. Yet if we but sift this material to find the moments when men and women were most articulate, we can hear what they wanted to say.

I begin with soldiers, for their secrets have been the best kept. The veterans hesitated to explain themselves, and historians have only infrequently challenged their silence. This book uses the testimony from soldiers that has been overlooked or, when noticed, not listened to carefully: the Indian fighter's statements about tribal society, George Patton's letters home, and the songs of the Lafayette Escadrille. I hope artifacts of these kinds can give the Americans in uniform a new voice; but this study seeks also to understand why soldiers could not speak more loudly and why other Americans remained reticent or untroubled about so many questions of war. What fears could not be expressed? What faith closed off darker thoughts?

Basic to this inquiry is an assessment of the heroic pose that Americans at war have so often held. In their memoirs the veterans of the Civil War insisted that they had fought an orderly and humane war. They remembered the form of combat, not the disorientation or terror; they spoke of the restraints on violence, not the excesses, and of the benefits of war, not the lasting wounds. The old soldiers called the enemy they had sought to kill "comrades." They encouraged a new generation to think that the battlefield was the crucible that tested character. American prophets of war assured themselves that war with the complicated new weapons was still ennobling and, indeed, that the terrible power of the arsenal ensured that less blood would be shed.

I wish to measure the cost of these points of view, but I do not wish to denigrate them. There was some truth in these myths and simplifications. War is not always hell. Even the bitterest veteran can, if he is honest, recall moments in combat when he acted easily and naturally. Americans have often respected their enemy and, at times, empathized with the opposing cause. Nor did the modern arsenal make soldiers simple cogs in industrialized warfare. The idea that machine guns, shrapnel, and poison gas were lifesaving innovations has proven wrong, but it was not always an absurd view.

It is the optimists and good soldiers themselves who show us the limitation of their faith. Some who saw the new arsenal as keepers of the peace were excited by the prospect of cataclysmic battles. Those prophets wanted to replace freedom with the discipline of a technological world and prescribed the purgation of combat for a corrupt society. The men who fought the wars reasoned less abstractly—but they sometimes doubted that war was humane, ennobling, or even comprehensible. Some of the stoical soldiers who had burned the crops of the Confederacy, seized the Indian lands, or crushed (after aiding) the guerrilla wars for independence against Spain anticipated the skepticism that finally dominated American war literature in the 1920's.

To restore this ambivalence to the history of America's first modern wars is to begin to discover what the statues have hidden. In fact Americans killed in compassion as well as anger; they were fascinated and blinded by their ability to destroy; they longed to punish the society they risked their lives to protect. In America, infatuation with war has often masked sorrow about battle; anti-war arguments have often been made by those with affection for the campaigns. But rarely, as in the best novels of the 1920's, has this ambivalence added subtlety and power to American discourse on war. It is not too late to change this.

The pattern of ambivalence is worth recovering because, most obviously, debate over these wars has not ended. Americans live with the imperial relationships abroad and the reservations at home that were created during the half-century after Reconstruction, when the modern armed forces were born, the last Indian battles fought, and the first wars for "civilization" prosecuted overseas.

An historian's answer can be dangerous. Revisionist scholars of World War I, after all, drew moral lessons that were probably more pernicious in the 1930's than the original sins they discovered. Yet I think the following pages tell of a "usable past" with no such potential for disaster. This is not a history of other people's blunders with the announcement that we now see the light. Rather, it is a study of how Americans, no more fallible than ourselves, came to think about war. I have wanted to see how another generation lived with the decisions it made: what the choices were, why they were made, and why there were not more choices in view. In war-making, Americans need to be aware of the hush so often thrown over combat, the ambivalence of antagonists toward enemies, and the fascination with destruction. With such awareness more choices may be imaginable.

# I
# THE
# BLOOD
# WASHED AWAY

*Talking about the Civil War proved to be almost as difficult as fighting it. In the late nineteenth century the restraint in discussions of the ordeal was both politic and deeply felt. This peace brought two paradoxes. Reticence made Americans innocent about the destructive course of the modern warfare they had, in fact, pioneered. Reconciliation with old enemies, moreover, encouraged ambivalence toward new ones, in the campaigns in the West, Cuba, the Philippines, and France.*

# 1

# THE
# ENDURING AND THE
# FORGOTTEN WAR

The outpouring of books on the Civil War in the half-century after Appomattox is as impressive as the national production of wheat, coal, and pig iron. To grow up in this period was to wonder over the embossed covers and steel engravings of these volumes while listening to elders dispute their contents. We do not find memoirs of the Civil War with uncut pages.

The recollections enshrined in the nineteenth-century books tell of a clean and uplifting war. Survivors spoke about the form of battles, not the blood and disorder they had seen. Veterans remembered the self-control that had mitigated violence, not the terror of life under fire and the scorched earth campaigns. And the old soldiers commemorated the concrete achievements of peace, little noting the issues and emotions unresolved by the war.

The most important thing about these books is what the veterans did not say. After the Civil War, Americans, more than any industrial nation, could see what modern war was to be. Mass armies had been recruited by patriotic appeals, then supplied and killed off by the industrial system. Where the invading armies had met civilians, cities were burnt and crops destroyed. No war of the eighteenth century had been like this; no war of the nineteenth century pointed more clearly to the future. Americans, however, failed to grasp this lesson, and their failure began in the personal narratives.

Had the first students of the Civil War paid attention to Karl von Clausewitz, they would have done more justice to their subject. That Prussian officer was more than a profound strategist; he knew how to *think* about war. He insisted that the chaos and terror of war had to be faced. Clausewitz loathed polite memoirists; the battlefield was no place for soldiers with good manners and weak stomachs: "Let us not hear of Generals who conquer without bloodshed." He was contemptuous of the eighteenth-century strategists who presented war as a clear, geometrical system and then limited its effects through tactical half-measures. "War is an act of violence pushed to its utmost bounds," Clausewitz wrote. A battle is a "stream of impressions," he stressed, "and in the uncertainty of all knowledge and of all science, more things occur to distract a man from the road he has entered upon, to make him doubt himself and others, than in any other human activity." *On War* is in part a psychological guidebook for men about to enter the calamity of battle in the industrial age.[1] It is the best handbook for a war reporter published in the nineteenth century.

It was advice that Americans did not hear, for virtually no one in the Civil War era read Clausewitz. Mid-nineteenth-century American military strategists lived in a different world. They relied on a Swiss authority, Baron Henri Jomini. His work provided a more orderly, less terrifying picture of war.[2] It is difficult to overstate the impact that Swiss scholar made in Washington and West Point—even his American translator was shocked by the Americans' slavish acceptance of his authority. Jomini taught warriors to ignore the violent emotions and results of combat, to put the sights and sounds of battle out of mind. His soldiers fought for formal advantages as abstract and bloodless as the moves on a chessboard. Jomini, and the Americans who followed him, produced texts on the military art that read like geometrical exercises. This was war without the smell of powder or the passion to finish off the enemy. American strategists agreed that war against civilized opponents should be a limited, even polite affair, marked by "mutual kindness and courtesy on the battlefield." The Union army marched into battle with instructions against "perfidy" and "bad faith" in combat. "Modern wars are not inter-necine wars," soldiers were taught, "in which the killing of the enemy is the object." [3]

We do not have to choose between the contrasting views of nine-teenth-century warfare that Jomini and Clausewitz offered. This war was, at turns, orderly and chaotic, chivalrous and cruel. The tradi-tional "elaborate quadrille" battles of 1861–62 gave way to scorched earth campaigns. Mutual respect, friendly bartering, and even over-night visits to the enemy on the front lines were as much a part of the war as the frenzied hatred other fighting men felt for their ene-mies. Nothing is clearer from the letters and diaries of Civil War sol-diers than that combat prompted the widest variety of feelings. The blood and confusion stirred men to duty and desertion; saintliness and debauchery; cynicism and idealism. [4]

American writers in the last three decades of the century did make a choice about which of these experiences was the real war. In their desire for reconciliation between North and South, they offered an outline of the action that made the war seem comprehensible, hu-mane, and efficacious. Few went as far as Andrew P. Peabody of the American Peace Society, who recalled that the Northern cause had been so noble that the fight of the men in blue "had none of the moral characteristics of a war." But in popular memoirs, the violent experience of the conflict was idealized until the bitterness and con-fusion of fighting nearly disappeared from the printed record. "The veterans," the historian Paul Buck found, "had forgotten their night-mares." [5]

The clarity of the Civil War memoirs may be their most signifi-cant feature. There was disagreement among the generals, of course, but they all assumed that there was a point of view (their own) that revealed the cause and credit for each battle. They seldom described bloodshed with any vividness.

Their reticence was not the result of ignorance of literary artful-ness, and it was often a self-conscious choice. General John Gibbon, for example, read vivid reports of the war, but he thought it was not the "soldierly way" to write them. Gibbon was wounded at Gettysburg, and a civilian writer asked him about the fight. This writer created a fictional, but quite realistic, letter to a Baltimore paper giving the confused impressions of a fighting man in the battle. Gibbon included the letter in his memoirs, but none of his own writing about the war showed that perspective.[6]

The popular view of combat was aimed above the bewildered and bleeding men to the questions of strategy and tactics. In the 1880's, for example, the *Century* magazine enlisted military men from the North and South for an epic replay of the war years. *Battles and Leaders of the Civil War* was a popular triumph and a signal of the inexhaustible American appetite for formal military history (the series eventually found room for the exploits of Civil War horses). These memoirs were in the tradition of Jomini, not Clausewitz. The grand strategy of victory and defeat was emphasized, not the human costs. Suffering was ignored or treated laconically—to illustrate some military virtue. The slaughter of the Union army at Bull Run, for example, was barely noted—there was more drama in the wounding of Stonewall Jackson:

> "General, how is it that you can keep so cool and appear so utterly insensible to danger in such a storm of shell and bullets as rained about you when your hand was hit?" He instantly became grave and reverential in his manner, and answered, in a low tone of great earnestness: "Captain, my religious belief teaches me to feel as safe in battle as in bed. God has fixed the time for my death. I do not concern myself about *that*. . . ."[7]

We have no reason to doubt such anecdotes, but they certainly simplified the experience of combat. They achieve clarity by subduing any sense of tragedy. War, in these memoirs, is reduced to a brisk, technical account of armies on the march. There is no room for complicated feelings.

General Grant used this simplicity to great dramatic effect, but his *Memoirs* too lack depth. Grant, by all accounts, was calm under fire—so stoical that he kept any maxims to himself the two times he was nearly killed by stray bullets. His almost casual courage and the dramatically paced record of his campaigns won his *Memoirs* great popular acclaim, but at a high price. The "fearful lesson" of the war that he had hoped to teach does not emerge from his narrative. In all the two volumes, only one sentence describes the destruction of Atlanta. "Grant's method of describing the war," Edmund Wilson noted, "always works to eliminate its tragedy. His mind seems so firm and clear that no agony or horror can cloud it." [8]

By the mid-1880's, when Grant's *Memoirs* was a best seller, veterans rarely spoke publicly of brutal or tragic elements of the conflict. "In the lapse of years," one general told a reunion of the Army of the Potomac, "the war recurs to us as a picnic on a large scale, somewhat long drawn out and arduous at times; but, after all, we recall more of joy than of sorrow, more of play than work." The war, a Confederate general recalled, was "the mildest and most humane ever fought." And gestures and jokes helped wash the blood away as surely as the solemn speeches. When Major John Wesley Powell, his right arm lost at Shiloh, encountered a Confederate officer who had lost his left arm in the same battle, they became fast friends. For years, whenever either bought a pair of gloves, he sent the one he did not need to his former enemy. One Southern advocate of reconciliation could jest with Atlantans that General Sherman was a "kind of careless man about fire." [9]

There were many in the South, of course, with considerably darker memories of the war, and when Confederate soldiers finally organized in the 1890's, their oratory gave a bloodier view of combat than the Grand Army of the Republic allowed themselves. But candid Southerners rarely found a national audience in the quarter-century after Appomattox. Richard Taylor's *Destruction and Reconstruction* (1879) is the exception. That Confederate Lieutenant-General, the son of President Zachary Taylor, recalled the ravaged South. Cruelty was as conspicuous in the Shenandoah Valley as in the Palatinate during the Thirty Years' War; and Sherman and Sheridan, spattered with Southern blood, were throwbacks to a barbarous age. And yet Taylor seems to have resented Southerners as much as Yankees. There were not many martyrs in his Palatinate. Attended by his servant in the field, he was not often impressed by other Cavaliers; his acid portraits of his comrades in arms give the impression that he was slumming for a noble cause. Taylor's memoirs, like Mary Chesnut's famous diary of those years, shows the collapse of the Confederacy as the result of backbiting rather than Northern bayonets. *Destruction and Reconstruction* is snide, embellished with literary allusions, and so amusing that no reader of it could believe that war was hell. The "close and fatal" fire sent rebels to "Valhalla" and gave Taylor anecdotes:

> Many men fell, and the whistling of shot and shell occasioned much ducking of heads in the column. This annoyed me no little, as it was but child's play to the work immediately in hand. Always an admirer of delightful "Uncle Toby," I had contracted the most villainous habit of his beloved army in Flanders, and, forgetting [Stonewall] Jackson's presence, ripped out, "What the h—— are you dodging for? If there is any more of it, you will be halted under this fire for an hour." The sharp tones of a familiar voice produced the desired effect, and the men looked as if they had swallowed ramrods; but I shall never forget the reproachful surprise expressed in Jackson's face. He placed his hand on my shoulder, said in a gentle voice, "I am afraid you are a wicked fellow," turned, and rode back to the pike.[10]

"Waving the bloody shirt"—that mainstay of Republicans in the first two decades after the war—revealed remarkably little about the years of battle. The spellbinders, such as Colonel Robert G. Ingersoll, focused on the current arrogance of the South and the past sins against blacks. He spoke with feeling about the fate of Northern prisoners at Andersonville, but not about the horrors that most old soldiers had known. (Ingersoll was usually content to make the point that everyone in his audience with a wound had received it from a Democrat.) Beginning with bitter words, Ingersoll turned the war saccharine: every veteran in the audience was a hero and "every promise made in war has now the ring and gleam of gold." Some Republicans had no stomach at all for the war issue. As early as 1867 Congressman Ignatius Donnelly, who was later to display his fervid view of technological warfare in a novel, closed his ears to the revelations about Andersonville: "I have not the heart to remember anything save only that these [Southern] people are human. . . ." [11]

In part, passions subsided because the results of the war were idealized: the value seemed so much greater than the price. Mutilated veterans, sharecroppers' bleak cabins, redeemer and redneck political machines—few Americans allowed *that* heritage to mar their sacrifice of the 1860's. Different images expressed the pervasive sentiment that the war had unlocked American energies and produced a glorious period of national growth. Smoking factory chimneys, rails across the continent, free settlers in the West—that was the popular iconography. [12]

But most often Americans talked of the intangible benefits of the war. The Civil War was doubly blessed, for it had saved the soul of the nation it made rich. It had provided the opportunity (so rare in America, many said) for the nation to learn obedience to law. Armed conflict swept away the weak or divided loyalties to civil authority. It was in these terms that, as the years passed, many Southerners found virtue in their defeat. "I can clearly see that the suffering of the Confederacy was an inestimable blessing," young Woodrow Wilson wrote in North Carolina. *"Because* I love the South," he later told the nation, "I rejoice in the failure of the Confederacy." Wilson, like many others, revered the discipline—the bending to force—that the war had taught. Discipline—understood as the vindication of the law of the Union and the endurance of personal pain—gave the war purpose, and a sort of majesty, for late-nineteenth-century Americans. [13]

But the facts of the war were not all so uplifting. The men in uniform had known more about diarrhea than saber charges. A half-million men had deserted. One soldier had died for every six slaves freed. Yet by the 1880's, few Americans had escaped the image of a comprehensible and humane Civil War. Republican orators (even as they baited the contemporary South) struck those themes before each election; veterans came together annually to remind the nation of their glorious sacrifice; and a barrage of stories and articles stressed the accomplishments of resort to arms. The 1860's became a golden age. Though apologists, indeed, felt deeply about the conflict, they showed great restraint in recalling their experiences. Few confessed any confusion, hatred, or fear in battle; none dared suggest that the North or South had made an empty sacrifice. The standard literature is sometimes thrilling, but never revolting. Often it reveals a sectional bias, but it is never disrespectful to the fighting men of either side.

The veterans remembered what they needed to fit into the society that welcomed them home. Victorian America waited to hear cheerful and orderly stories, not tales of trauma and holocaust. Everyday life in nineteenth-century America provided many opportunities to learn stoicism. The veterans, unpracticed as literary realists, knew far more than modern readers about the screams that doctors could not quiet and the silent bodies laid out in the family parlor. These were not matters to dwell upon. And the orderly memory of the war was also a product of more subtle feelings Americans had about how their society worked. As professions and bureaucracies grew in power, it was natural to see the war as the unfolding of organizations and procedures. As social ethics and law were claimed to be processes of formal deduction from eternal principles, the war was examined for abstract lessons, not subjective experience. As human struggle with nature seemed to follow scientific laws, probes of consciousness seemed a waste of time.

\*     \*     \*

Our own image of the Civil War is seldom found in the first beautiful books and lengthy speeches that commemorated the battles. No publisher brought together the major photographs of the campaigns in the nineteenth century—Mathew Brady's wet plates sat, forgotten, in a Washington studio. The first stories of the war rarely speak of the blind violence that Bruce Catton has dramatized; there is little hint of those haunted survivors that William Faulkner studied. Even our archives can mislead us about what the war meant to the veterans. The war in the memoirs was not the war that many common soldiers had written home about from the field. The enduring war was not a tale of mud, sickness, and lost years.

Yet we can recognize the twentieth-century view of the Civil War in some nineteenth-century books. The "real war" that Walt Whitman felt "will never get into the books" is in the memoirs of some of the men who lived with the sound of guns. A small group of officers and novelists did remember the terror on the battlefields that most Americans wished to forget.[14]

Winter Sport in a Confederate Camp
*(Battles and Leaders of the Civil War*, 1887)

There was, however, no literature of disillusionment. Writers who denied the orderliness, or mildness, or effectiveness of the conflict usually stressed the importance of the values that remained. Knocking out any panel of the American triptych on war made the others more venerated. Some officers celebrated their control of the campaigns and the blessings of the war at the same time they admitted the need for harsh measures to win it. Literary realists praised the war's discipline even as they rejected the comprehensible and humane war that most Americans cherished.

Clausewitz criticized what governments thought war should be—a restrained and dignified test of armies in the field. He foresaw (and feared) what war might become—the mobilization of entire societies with few checks on violence. What held people back from intense warfare, Clausewitz stressed, was the dead hand of military tradition, "an unconsciousness of what is possible." [15] Sherman and Sheridan were the first American officers conscious of that vast new power. Sherman's swath of destruction on his march to the sea; Sheridan's devastation of the Shenandoah Valley—it was (as the South bitterly complained) a new kind of warfare to inflict on a civilized opponent. Northern commanders set few limits on the blood or resources they would spend to crush their enemy. Sherman told secessionists that the Union had a right "to take their lives, their homes, their every thing . . . war is simply power unrestrained by constitution or compact." And Sheridan believed that "the people must be left nothing but their eyes to weep with over the war." [16]

Harold Lasswell has called this outlook "satanism": the spirit that would bring the total war of the twentieth century. But Sherman and Sheridan were, in fact, incomplete architects of terror. Their violence had limits. They did not like to look at the land they had burned; they shed blood for specific purposes; and they tempered their severity with compassion for the victims. Neither man recorded bloodshed realistically. They described an orderly, comprehensible war in which terror against civilians always served rational ends. Punishment, Sherman emphasized, upheld law and rehabilitated the victims. He compared secessionists to "Satan and the rebellious saints of heaven"—but if they would yield and repent in the fire, he would save them. After threatening Atlanta, he held out the beauty of surrender: "You may call on me for any thing. Then will I share with you the last cracker, and watch with you to shield your homes and families against danger from every quarter." Sheridan, similarly, did not lust after vengeance. Bringing terror to civilians was simply the best way to teach the enemy to appreciate the value of order:

> I do not hold war to mean simply that lines of men shall engage each other in battle, and material interests be ignored. This is but a

duel, in which one combatant seeks the other's life; war means much more, and is far worse than this. Those who rest at home in peace and plenty see but little of the horrors attending such a duel and even grow indifferent to them as the struggle goes on, contenting themselves with encouraging all who are able-bodied to enlist in the cause, to fill up the shattered ranks as death thins them. It is another matter, however, when deprivation and suffering are brought to their own doors. Then the case appears much graver, for the loss of property weighs heavy with the most of mankind; heavier often, than the sacrifices made on the field of battle.[17]

In war, then, the cure must be harsh so that it might work, and violence was a cure: a rational procedure for setting the body politic in order.

This insistence that the bloodiest tactics were part of the military's healing art echoed through textbooks during the rest of the century. After Sherman and Sheridan, efforts "to crush a population," or "to bring the war home to a people" by destroying "the necessaries of life" were permissible. It was now simply a matter of terror's effectiveness: "The advancing spirit of the age does not condemn any mode or means of war simply because it may be extremely destructive, but only if it be *uselessly* or *unnecessarily* so." [18]

No one in nineteenth-century America considered what those principles would mean in practice. Civil War gallantry dominated the nation's view, not the specter of burned fields and empty cities. But while Americans clung to romance, Europeans learned from the ordeal. The Spanish government in 1897 cited Sherman and Sheridan to justify the scorched earth campaigns in Cuba. German strategists in the 1930's studied the Northern tactics to learn how to make war more devastating. The legacy of the Civil War could be softened and forgotten, but only for a time.[19]

\*    \*    \*

The Northern commanders brought the war to Southern civilians, but the literary realists succeeded in bringing the horror of battle to many more American homes. The generals' new tactics had touched only the South, and in their memoirs they withheld the full picture; the realists forced their readers to look at the dazed Americans whom the Northern armies had left behind.

The realists, of course, saw much less of the war than the Northern commanders did. Yet they found it charged with mysteries the officers never mentioned. Grant, Sherman, and Sheridan had put the war behind them; the realists—even those who had not seen a battle—were obsessed by it. They hurried their work, as if in a race with the Southern springs that transformed these battlegrounds into Arcadian fields for tourists. Those writers were impatient with "the old fashioned, upholstered, historical form," as Joseph Kirkland called it, "—charging battalions, triumphant tactics, masterly combinations and other stuff." Albion Tourgée pictured a wounded soldier so suffocated by such reports that he could not believe he had, in fact, fought at all. [20]

Realists agonized over how much they dared tell and never stopped questioning if what they said was the truth. Ambrose Bierce endlessly reworked his tales of horror and often tramped over the battlefields of his youth to reconsider his personal nightmare. Stephen Crane, born too late for the campaigns, rushed to wars around the world to see if the Civil War he had imagined was true to life. Realists, then, fought two different battles: a struggle with literary form and the more harrowing one of coming to terms with the scenes they portrayed.

Visions of war in our century rely so heavily on the perspectives of these realists that it is easy to take their victories over convention for granted. Realists fought to escape the "epauletted history" and to see the battle as the common soldier saw it. In their accounts they focus on the ordinariness of men at war—the daily search for food and sleep, the routine of guard and drill, the matter-of-fact talk about home and the enemy. They draw the reader into war and heighten the shock by thrusting extraordinary scenes and emotions into the narrative—doubt and wild retreat, great courage and self-sacrifice, pools of blood and cracking bones.

It is the juxtaposition of the attractive with the doomed, the familiar with the grotesque, that so shocked readers in the last quarter of the nineteenth century. John DeForest wrote:

> . . . a brave, handsome boy of Company D, gay and smiling with the excitement of fighting, disdaining to cover himself, was reloading his rifle when a ball transversed his head, leaving two ghastly orifices through which the blood and brains exuded, mingling with his auburn curls.[21]

Similarly, Bierce's short stories of horror built on the familiarity of the victims; corpse embraces corpse, and the family reunions occur in blood.[22]

The realists frequently described a war beyond the comprehension of the common soldier. The smoke and debris blind him: he is unaware of the clever maneuvers planned at headquarters. They often saw the war as a clash of undifferentiated masses in which individual actions lost significance. "The regiment whose history I was asked to write," Tourgée said, "was one in which personal adventure cut a remarkably small figure. In its whole history, there is hardly an instance of individual contact with an enemy. There are no startling experiences to relate, no deeds of special daring." In *The Red Badge of Courage* Henry Fleming was dazed by the drill and boredom of life at the front: "He had grown to regard himself merely as a part of a vast blue demonstration. . . . For recreation he could twiddle his thumbs and speculate on the thoughts which must agitate the minds of the generals." The realists' soldiers had forgotten (if they ever knew) why they were fighting. Though their pain and panic are described in detail, their sacrifices often appear empty—a "useless slaughter" some judge; an ironic test of courage, Henry Fleming finds; and merely "wearisome *ennui* and deplorable *désoeuvrement*," others conclude.[23]

When realists showed fighting men mutilated, doubt-ridden, and inarticulate in battle, they provoked the wrath of Americans who remembered a comprehensible and humane struggle for the Union. *The Red Badge of Courage* was denounced as "a vicious satire upon American soldiers and American armies. . . . Nowhere are seen the quiet, manly, self-respecting, and patriotic men, influenced by the highest sense of duty, who in reality fought our battles." But such conservative critics jumped to the wrong conclusion about the realists. Joseph Kirkland, after pages of grotesque battle scenes and scathing portraits of cowards in the ranks, closed out his story with a bow to convention: "On the whole, the fighters, dead and alive, ought to be very thankful that things have turned out so well; and to feel entirely satisfied with the general result." *The Red Badge of Courage* was certainly not a novel of disillusionment; Crane, so frequently the poet of a universe "flatly indifferent" to human struggle, allowed Henry Fleming to return to his regiment "with a large sympathy for the machinery of the universe. With his new eyes, he could see that the secret and open blows which were being dealt about the world with such heavenly lavishness were in truth blessings. . . . He was a man." [24]

The themes of initiation and acceptance were prominent in the realists' conception of war. Americans faced the terrible bloodletting and confusion and endured—all of the writers found great value in this. They resented the tendency to soften and romanticize the Civil War, only to surrender to the popular view that it had disciplined the national character.

The realists, despite their accounts of battle, confessed to a fascination with life under arms. Kirkland's main character was "spellbound by the romance of the gleaming fires, the white tents, the deep shadows, the lines of silent, slow-marching sentinels." Similarly, Bierce and Tourgée did not hide their sense of the beauty of their long marches across the South. When battle interrupted such reveries, the realists often found war attractive. That "hideous" sound of guns, Kirkland's hero admitted, "is the sweetest music my ears ever listened to." DeForest found bombardments "sublime" and even when in danger recognized a "joy of battle." Tourgée concluded that "poetry and war are almost inseparable." Combat had a lyric quality:

> He remembered once, when he had led a charge on a hostile battery, through the brown autumn woods ahead of his line, with flash-

ing sword in one hand and plumed hat in the other, how the blood danced through his veins as if the very elixir of joy had inspired its impulses.

Stephen Crane was so excited by the aesthetic dimension of battle that we often lose sight of Fleming in the "blue demonstration" of war. When Crane finally witnessed a bombardment, he was captivated by the scene: "It was the most beautiful sound of my experience, barring no symphony. . . . This is one point of view. Another might be taken from the men who died there." [25]

The realists were connoisseurs of the violence endured, but not of the violence inflicted. No one proved their courage by killing or wounding rebels. These writers stressed the common sacrifice and comradeship of fighting men. The legend of the Blue and the Gray bound together in noble work on the battlefield survived in this literature. Character, not uniform, mattered. Given the shocking and grotesque conditions in combat, can the fighting man stand it? DeForest took his characters to the limit of their ability to cope with the horror, and then exulted in their stoical discipline:

> It will be asked, perhaps, whether I . . . preserved my staunchness under these trials. I must confess, and I do it without great shame, conscious of being no more than human, that in my inmost soul I was as insubordinate as the worst men were in speech and behavior. In my unspeakable heart I groaned and raved. I wished the bridges would break down—I wished the regiment would refuse to take another step—it seemed to me that I should have been silent in the face of mutiny. But nothing of all this passed my lips, and none could suspect it from my actions. [26]

The frank admission of panic and pain by realists did not overturn the popular faith in the efficacy of the war. The darker side of combat only highlighted lessons of discipline for the men that endured. All the realists looked back fondly on the "intensity of character" Americans developed in "those days of miracle and self-forgetfulness." [27]

By the end of the century three points of view marked recollections of the Civil War. The most popular memoirs softened and idealized combat and uncritically applauded the results. Some articulate military theorists remembered that the South had been ravaged, but they did not challenge the convention that the struggle had been a noble one. The realists evoked the violence in order to praise the men who endured it. The latter two groups—the reluctant prophets of total war and the imaginative writers so eager to describe the terror of battle—both departed from the conventional focus on the structure of the war. For them war was terrifying, confusing, and revolting. And yet there remained a hidden war, one the veterans had not forgotten, but one that even the realists found so mysterious that they could not fully describe it.

# 2

## "THE SILENCE WITH HIM AND OF HIM"

The war books rolled from the press, the toasts at military banquets lasted well into the night, and each Decoration Day the orators gathered at the cemeteries. Yet in some ways the most important legacy of the war was silence.

Reticence never seemed too high a price to pay for reconciliation. Talk of wounds appeared to enflame the attitudes that had, after all, caused them. Many, however, had a more personal reason for silence. Soldiers did not speak of the blood and terror simply because literary conventions and squeamish civilians stood in their way. They often could not say what they felt, and some bore emotional wounds that made speech impossible.

That silence was costly. It broadened the gulf between the victims of the war and the civilians who had not experienced it. Reticence set an example for the generations preparing to fight and discouraged them from probing their own feelings about war. Americans were led to talk only about the spiritual uplift of combat. And, having been told that old enemies were comrades, the American soldier found the enemies of later wars confusing.

＊　　＊　　＊

Civil War literature has no more serious theme than the recognition that silence is the most reverent response to combat. In trying to find a new language to describe war, realists found that communication broke down. Bierce's men never fully awakened from their nightmare; Crane's numb country boys mistook delirium for courage; and all of the realists' characters were failures at explaining themselves. In fact, these writers, like the men they described, doubted they grasped the psychic reality of combat. No American, DeForest complained, "has written the whole truth about war and battle. I tried, and I told all I dared, and perhaps all I could." Tourgée, similarly, left the field at Bull Run, humble and mute:

> Of course there was a good deal of noise and, in a certain sense, much confusion; but the noise of battle is not like the tumult of the storm, when one stands on the shore and feels the north wind pile the breakers on the beach, and sees the lips of his friend move, an arm's length away, and knows that he is speaking, but cannot hear a word. The roar of battle is over and above the soldier, but with him who fights there is a sort of silence which seems all the more terrible from the fact that it seems unnatural. You hear what a comrade says when he is stricken; you answer an inquiry of one on your right as to the enemy, and of one on your left as to how many cartridges you have left, without for a moment ceasing to fire. The roar of battle is terrible, but its silence is still more fearful. The turmoil is above and about the soldier, but the silence with him and of him. [1]

Even the most articulate memoirists, so loud in their commemoration of the days under fire, at some point drop their pens. Oliver Wendell Holmes, Jr., called on the nation to revere "the soldiers' faith," but he also preached that there was something more to accept than the obedience and pain that had tempered his generation—"Having known great things, to be content with silence." [2]

Walt Whitman began the war with booming chants for the Union, but he grew quiet as he learned of the ordeal. *Drum-Taps* celebrates the exuberance of the men in blue who marched south in 1861 ("Year that suddenly sang by the mouths of the round-lipp'd cannon . . .") but we can date his poems by his gathering hush in the bivouacs and hospital wards. The cacaphony of "Beat! Beat!

Drums" (1861), deafening citizens with the call to arms, yields to "The Wound Dresser" (1865):

> (Arous'd and angry, I'd thought to beat the
>     alarum, and urge relentless war.
> But soon my fingers fail'd me, my face
>     droop'd and I resign'd myself,
> To sit by the wounded and soothe them, or
>     silently watch the dead;)

Whitman's notebooks in *Specimen Days* commemorate the marching troops who ceased their shouts and the young men in invalid's dress who remained quiet about their heroism. The poet, perhaps like the ragged soldiers he loved, overcame his nausea at the blood and his doubts about the rhetoric from Washington. But in celebrating the war, Whitman hoped to teach the nation to be most reverent about the men who had died "unknown," waging a battle that now "in the mushy influence of current times" could not be put in books. [3]

Whitman was right: the hush in war literature continued through the first three decades of the twentieth century. Well-behaved Cavaliers and Yankees were prominent in popular fiction, winning improbable glories on the battlefield and uniting families in still more improbable marriages after they laid down their arms. When these heroes entered the parlor, they forgot the war. The abler writers who broke new ground studied men and women who could not comprehend or explain the war they had fought.

Harold Frederic and Francis Grierson were too young to fight for the Union. Frederic, in Oneida County, New York, and Grierson, in Sangamon County, Illinois, listened to the war unfold around the village post office and homestead. Both men made a career in Europe, but they were cosmopolitans who were spellbound by the ordeal of their native land. Frederic and Grierson labored to tell about an inner war, a war that civilians could not understand and that returning soldiers could not express. They recaptured a childlike sense of wonder and magic about the war. In their stories we do not often visit the bivouac or trench, and, indeed, the reader is left as dumbfounded about the meaning of the sacrifice as the baffled farmers who waited for the news of death.

In Frederic's upstate New York one of the few men who has seen a battle and returned to the village was a man who could not be heard: "shot straight through the tongue. . . . Whenever he attempted conversation, people moved away, or began boisterous dialogues with one another to drown him out." The man's wound speaks for him, as do the photographs of the town's sons, wearing higher boots after each season in the Southern mud . . . and the very carpets in the parlors, that grow darker each year as the home loom is fed more useless Union blue and mourning cloth. The deserters and dissenters are the most admirable men in Frederic's stories, but he was more interested in probing the minds of uncomprehending men and women behind the lines than in vindicating upstate Copperheads.[4]

Francis Grierson, in *The Valley of Shadows* (1909), made the war an affair of gunslingers and shamans. He remembered Midwest fire-eaters and holy men who left their log cabins in a trance and in "the 'silence' that belonged to the prairies," prepared their souls for war. Grierson's story is partly a fanciful narrative of shoot-outs and raids, partly an attempt to evoke the magical transformation of personality in this war. He respected the sacrifice of the ruffians and the holy men, but he left their motives and ideals a mystery. The soldiers' faith cannot be probed too far, though Grierson hoped their "silently fatal" faces might shock dull Americans who were too comfortable in peace.[5]

\*     \*     \*

In the 1880's and 1890's reticence about war increasingly became part of political etiquette. Albion Tourgée did all he could to make Americans face embarrassing questions about the Civil War—those issues that had been cloaked in silence. Tourgée, who enlisted before Sumter and kept watch on the rebels until 1905, waged the longest campaign in American letters. He had been shot, and, for a time, paralyzed and imprisoned: no writer endured more for the Union. As Tourgée's wounds healed, he watched the nation attempt to forget the war. He was silent about some things. Though contemptuous of the gilded picture of the war, he was not invariably a realist and he seldom told of the battles in his books. Tourgée had not forgotten any of his harrowing steps from Bull Run to Chickamauga, but he did not describe them in detail because he feared his readers might only feel pity for the Union soldier and forget the cause that he had bled to save. In the 1860's, even as he watched the bones of his comrades bleach in the sun, he checked his grief. Death was a privilege, and the patriot was defiled by tears: "He who mourns above his verdant grave when the cause for which he fell has proved triumphant, offers insult to his memory." [6]

"Memorial Day" became Tourgée's special grievance. He noted that the "jubilant remembrance of victory" of Decoration Day was being replaced in the 1880's by a new, sentimental day when "only the manhood and valor of the dead were to be commemorated." This to Tourgée seemed mindless. He endorsed the "grace" extended to the South, but he was angry with Northerners who had forgotten why they fought. Forgive the South and put away the battle registers and banners, Tourgée said. Then, he hoped, the nation could hear the true requiem for the Union dead:

> All that it is needful for the citizen and the statesman of today to remember of the great war of yesterday is, *not* the battles, the marches, the conflicts,— *but only the causes that underlay the struggle and the results that followed it.* [7]

Tourgée dared to say that it had been a war about race—and that on Memorial Day Americans now whistled as they hurried past the graveyards, pretending that the issue was as dead as the interred combatants. But the Blue and the Gray could only be memorialized by a campaign for the blacks; he would listen to nothing else.

Eventually it became good manners in America to speak with circumspection about new wars lest old soldiers be discredited. Some Civil War veterans were enraged that the anti-imperialists dared to complain about the Army's "water cure" of rebels in the Philippines. These veterans put painful memories of combat to rest as they declared that they did not care to look into this "Tophet." "Every time they make this great hub-bub about cruelties they are hitting back at those that were in the Civil War. . . ." Major-General Grenville M. Dodge told members of the Military Order of the Loyal Legion, "there is no officer listening to me who did not see cruelties in the Civil War. Many of you have had to order them but you know you were never brought to account for them when they were acts of necessity." [8] Lifting the lid a bit on the problems that the Civil War literature hid, those old soldiers thought that the wisdom of again slamming down the cover on war would be obvious.

It may also have been necessary to find relief from remorse about those old battles, but in shielding their eyes from campaigns, the fighting men closed themselves off from the new generation of soldiers who, willingly or not, dealt in terror.

New soldiers did not expect candor from the thinning ranks of the Blue and the Gray. No veterans' organization arose to enable the generations that took up arms to swap stories. And no memoir of the Civil War seems to have interested the armies of 1898 and 1917. The young men did not reject their elders, they simply marked them as veterans of a war that could not be shared. The *Stars and Stripes* of May 24, 1918, ran "The Battle Hymn of the Republic" across the front page, but the doughboys, the paper noted sadly, could not be induced to celebrate Decoration Day. They fled the speeches for the baseball diamonds of France.

In the literature of World War I the story of the earlier crusade was lost. Decoration Day was seldom marked by doughboys, for the memories it evoked were incomprehensible to them. The Marines in Thomas Boyd's *Through the Wheat* (1922), for example, stand dumbly through the ceremony and then march silently away, the dust muffling their escape. There is also a hollow commemoration in Faulkner's first tour of Yoknapatawpha County. Faulkner's characters carry memories of the Confederate dead with them as they move amidst the stately buildings and statues of the Lost Cause. But

Southerners could not understand that sacrifice any more than they could comprehend the wild young men who had just come home from France. The Civil War, in *Sartoris*, is remembered as absurd vignettes (one a gallant raid for anchovies). The two old men who rake over memories are both deaf. In the uproar of their voices they say nothing:

> "what the devil were you folks fighting about, anyhow?"
> "Bayard," old man Falls answered, "be damned ef I ever did know." [9]

However, the two generations of fighting men are copying each other. Young Bayard is as mute (if not physically as deaf) as the earlier Sartoris warriors. So too in later American crusades, soldiers were gripped by the same impulse to simplify and soften their sacrifice. Uneasy with the old commemorations of valor, they could not explain what they themselves fought for.

Theodore Roosevelt's *The Rough Riders* is the high point of these post Civil-War memoirs—a genre that almost convinces the modern reader that putting on the uniform turned men to stone. As he led his men through the stinking camps and up the bloody slopes in the improvised campaign, Roosevelt recorded neither the anguish nor the faith of his troops. He strongly rejected the psychological perspective of writers like Stephen Crane. The Rough Riders both awed and puzzled Crane. In combat, they "lashed themselves into a delirium that disdained everything . . . one could hardly imagine that they were the silent, stealthy woodsmen, the splendid scouts of the previous hours." But Roosevelt was never confused:

> I did not see any sign among the fighting men, whether wounded or unwounded, of the very complicated emotions assigned to their kind by some of the realistic modern novelists who have written about battles. At the front everyone behaved quite simply and took things as they came, in a matter-of-course way.

Roosevelt made all casualties stoics: "Occasionally one of our men would crumple up. In no case did the man make any outcry when hit, seeming to take it as a matter of course; at the outside, making only such a remark as, 'Well, I got it that time.' " Such simplicity seems contrived, and probably was; one of the reasons Roosevelt wrote *The Rough Riders* was to counteract the early reports that the company had walked into an ambush—rumors spread by panicky Rough Riders after they took their first casualties. Not surprisingly, other witnesses reported more emphatic remarks as men were struck down by the Spaniards' Mauser bullets.[10]

Roosevelt also toned down the exuberance he felt in battle, so clear in his own war letters. We hear nothing in *The Rough Riders* of his joy in killing a Spaniard with his own hands; nor does he admit that he stripped an enemy corpse of cartridges "for the children." Perhaps his greatest failure is that he does not even hint at his masterful profanity; Roosevelt's oaths were so remarkable that John J. Pershing, after twenty more years of Army life, could still recall them exactly.[11]

But it is the political silence that haunts *The Rough Riders*. In the summer of 1898 Roosevelt suddenly became mute on the goals and purposes of the war with Spain. *Cuba libre*, the *Maine*, the *reconcentrados*—all the appeals and symbols that Roosevelt believed in as he promoted American action, dropped from his vocabulary. The celebration of expansion and peace-keeping was adjourned. *The Rough Riders*—and Roosevelt's correspondence as a soldier—demonstrates an extraordinary moral silence. He says nothing about the declaration of war; nothing about the Cuban insurgents; nothing about the political character of the Spanish. And Roosevelt leaves the impression that neither his Eastern college youths nor his ruffians from the Southwest speculated on those matters.

If modern readers believe that the Rough Riders from the frontier were simply adventurers without political notions it is probably because they have spent too much time with the "westerns" that Roosevelt helped to foster in the East. But the specter of a tyrannous Spanish power was not a new idea in the Southwest. Cuban "patriots" had lectured throughout Arizona and helped to turn the Territory in favor of intervention before the *Maine* sank. And not a few "cowboys" volunteered as much to force Washington to accept Arizona as a state as to force Madrid to cede Cuba. No one could mistake the Rough Riders for a political cadre, but few were ignorant of practical politics or deaf to the idealism of the war. Their songs proclaimed their political objectives. One evening in camp, the Rough Riders gathered to hear a forty-five minute oration on "The Brotherhood of Man" they had asked a sergeant to deliver. Roosevelt attended, but makes no mention of that evening. Indeed, he found almost no place for the reflections of his men, merely noting, for example, one Arizonan's attempt to draw him into conversation about "the mysteries which lie behind courage, and fear, and love." Mr. Dooley's title for *The Rough Riders*—"Alone in Cubia" is a fair judgment of how the characters of Roosevelt's men faded as he attempted to glorify them.[12]

At the turn of the century, few Americans wished to lift the curtain Roosevelt had placed in front of fighting men. John Fox was a correspondent in Cuba; he wrote to his family that he could not stand to look at the bloodshed. Fox, however, concluded that soldiers were immune to such harrowing scenes. In his great triumph of 1903, *The Little Shepherd of Kingdom Come*, he ignored everything he had witnessed in real war, and created the tale of a Unionist "shepherd" from Kentucky who won his manhood with a "beautiful sabre cut across his right cheek" and had found "no passion during the war" to mar his kindly face.[13]

It is tempting to regard such genteel views of war as curiosities of the Victorian parlor. Yet that vision of combat endured, and it influenced much later arguments about war. Before the 1930's, old soldiers clung to the stoical mode in their memoirs. No reader learned much about the modern battlefield by listening to the officers who had fought there.

General Pershing's *My Experiences in the World War* (1931) marked the twilight of this stoicism. Pershing was not a pompous man—he confessed his blunders with the French and his embarrassment when Pétain kissed him. Nor was he insensitive to the destruction. He recorded his hospital visits and noted the dazed civilians driven from their homes. In the last battles he grew melancholy as he realized that his men would fall near the lines of white crosses where the army of 1914 rested. Yet it was a picture that Pershing did not want to complete. He called the wounded simply either "convalescent soldiers" or "poor fellows . . . quite beyond hope," hurried his visits, and never listened to their stories. Pershing found no place in his two volumes for the shell shocked, the mud, or the lice. He reported that the war was rarely discussed at the officers' mess.

Pershing must have felt ill-used by the "rulers and governments" he so vaguely condemned. And by 1931 his faith in the American crusade for Wilsonian principles was muted indeed. But his "inner war" remains as inaccessible in *My Experiences* as in the other bulky volumes that had helped Americans to relive (and forget) earlier wars. Only once in the memoirs did Pershing break the code of silence and speak personally of combat. At the dedication of the Ossuary near Verdun—a mammoth depository of human bones—he confessed that "my triumphant sense of victory has been entirely overwhelmed by my sympathy for the men who fell. . . ." Pershing then spoke of Pétain with words that have the force of personal conviction: "The fall of each one of your soldiers was a stab in the heart of his general and the impassive expression under which you hide your feelings masked constant and unremitting grief." [14] This is what the stoical mode had always hid. It remained for a new generation of fighting men to put their speech in the first person.

*     *     *

Americans in the peace movement were as wary of realism as the old soldiers were. The American Peace Society had shelved its antebellum plans for a painting in the lobby of the War Department showing mutilated citizens on a battlefield strewn with weapons and bleaching skulls. That approach seemed ineffective and uncouth. Jane Addams thought that such paintings looked terribly dated. War, in this modern view, "eclipses the imagination, rendering words impotent to describe it." And the Mohonk Conferences, the largest forum for the discussion of peace held before World War I, actually prohibited mention of any unpleasant details of battle.[15]

The angriest critics of war were at a loss for words. Against the manly endurance the apologists remembered in combat, some peace workers attempted to describe licentiousness in uniform. The "strenuous life" turned out to be a spree of sex, drink, and crime. *The Advocate of Peace*, for example, conceded that Theodore Roosevelt's appeal to the martial virtues was "brilliant," but sought to show that war was the wrong way to achieve those ideals, what with "the loathsome pollutions of camp life . . . the vulgarity and profanity of the mêlée of fighting which the Governor of New York knows all about." [16] The corruption, though, was more heavily veiled than the insult. Year after year peace workers hinted that drunkenness, venereal disease, sodomy, and crime were part of basic training.

Yet these moral watchmen could not bring themselves to give realistic portraits of the fallen men. The vices they spoke of invariably "exceeded description"; the military was good at keeping secrets. In this "hideous nether side of war" brothels are guarded by troops, the figures on venereal disease are suppressed; the *"Perverted* Sex Appetite, has a vile festival weeks at a time" in the privacy of ship's company; and, behind the walls of the Naval War College, "naked society women cavorted around patriotically clad in silken American flags." [17]

On this issue of licentiousness the peace movement did join issue directly with the apologists for war. But in accepting that issue, peace workers also accepted the mystique of silence about what fighting men actually did. Disembodied vice replaced disembodied heroism, and simple lassitude replaced simple glory. We do not see the soldier any more clearly when he breaks all the rules than when he upholds them.

There was a case to be made for the vow of silence about battle. Evoking war—as the realists dared to do—might actually incite men to bloodletting: "The horror makes the thrill." But by standing mute about life under arms, the peace movement could not argue effectively against the abundant testimony that war was the sure test of true manhood. More seriously, the peace workers were led to close their eyes to what might happen on the modern battlefield.[18]

\* \* \*

The men who were asked to march onto new battlefields paid most dearly for this pervasive silence about war. Because of the winnowed memory of an ennobling war, campaigns could easily appear as the rite of passage for heroes—and martyrs. In some cases there was nothing intellectually dishonest in calls for this sacrifice. Oliver Wendell Holmes, Jr.,—who had paid in blood for Northern bungling and Southern bullets—commended his experience to a new generation in his famous affirmation:

> In the midst of doubt, in the collapse of creeds, there is one thing I do not doubt, that no man who lives in the same world with most of us can doubt, and that is that the faith is true and adorable which leads a soldier to throw away his life in obedience to a blindly accepted duty, in a cause which he little understands in a plan of campaign of which he has no notion, under tactics of which he does not see the use.[19]

But in most discussions of peace and war early in the century, this sensibility stemmed from books, not personal ordeal. A tradition of reticence encouraged a taste for martyrdom by making that martyrdom less real. It was the legend of the Civil War that raised the courage of Woodrow Wilson and Albert Beveridge and made them "envy" the dead and mutilated of the Blue and Gray.[20]

To wash the blood away after Appomattox meant that vital questions about shame and guilt disappeared. Neither shame—the hatred of what we have *become*—nor guilt—the agony over what we have *done*—intrudes in Civil War literature. In the national celebration and mystique of the benefits of the war, these emotions were denied rather than resolved, as they might have been through appropriate acts of confession, purgation, and forgiveness.

The toasts at military banquets to "foemen worthy of our steel!" and the Civil War memoirs with their engravings of "Our Friends the Enemy" blurred the emotional lines between comrades and victims. In the celebration of the 1860's both the North and the South drew inspiration from the aggressive acts of their former enemies. With the peace, the "manly virtues" on the battlefield were transformed into "the common property of us all." The scholarly "Grant worshippers" in the Old Confederacy had their counterpart in the Union soldiers who recalled that as the men in gray had charged "there was thrill of pride that these brave men were, after all, Americans." [21]

It seemed, now, that the North and the South had been on the same side and wished to relive the battles as comrades. On Broadway in the 1890's audiences shook the house as Sheridan's cavalry charge was put on stage in *Shenandoah* and then stayed to stamp and cheer through the curtain calls as the band played "Dixie." [22] Through the camera of D. W. Griffith, the Blue and the Gray looked about the same; skin color, after all, was the mark of the enemy in *Birth of a Nation* (1915). Griffith's audience saw a boy from the North and a boy from the South die on the battlefield in each other's arms. Now the theater rang with shouts as the reconciled white race fought blacks.

It seemed that the old soldiers had not been enemies at all. Woodrow Wilson, speaking to the Grand Army of the Republic, stated boldly what a generation of memoirs and Decoration Day speeches suggested: "You feel, as I am sure the men who fought against you feel, that you were comrades even then, though you did not know it." [23] The Blue and the Gray were asked to block out their memories of the wounds they carried, their friends who had fallen beside them . . . and the lives they had themselves cut short.

The enemy thus was simplified. He was a gallant figure in a legend, not the complicated threat that soldiers faced with a mixture of anger, fear, and admiration. There is, surely, some substance to the idea that enemies are comrades. Everyone on the battlefield

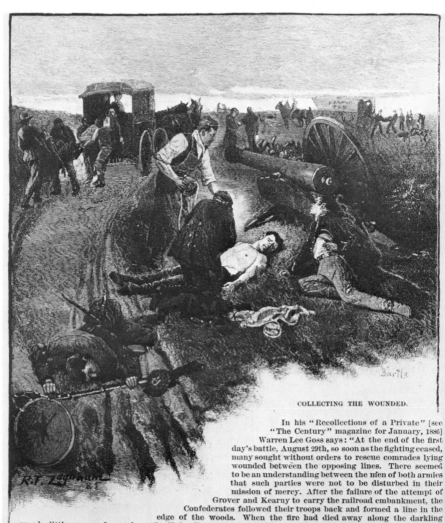

COLLECTING THE WOUNDED.

In his "Recollections of a Private" [see "The Century" magazine for January, 1886] Warren Lee Goss says: "At the end of the first day's battle, August 29th, so soon as the fighting ceased, many sought without orders to rescue comrades lying wounded between the opposing lines. There seemed to be an understanding between the men of both armies that such parties were not to be disturbed in their mission of mercy. After the failure of the attempt of Grover and Kearny to carry the railroad embankment, the Confederates followed their troops back and formed a line in the edge of the woods. When the fire had died away along the darkling woods, little groups of men from the Union lines went stealthily about, bringing in the wounded from the exposed positions. Blankets attached to poles or muskets often served as stretchers to bear the wounded to the ambulances and surgeons. There was a great lack here of organized effort to care for our wounded. Vehicles of various kinds were pressed into service. The removal went on during the entire night, and tired soldiers were roused from their slumbers by the plaintive cries of comrades passing in the comfortless vehicles. In one instance a Confederate and a Union soldier were found cheering each other on the field. They were put into the same Virginia farm-cart and sent to the rear, talking and groaning in fraternal sympathy."

(*Battles and Leaders of the Civil War*, 1887)

shares the risk and may admire the skills of his opponent. The danger of that empathy is that it makes new enemies difficult to understand and harder to fight.

On the Great Plains and in Spain's island empire, American soldiers continued to convert their enemies into comrades, just as the Civil War legend had taught. There were new reasons to empathize with the enemy in those wars. Officers frequently thought that the government's orders were contradictory; civilian ideals, empty. Some officers grew estranged from the society that ordered the campaigns, and at times they identified with the enemy's cause.

In the years after Appomattox the pervasive reticence about war had the consequence of making new campaigns inviting; as Americans became reconciled with their old enemies they found their new foes harder to fight. Violence, it must be emphasized, was not often checked by this blurring of the distinction between friend and foe. In some instances the enemy's perceived virtues, or his puzzling refusal to be helped, made the soldiers more willing to shed blood.

# III

# THE EVANESCENT ENEMY

*American soldiers, with no say about whom they were to fight, speculated freely on the nature of their enemy. They found, especially in the Indian, a worthy enemy who both raised questions about the American cause and confirmed the virtues of the armed forces.*

# 3

# RED,
# WHITE, AND THE ARMY BLUE

The peace at Appomattox meant war for the Indian. In the next quarter-century 6.5 million settlers upset the precarious balance between 2 million pioneers and their 100,000 "hostile" red neighbors. The industrial energy that had flowed into the war now pushed rail lines across hunting grounds. Some 25,000 soldiers were sent west to meet the ever-more-insistent demands for protection coming from the stockmen and miners spread out between the Staked Plain and the lands watered by the Powder, Bighorn, and Yellowstone rivers.

Those Indian fighters have at last been knocked out of the gallery of heroes created by western novels and movies. A granite mountain outside of Custer, South Dakota, is being sculpted in the shape of Chief Crazy Horse. The decanonization of the Army's Indian fighters is a good thing, but not if critics are so self-righteous as to think they have nothing to learn. Recapturing the Indian's side of the winning of the West does not mean that the white Americans' story is a simple tale of greed and brutality and not worth recounting. On the contrary, the story of the officer corps in the final Indian wars is complex, and impassioned with accusations which the Army still makes against the civilians who send it to fight.

It was ironic that the men who had shed blood to keep their own society together now were ordered to dismember the culture of native

Americans. The officer corps did not relish its double assignment of pushing Indians back from lands claimed by whites and, for good measure, "redeeming" native Americans from "barbarism"—for Christian civilization. The letter books and official reports that these men kept so meticulously (in the boredom of the isolated outpost, record keeping was a cultivated art) are a continual lament: civilian officials and opinion-makers, it was said, only cut budgets and gave contradictory directions. The rules of war demanded restraint and a fine regard for the enemy's rights, but the same civilians who laid down those rules wanted quick victory on the battlefield. The Federal government itself broke treaties that promised the Indians land, yet expected the Army to keep the peace through mutual trust. At the same time that Western settlers clamored for protection, their land grabs provoked Indian retaliation.

From the East came word that as the frontier moved west, the Indian would simply "vanish" and that, in the meantime, "this copper-colored sphinx . . . when broken down by the military power of the whites . . . becomes the most commonplace person imaginable." The Army had to fight an enemy which did not expect extinction and was not pliant. "Friends" of the Indian—those who talked of a "conquest by kindness"—were a special annoyance. Eastern philanthropists such as Edward A. Lawrence damned the officers when blood was shed—and were among those who chillingly approved the "swift retribution" meted out to General Custer by the Sioux. Not incidentally, Army officers endured the torture of the annual congressional debate over how much their pay should be cut, and seethed as frontier bankers charged 12 to 40 per cent to convert their government paper into specie. Frontier forts rarely had the long, timbered stockades beloved by Hollywood set designers—but we sense that officers longed for a massive wall, high enough to repel civilians as well as Indians. [1]

By 1870, General William Tecumseh Sherman doubted his men could fight with honor on the plains. The American in blue who stood between white and red "gets the cuffs from both sides." But Sherman might have been envied by General Philip Sheridan, who mused upon a shattered reputation as he watched whole frontier towns turn out to hang him in effigy.

To officers so provoked, action seemed the thing to sweep away the complications of the Indian problem: to strike at the red man again and again seemed not only the quickest way to dry up civilian complaints, but the just way to punish an incomprehensibly wild enemy. General Sheridan pleaded with Sherman for the authority to act upon the appalling reports that crossed his desk each week:

> Since 1862 at least 800 men, women, and children have been murdered within the limits of my present command, in the most fiendish manner; the men usually scalped and mutilated, their [he omits the word] cut off and placed in their mouth; women ravished sometimes fifty and sixty times in succession, then killed and scalped, sticks stuck in their persons, before and after death.

Sheridan said it was now a question of who was to remain alive in his district, red or white. As for himself: "I have made my choice." It was, in fact, Sheridan who announced the epitaph of the red man: "The only good Indians I ever saw were dead." [2]

General Sherman appreciated his friend's feelings because he had come to about the same view. The most extravagant threats of "exterminating" the Indian mark much of Sherman's discussion of the West under his command. Both of those old soldiers proposed that native culture be obliterated . . . the red man himself, his wife, and his children, they suggested, were just as expendable. Each was inclined to weigh, quite literally, the destruction of Indian civilization against the material achievements of the frontier—the things that can "be counted, taxed and governed by the laws of nature and civilization." Each often claimed to have made his choice. [3]

That choice, made in passion, proved extraordinarily difficult to carry out. For the Indian fighters were troubled by various kinds of respect for their enemy. In the first place, no commander in the West could conceal his admiration for the red man's fighting skill. "Experience of late years," reported one commander to his colleagues, "has most conclusively shown that our cavalry cannot cope with the Indian man for man." Though these seasoned veterans and heroes reported a very favorable official casualty ratio, in their more candid moments they admitted that Indian fighting was the most difficult combat American soldiers had ever faced. It followed that so high an estimate of the enemy's tenacity undermined the Army's pride in its own competence. Sheridan berated the inefficiency that made campaigns in the West "a series of forlorn hopes," and Sherman wrote in so many words to the Secretary of War what had haunted his fellow officers: ". . . it seems to be impossible to force Indians to fight at a disadvantage in their own country. Their sagacity and skill surpass that of the white race." Victory against such valiant opponents was also bittersweet: both Sheridan and Sherman confessed to pity and compassion for the native Americans they had set out to destroy. As Sheridan wrote:

> We took away their country and their means of support, broke up their mode of living, their habits of life, introduced disease and decay among them and it was for this and against this they made war. Could anyone expect less? [4]

The tension between civilized and primitive society was felt most intensely by the field officers who served under Sheridan and Sherman. In the West, the Indian often seemed more than a worthy opponent: he cast doubt on the value of war for civilization itself. Empathizing with the red man while fighting him was an unsettling experience, and officers resolved it in very different ways. The Army's apologia for its enemy has to be interpreted carefully—but it can tell us much about the military's attitude to the society it was fighting to protect. And these observations on Indians presage the response of fighting men to their enemies in the first decades of the twentieth century.

Few officers escaped a sort of wistful appreciation of their primitive enemy in what they took to be his insatiable appetite for war—and not a few whites celebrated this unrestrained aggressiveness. Indeed, peaceful assimilation seemed not good enough for the Indians. A fight to the death seemed inevitable and strangely exciting to these

men . . . even to General Charles King, who had been hit by an
Apache bullet:

> Oh, what a stirring picture you make as once more I fix my glasses
> on you! Here, nearly four years after, my pulses bound as I recall the
> sight. Savage warfare was never more beautiful than in you. On you
> come, your swift, agile ponies springing down the winding ravine,
> the rising sun gleaming on your trailing war bonnets, on silver
> armlets, necklace, gorget; on brilliant painted shield and beaded leg-
> ging; on naked body and beardless face, stained most vivid ver-
> million.[5]

King's glorious, doomed Indians seem much like the red men of
twentieth-century popular culture, as indeed they should, since after
leaving the Army King wrote several dozen novels which helped es-
tablish the genre.

Similarly, one of Sheridan's favorite generals sought a large audience to explain the temptations of native American culture:

> To me Indian life, with its attendant ceremonies, mysteries, and
> forms, is a book of unceasing interest. Grant that some of its pages
> are frightful, and, if possible, to be avoided, yet the attraction is
> none the weaker. Study him, fight him, civilize him if you can, he
> remains still the object of your curiosity, a type of man peculiar and
> undefined, subjecting himself to no known law of civilization, con-
> tending determinedly against all efforts to win him from his chosen
> mode of life.
>
> If I were an Indian, I often think that I would greatly prefer to cast
> my lot among those of my people who adhered to the free open
> plains, rather than submit to the confined limits of a reservation,
> there to be the recipient of the blessed benefits of civilization, with
> its vices thrown in without stint or measure.

General George Custer met the object of his interest at the Little Big
Horn two years after his gratuitous advice was published.[6]

General Nelson A. Miles, one of the officers who chased the
Sioux after Custer's fall, had a personal reason for revenge: an Indian
had taken a point blank shot at him during an awkward moment in a

peace parley. But Miles's reflections show the remarkable extent to which these men transcended their anger with the enemy. The general spoke of the Indian's "courage, skill, sagacity, endurance, fortitude, and self-sacrifice of a high order," and of "the dignity, hospitality, and gentleness of his demeanor toward strangers and toward his fellow savages." Miles was inclined to think that lapses from this standard meant only that Indians had "degenerated through contact with the white man." Miles's colleagues found him to be an arrogant man, but he made few boasts when he wrote about Indians. Reflecting on the Custer debacle, he accepted Longfellow's contrite judgment ". . . that our broken faith / Wrought all this ruin and scathe." [7]

Miles was not an eccentric in the sympathies he expressed. The officer who came to bury his comrades at the Little Big Horn 48 hours after Custer's disaster had the same turn of mind. Colonel John Gibbon paid respect to the "strategic ideas" of the Sioux, and he seems to have been more angry at the "human ghouls" in the Army who had disturbed some Indian graves than at the warriors who had killed and mutilated his colleagues. The white man's desecrations, he thundered, "impress one with the conviction that in war barbarism stands upon a level only a little lower than our boasted modern civilization." By Gibbon's lights, the record of white hostility and treachery would force any man to fight: "Thus would the savage in us come to the surface under the oppression which we know the Indian suffers." Like so many Indian fighters who addressed the perennial "Indian question," Gibbon raised more questions about his own culture than he answered about his antagonists'. [8]

To many of the Indian fighters the courage and bearing of the red man suggested a purer way of life before the coming of white Americans, and the military frequently searched for Greek and Roman analogies to suggest the virtues of its enemies. Heathens though they were, they had nobility. Even the Indians' faults might be excused by their manifestly lower stage of cultural evolution.

General George Crook was in a good position to speak of the red men's virtues, for, as a fighting man, he resembled them. In the field he dispensed with the Army uniform and enjoyed the life of the nomad. Crook left one post, he tells us, "with one change of underclothes, toothbrush, etc., and went to investigate matters, intending to be gone a week. But I got interested after the Indians and did not return there again for over two years." In the harsh campaigns in the Southwest, Crook taught his men to move over the land like Apaches, and when white men failed him, he was adept in recruiting Indians for Army service. "He's more of an Indian than I am" marveled one Apache chief. Crook repaid such compliments. He extolled the classical bearing and demeanor of the men he hunted down, and when he went back to West Point to give a graduation address, he may have shocked many with this observation:

> With all his faults, and he has many, the American Indian is not half so black as he has been painted. He is cruel in war, treacherous at times, and not over cleanly. But so were our forefathers. His nature, however, is responsive to a treatment which assures him that it is based upon justice, truth, honesty, and common sense. . . .

Crook hesitated to condemn even the most ferocious Apaches, because he respected their spirit and had come to conclude that "we are too culpable, as a nation, for the existing condition of affairs." [9]

In a curious way, even the Army's darkest views of native Americans strengthened this expression of compassion and guilt. Colonel Richard I. Dodge, for example, balanced some benign allusions to hostile Indians as Greeks and "natural men" with a harsh critique of their culture. His enemy was bereft of any sense of law or right—"a barbarous, cruel, ignorant, shiftless race." Dodge's criticism was so thorough, however, that he was left with deep pity for his enemy. The "wild" Indian, Dodge argued, was not accountable for civilization's concept of "crime." Moral responsibility seemed to rest entirely with whites. Even "the killing of soldiers in battle," Dodge explained, "is not to be regarded as murder or outrage. It is simply the necessary adjunct to our pernicious system of Indian management." Dodge's critique of white responsibility became so vitriolic that he was left with few banners of civilization to carry. American violations of treaties were "more barbarous than anything . . . [the Indians] have done against the whites." The West had become a giant Andersonville for Indian captives—and every American citizen shared the guilt of the crime. Dodge could not see much difference between Indian torture and the evil of his own society: "Barbarism torments the body; civilization torments the soul." [10]

Some officers went further. Henry B. Carrington was one of the field officers who supplied General Sheridan with maddening accounts of Indian outrages. Carrington's official report of the 80 fallen soldiers under his command in the Fetterman incident of 1866 made grisly reading:

> Eyes torn out and laid on the rocks; teeth chopped out; joints of fingers cut off; brains taken out and placed on rocks, with members of the body; entrails taken out and exposed; hands and feet cut off; arms taken out from sockets; eyes, ears, mouth, and arms penetrated with spearheads, sticks, and arrows; punctures upon every sensitive part of the body, even to the soles of the feet and palms of the hand.

Carrington's own response to this carnage was not vengeful but reflective, even scholarly. A year later, Margaret Carrington, the Colonel's wife, published *Ab-sa-ra-ka*, a study of the land the Army had fought to control. In her book, Mrs. Carrington treated this act of war with impressive open-mindedness, never directly condemning it. She did note that "the noblest traits of the soldiers were touchingly developed as they carefully handled the mutilated fragments" from the battlefield—but she also praised the Indian: "In ambush and decoy, *splendid*." Close observers, she wrote, transcended anger to become reconciled, even sympathetic, to "the bold warrior in his great struggle."

Colonel Carrington brought out enlarged editions of *Ab-sa-ra-ka* in the 1870's, and he expanded on this theme of noble resistance. To him, the barbarities of the whites, in their "irresponsible speculative emigration," overshadowed the red "massacre." Carrington confessed, like Custer, "if I had been a red man as I was a white man, I should have fought as bitterly, if not as brutally, as the Indian fought." And standing before the American Association for the Advancement of Science in 1880 to read his official report of the Fetterman mutilations again, Carrington explained to the scientists how the Indian's disposition of enemies was intended to disable his foe in the afterlife, and so was quite understandable. Nor did he disparage the red man's values, but rather closed his address by suggesting some inadequacies on his own side: "From 1865 until the present time, there has not been a border campaign which did not have its impulse in the aggressions of a white man." [11]

Few men in the West raised more unusual questions about both cultures than did Captain John G. Bourke. He entered the campaigns, he wrote later, "with the sincere conviction that the only good Indian was a dead Indian, and that the only use to make of him was that of fertilizer." But the notebooks of this odd, inquiring soul soon reveal a man haunted by the details of the enemy's life. After mastering several Indian languages, Bourke produced an impressive series of monographs on native religious ceremonies, and in 1895 he became president of the American Folklore Society. Learning proved corrosive to his early cultural pride, and at the end of his Army service he was willing to admit that "the American aborigine is not indebted to his pale-faced brother, no matter what nation or race he may be, for lessons in tenderness and humanity."

Admittedly, Captain Bourke's appreciation of native culture was more complex than was the respect paid by other Indian fighters. Acknowledging the red man's fighting prowess and noble mien, he was more deeply interested in Indian snake ceremonies and scatological rites—mysteries thoroughly repulsive to most white sensibilities. Indeed, his interest in those ceremonies was as intense and sustained as were his protestations of "horror" during each "filthy" and "disgusting" rite. He put all this scholarship and, possibly, prurience to work in *Scatalogic* [sic] *Rites of All Nations*, where he observed such "orgies" throughout the development of western civilization, even surviving in nations of what he called "high enlightenment." Here was no sentimental accommodation with Indian culture but a panoramic reminder to the white race of its own barbaric past. Thus the Indians' vices, no less than their virtues, set up a mirror before the advancing whites. [12]

It did not, of course, deter them. However noble they may have painted the savage, all of those Indian fighters held to a fundamental conviction that the price of civilization was not too high. Aware as they were of the ambiguities of their mission, their sympathies and remorse never swayed them from their duty, and no officer of tender conscience was provoked to resign his commission.

How could such ambivalence be sustained? The military's apologia for the red man answered certain professional and psychological needs of the workaday Army. Some of these men, for both noble and ignoble reasons, wanted to take control of the Indian affairs that had been held by civilians—and at times the officers' good words for the long-suffering red man smoothed the way to that goal. Further, by praising the Plains Indians as relentless and efficient warriors, the military justified its own ruthless strategy—and setbacks. Those officers said little about the ritualistic quality of native American warfare. One learns almost nothing, for example, of the *coup* rituals that turned some combat into bloodless games of honor. Nor did the military emphasize that their enemy retired from the field during unsuitable weather and ceremonial periods. Most of all, these officers did not see the difficulties that the Plains Indians faced in turning the white man's cultural offerings into weapons to defend native interests. The horse and the rifle, for example, were startling innovations that no tribe had fully integrated. The Plains Indians—themselves sometimes first-generation immigrants from the East—struggled with a culture in some ways as unsettled as that of a white boom town. The Army preferred to emphasize the Indian's strength rather than show sympathy for his military weaknesses. [13]

Nor was the officers' study of Indians exactly disinterested; on the frontier close study of native Americans was nearly always linked with military advantage and cultural conquest. And while empathy for the enemy clearly made the assignment to "redeem" the Indian more painful, there were some emotional satisfactions to be derived from even the most generous cultural relativism.

In some instances an officer's respect for the primitives' unfettered aggressiveness unloosed his own. Thus General George Schofield, commander of the Department of the Missouri, could confess that "civilized man . . . never feels so happy as when he throws off a large part of his civilization and reverts to the life of a semi-savage." When Schofield acted on his own advice on a long hunting trip, he returned invigorated, writing that "I wanted no other occupation in life than to ward off the savage and kill off his food until there should no longer be an Indian frontier in our beautiful country." A similar ominous conclusion from relativistic premises was drawn by one of General Sherman's aides, who praised General Miles's sympathetic account of Indian culture, and the nobility of Indian religion in particular, and went on to say:

> There is no doubt the Indians have, at times, been shamefully treated. . . . And there is no doubt a man of spirit would rebel. . . . However, it is useless to moralize about the Indians. Their fate is fixed, and we are so near their end, it is easy to see what that fate is to be. That the Indian might be collected, and put out of misery by being shot deliberately, (as it would be done to a disabled animal), would seem shocking, but something could be said for such procedure.[14]

Such aggression, accompanied as it was by grief and guilt, is surprising only if we forget how central anger is to all three emotions. This most ambivalent response was born of the frustrations the Indian fighters endured in subduing the native cultures. The Indians' tactics seemed horrible, yet ingenious. Their culture was repellent, but also alluring for its integrity. At the same time, there is evident in the reports and memoirs of these officers a disturbing sense that they had been abandoned by their own unworthy civilization. If Army training and experience prevented the whites from acting on their anger, some of that anger was internalized and expressed in the mourning and guilt they exhibited so frequently. Their appreciation of the native Americans for what they had been was combined with a determination to punish a society for what it refused to become. Their fight for civilized settlement as it should be was troubled by their anger that some virtues, retained by the primitives, were slipping away from the white man.[15]

The pull between the civilized and the primitive is likewise evident in the white man's conflicting strategies to win the West. Many of the Army agreed with General Sherman that under certain conditions of battle the whites were inferior to the Indians "man for man." Organization and technology, then, might carry the day. Thus General Sherman in retrospect considered a machine—the railroad—the hero of the winning of the West. "In the great battle of civilization with barbarism," Sherman judged, the railroad deserved more credit than the men on the frontier, and accounted "fully for the peace and good order that now prevail throughout our country." General Custer also spoke more warmly of the railroad than of his enlisted men, and General Miles credited his victories to "superior intelligence and modern appliances." Miles relished one curious triumph over the Indians who had killed Custer: he allowed two groups of Sioux to talk to each other on the telephone. Here were "men who had been through the sun dance and taken an active part in the Custer massacre [yet] their hands shook visibly, their bodies trembled with emotion, and great drops of perspiration rolled down their bronzed bodies."[16]

But the military's celebration of technology was far from unanimous, and some military observers found the Indian's unorthodox warfare a positively admirable defiance of America's slavery to technology. The red enemy, Captain Bourke explained, "will not brook the restraints which, under our notions of discipline, change men into machines." The Carringtons, similarly, saw the Indian's fight as a warning: his "sense of freedom and independence brings such contrast with the machinery and formalities of much that is called civilized life." Even General Crook officially reported that war against the Apaches was stalled because the American soldier had become a "machine. . . . His individuality is completely lost in his organization." Bourke and Crook followed the logic of their criticism to its extreme, urging that "the civilized soldier must be trained down as nearly as possible to the level of the savage." [17]

If we appreciate the military's doubts—of its mandate, of its ability, of its justness—as well as of its commitments to civilization, to duty, and to progress, the tragedy of the West does not go away. It deepens. Was there an escape from the emotional trap in which the Army found itself? To refuse to win the West would have required a conversion to primitivism hard to imagine inside the Army and scarcely imaginable in ordinary men living ordinary lives outside it. But the cultural odyssey of one lieutenant in the Nez Percé war illustrates that such a transformation was possible.

Charles Erskine Scott Wood (1852–1944) served on General O. O. Howard's staff, and it was he who recorded the moving speeches of the defeated Chief Joseph. Wood's reflections on the Nez Percé campaigns, published in the early 1880's, struck the conventional balance between remorse and pride. Surveying the shameful record of white treaty violations, he warned his Army colleagues that retribution might follow. Yet necessity seemed to excuse bad faith: "forces" were "silently at work beyond all human control," against the red man's survival. True, Wood, a gifted literary man would eventually join the crowded celebration of the culture he had worked to destroy, writing of the Indians' vividness and nobility, qualities that seemed the more poignant because of their passing. But in all this, Wood declined to indict directly the civilization that had corrupted and supplanted the Indians, and he sounded much like General Custer.[18]

But Wood was, in time, to change greatly. He quit the Army, and entered the Columbia Law School. Now dissatisfied with the state of letters and the law in his time, Wood allied himself with the radical Industrial Workers of the World and searched for a literary form to express his increasingly anarchistic temperament. The fruit of this veteran's singular rehabilitation was a long experimental poem, *The Poet in the Desert* (1915 and 1918), an affecting personal renuncia-

Charles Erskine Scott Wood at West Point
(Photo courtesy of Katherine Caldwell)

tion of "civilization" and a call for the revolt of the masses against privilege. The "forces" now at work, anything but silent, seemed the roar of a machine-like civilization that drove men to war. Gripped by his vision, Wood recollected his part in the Indian campaigns and expressed his allegiance clearly:

> I have lain out with the brown man
> And know they are favored.
> Nature whispered to them her secrets,
> But passed me by.
>
> .     .     .
>
> I sprawled flat in the bunch-grass, a target
> For the just bullets of my brown brothers betrayed.
> I was a soldier, and, at command,
> Had gone out to kill and be killed.
>
> .     .     .
>
> We swept like fire over the smoke-browned tee-pees;
> Their conical tops peering above the willows.
> We frightened the air with crackle of rifles,
> Women's shrieks, children's screams,
> Shrill yells of savages;
> Curses of Christians.
> The rifles chuckled continually.
> A poor people who asked nothing but freedom,
> Butchered in the dark.[19]

Wood's polemic was more straightforward, I think, than many asserted today on behalf of the native Americans. He learned—and his colleagues in the Army demonstrated—that respect and compassion for another culture are unsure checks on violence. In this one case, the white man's enemy won the intellectual battle on the frontier.

European nations have long known the dangers of contagion by the enemy's faith. Statesmen trembled as the armies that stopped Napoleon contracted liberalism, just as they have more recently as the counterinsurgency troops in third-world lands have picked up the rebels' Marxism. America's frontier officers had put the Civil War behind them and were not ready to turn on their society to save the red man. We must remember also that the American Indians never sought to "redeem" the men in blue from civilization.

# 4

# IN SEARCH
# OF A WORTHY ENEMY

The officers' apologia for their first enemy after Appomattox did not flow simply from literary conventions, nor from opportunism. The soldiers had read little of James Fenimore Cooper (though Custer, when a student, had read him avidly). Still less did they pose as the red man's friend simply to curry favor in Washington. What the soldiers said publicly they said in private, and they spoke up for the Indian when they had no chance for gain. Empathy for the red man had appeared many times before the last battles for the frontier, but on this occasion it was spurred by the national mood of reconciliation after the Civil War.

The last Indian campaigns began a half-century search to find an enemy as worthy as the noble antagonists in the legend of the Civil War. The opponent had to be formidable, so that the blood shed to defeat him would be justified and victory sweet; he had to be committed to a defense of his culture, so that fighting men might prove their faith in their own; and, finally, he had to be forgiving, so that the antagonists could be reconciled when arms were laid down. But the red man failed to validate the war on the frontier in those ways. The white man, from the first, had held too many advantages; and in the end, the Indians were not encouraged to forgive. No picture of the Civil War is as sobering as the scene of the frozen corpses

of native Americans of both sexes and all ages in the pasture at
Wounded Knee. Indefatigable in their admiration of their victims,
the Army pressed a massive plan for Indian recruitment in the early
1890's; however, the Indians on the reservations had little enthusiasm for a life in Army blue.[1]

Union Soldiers Sharing Their Rations with the Confederates
(*Battles and Leaders of the Civil War*, 1887)

The search for a worthy enemy continued among many soldiers.
The concept of the enemy as a despised, threatening force—so often
the notion of civilians—was rejected by many fighting men as they
struggled to find an adversary worthy of their own self-affirmation. If
the search was not inevitable for American warriors, it was, as the
most articulate soldiers tell us, compelling. Our poets of combat,
such as Stephen Crane, recognized the small room left for hatred between enemies in modern battles, but it was Friedrich Nietzsche who
most sharply defined that evanescent enemy who can be glimpsed in
the hasty letters home and the long-winded memoirs of the men who
fought:

How much reverence has a noble man for his enemies!—and such reverence is a bridge to love.—For he desired his enemy for himself, as his mark of distinction; he can endure no other enemy than one in whom there is nothing to despise and *very much* to honor! [2]

Albion Tourgée left a record of the desperate lengths a veteran might go to find this enemy. Tourgée's wounds from the war had no sooner healed than he joined in a tumultuous battle against the Ku Klux Klan in North Carolina. The old soldier stood in awe of the Klan. During Reconstruction he carried no grievances against the men of the defeated Confederacy, and he even came to praise his tormentors in nightshirts—the Klansmen who threatened his life.

The war for the Union had differed "from all other conflicts based upon divergence of belief, in this one element—its force was directed solely against the *idea* which it opposed, and not at all against the individuals by whom the idea was upheld." Tourgée recalled that "before we first entered into battle our souls had been shrived clean of hate." So too, when crushed by the Klan, Tourgée claimed to be free of *ressentiment*. His "unbounded admiration" for his enemy's "warlike instincts and regal pride" may make us believe that one of Nietzsche's noble men has returned from the Greek myths carrying a carpetbag. [3] Tourgée's call for a campaign against rednecks and Bourbons to defend the black man's rights went unheeded, of course.

Americans next took the measure of enemies as the nation sought to "liberate" the Cubans and Filipinos. But while America's first campaigns after Appomattox, fought for the Indians' domain, was tragedy; the second war, fought for remnants of the Spanish Empire, was farce. So, at least, was the impression of many contemporaries. Both the hawks and the doves of 1898 conceded that words such as "battle" had to be used in quotes in that war. It is the satires of the Spanish-American War that have endured—William Graham Sumner's "Conquest of the United States by Spain," Mark Twain's "Defense of General Funston," and the barroom analysis of Finley Peter Dunne's Mr. Dooley. In the eyes of Mr. Dooley, the heroes of the war were seedy, at best:

"If the'se wan thing I'm prouder iv thin another in me past life," said Mr. Dooley, " 'tis that whin me counthry called me to go to th' Spanish war, I was out. . . . Be hivins, Hinnissy, if a man's brought up befure a judge on a charge iv larceny, th' coort says: 'Any prevyous convictions?' 'No,' says th' polisman. 'Five years,' says th' judge. 'But he was a hayro iv th' Cubian war.' 'Make it life,' says th' judge." [4]

Caught up amidst the backbiting of their colleagues and recriminations of civilian dissenters, the men in uniform did not fare well. "The American people are so strangely indifferent to the genuine heroism" the New York *World* complained in 1899. The only soldier to win permanent glory at home was Theodore Roosevelt (and John J. Pershing privately attributed Roosevelt's fame to his gift for self-promotion). Pershing won great advancement in the war, but was besmirched by a whispering campaign that he had engaged in sexual misconduct on Mindanao.[5] Admiral Dewey's fall was precipitous. Touted for the presidency as he made his slow return from the South Pacific, Dewey's warm welcome soon soured. He was denounced as a simpleton almost as soon as he began to discuss public issues, and accused of financial sleight of hand with the home in Washington given to him by the welcoming committee. The "Dewey Arch," jerry-built for his arrival in Manhattan, sagged and was hauled away after the city lost interest.

The jests and apathy of the public were disheartening. Americans who were proud of the war found that kind words for the Spaniard helped preserve the dignity of the men who had captured Cuba and the Philippines. The professional military led the retreat from the passions of 1898. Naval officers had spent much of their careers pleasantly steaming into Spanish ports to make courtly visits. Even after the sinking of the *Maine*, these sailors felt no hatred toward the well-dressed Spanish officers who had made such a fine impression on American quarterdecks.

"Don't cheer, men; those poor fellows are dying," an American captain had cautioned as he looked at the decks of the doomed *Viz-*

*caya*, and the sentiment was quickly repeated and applauded throughout the Navy.

The day after the battle of Santiago was the Fourth of July, but officers on the *Iowa* toned down their celebration so as not to offend the sensibilities of their prisoners.

In Cuba, the Army had begun to fraternize with their prisoners soon after the ceasefire, praising their enemies for their determined and gallant fight to protect the island. *The Official Dewey Souvenir Programme* gave space to illustrate "the valor of the Spaniards," and Spanish testimonies of Yankee courage were widely reprinted in the American press. Even the popular press, which had treated Spaniards as swarthy butchers in the spring of 1898, repented by the end of that year. In this spirit, there was little opposition to the government's remarkable plan to smooth the way to peace: a clause was inserted in the treaty praising the bravery of Spanish (but not American) soldiers, and Washington paid over a half-million dollars to send the enemy to Spain.[6]

As sincere and forgiving as the Spaniards may have been, the troops who sailed home in this armada could not plausibly be called a formidable enemy. This was a campaign of a few weeks in which Americans took more casualties from camp sewage than from Mausers; the Navy lost but one man—and no ships—in the battles of Manila Bay and Santiago. Gentlemanly gestures to Spain could not hide the fact that she was not a worthy enemy who could confirm the value of the war. And, ultimately, the enfeebled enemy cast all of American actions of 1898 in an *opéra bouffe*. In Manila, Captain T. Bentley Mott felt uneasy as he watched American officers seize the governor-general's palace, "smoking their cigars with a comfortable air of proprietorship in these lofty rooms of viceroyalty." Above the smoke were the stern portraits of Spain's rulers and adventurers in the *siglo de oro,* and Captain Mott mused—he almost dared wish—that if those bold warriors in casques had stood before Manila that day, "there would have been more American soldiers left dead upon the fields of Malate." [7]

Anti-imperialists were not as magnanimous toward Spain as the Americans in uniform were. Critics of the war spoke up for the new enemy, the Filipinos, and made the Army's victories on their islands seem hollow. American dissenters pointed out that the rebels did not always have guns, and that the Army killed so many more natives than it wounded it was clear there was no fair fight. If there was any doubt about the moral character of the war, the anti-imperialists published the soldiers' own words from letters and dispatches to show their frenzied attacks on "niggers," using measures like the "water cure" to turn the land into a "howling wilderness." [8]

This was the reverse side of the conception of the enemy as comrade: to reduce him to an abstract, opposing force that must be crushed. William James, noting the more elevated language of the architects of the war in Washington, saw how the enemy had become a blur in these campaigns against guerrillas and he feared the violence that might be turned against them:

> The Filipinos have not existed as psychological quantities at all. . . . We have treated [them] as if they were a painted picture, an amount of matter in our way. They are too remote from us even to be realized as they exist in their inwardness. [9]

Theodore Roosevelt showed how rage could take command when the enemy failed to make himself understandable. Roosevelt did not always thirst for his enemy's blood—certainly not that of the Spaniards who had shot at him in Cuba, for they had won his respect as "brave foes, worthy of honor for their gallantry." But as native rebels turned against the American liberators, Roosevelt abandoned chivalric measures. The "bandetti and marauders," utterly "treacherous and cruel," were to be met with their own methods; the President condoned scorched earth campaigns and torture inflicted by the "hot-blooded and powerful young men" in the American Army. Roosevelt would not listen to the charges that the "severity" of the Army was a discredit to the service, yet the President conceded there had been "mild torture," and that "not a few of the enlisted men" had found it necessary in order to press the campaign. Clearly,

Roosevelt was uncomfortable in excusing torture—and often denied that it was his intention—but his language was reckless: "the Army should understand that I thoroughly believe in severe methods when necessary, and am not in the least sensitive about killing any number of men if there is adequate reason." [10]

What is striking about the campaigns in the Philippines is how impervious many officers remained to such incitements to violence; they could not view their enemy as a simple target for their rage. The Army hardly needed Roosevelt's encouragement to strike out at the rebels, the frustrations of pacification were goad enough. The rebels were a bewildering threat for they had been allies and they were expected to become wards; but in the meantime they met the invasion forces, at turns, as genial hosts and formidable resistance fighters. "The presidentes and town officials acted openly in behalf of the Americans and secretly in behalf of the insurgents," General Arthur MacArthur marveled in one report from the field, "and, paradoxical as it may seem, with considerable apparent solicitude for the interests of both." [11] In the final campaigns against the Moros, the Moslem *juramentado* who might interrupt a peaceful stroll to kill all the white Christians at hand epitomized the mercurial force the officers were ordered to crush.

As in the American West, the brutal facts of conquest and pacification did not rule out complex attitudes toward the enemy. Far from denying the enemy's "inwardness," the officers were often students, and sometimes connoisseurs, of the culture of the islands. As Dewey's fleet anchored off of Manila, volumes of the *Encyclopedia Britannica* were passed around so that the sailors could read the most recent scholarship on the native cultures. Throughout the initial, friendly contacts on shore as well as during the long and bitter occupation, officers of the Navy and Army sought out the Filipinos to observe their markets, sports, and ceremonies, and today the papers of those officers contain material enough for a travelogue. An invitation to kneel by the Koran on Mindanao seems to have been as eagerly sought as the privilege of attending a snake ceremony in Arizona. Here, John J. Pershing was not the icy presence known to a later generation of doughboys. In the Philippines he solemnly chewed the betel nut, placed his hand on the Koran, and thankfully accepted the religious office of *datto* in a Moro tribe.[12]

Often, the more desperately the rebels fought the more respect American officers paid them. John R. White came away from his long campaigns through Negros with none of Roosevelt's rage: "we felt, after we had chased an outlaw chief for a few months through the jungle, a spirit of not unfriendly competition." Beguiled by the haughty and determined Moros, Robert L. Bullard saluted their "superior bravery," discounted their reputation for thievery and lying, and predicted that they would do well for themselves in the free market he hoped to see under the Stars and Stripes. Considering what fond recollections Americans had for the Apaches, it is not surprising that in the officers' diaries and memoirs we often find warm words for the Moros, the Army's most intransigent enemy on the islands.[13]

The sympathies of the officers in the Pacific were not always clear-cut, however. Henry W. Lawton was the Major General of United States Volunteers; he arrived in the islands in the spring of 1899. But he had great doubts about the justice of pacification. He told a member of the Philippine Commission that the war was "unholy." [14]

Frederick Funston, the general whom Twain scorned for his treacherous capture of Aguinaldo, also illustrates the cross-currents of allegiance in the war. In 1896 Funston had been so moved by the Cuban cause that he left America and fought with the *insurrectos*. He was recuperating from the jungle campaign at his home in Kansas when the *Maine* sank, and Funston then volunteered to drive the Spaniards out of the Philippines. It was his guerrilla techniques, now turned against the Filipino rebels, that enraged Twain. Funston, however, did not sever his emotional ties to the *insurrectos*. He kept up his friendships with the Cuban rebels and never seems to have hated the Filipinos who fought him so desperately: he called the rebel who fired a Krag into his face a "plucky fellow" and in speaking of his prize catch, he said, "It was well known to all of us that Aguinaldo was a man of human instincts. . . ." Funston explained in his memoirs, "he is a man of many excellent qualities, far and away the best Filipino I ever was brought in contact with." [15]

General Arthur MacArthur always viewed the Filipino's plea for independence from the United States more sympathetically than the civilian administrators did. To the horror of Governor William Howard Taft, the general welcomed the captured Aguinaldo to the Malcaña Palace and pardoned the rebel. Not surprisingly, some officers resented "fighting a weak race whose only crime was a badly timed desire for freedom," and saw a tragic estrangement between "two brave and earnest peoples." [16]

Pershing referred to the natives as the "so called enemies" because they had started the war as allies against Spain and Pershing thought they would end the campaign as his friends, convinced of the American benevolence. John M. Gates, who has made the most thorough study of the Army in the Philippines, has concluded that Pershing's fellow officers were "progressives in uniform" who pursued uplift above either their own glory . . . or the natives' blood. Most officers would not tolerate military measures out of keeping with their view of themselves as cultural stewards of the Filipinos. In fact, Nelson A. Miles, the Commanding General of the Army, attacked *civilians* for allowing soldiers to go unpunished for "marked severities" in conducting the war. Barbarities such as the water cure were practiced by a minority of officers out of their anger that the rebels (in an unholy alliance with American anti-imperialists, it seemed) refused to accept the Army's plan for redemption. After the Filipinos' will to fight had been broken the Army in the Pacific closed ranks and reasserted the testimony of love for the Filipino and benevolent plans for his future. The officers at last had struck down an enemy they could not understand with a force they were reluctant to justify. [17]

In that world of professionals—a world in which irony was dead—the insurgents in the jungle were embraced as warmly as the Indians of the Plains had been. The Acting Military Governor of the Philippines in 1901 had fought the Sioux, the Cheyenne, the Arapahoe, and the Nez Percé, and he hoped that cordiality would continue to be part of American war-making: "let us so work that the more enlightened Filipino may, as did the savage Indian, look upon the army as an honorable and generous adversary when forced into war, and one always ready to be a staunch friend." [18]

It was a member of MacArthur's staff who finally summed up the officers' case on the conquest of the Philippines. With passion—and a thoroughness bordering on pedantry—James H. Blount used the testimony of the Army and Navy of 1898 to make a brief for Philippine independence. Blount, in 400 pages, showed how wise his fellow officers had been to recognize that the Filipino had the character for self-government. *The American Occupation of the Philippines: 1898–1912* (1912) appeared after the anti-imperialist protest had played out; the officers stood, nearly alone, supporting the cause of their old enemy.

\*      \*      \*

There were only brief encounters with enemies in the decade and a half after the pacification of the Philippines. The interventions in China, the Caribbean, and Mexico were hasty and, for the soldiers, bewildering adventures that did not enable Americans to take the measure of their foe.

Then, at last, in the European War, American soldiers found a worthy enemy in Germany: formidable, sincere and forgiving. The abstraction of the German into a contemptible "Hun" occurred largely on the home front. Many of the American volunteers who flocked to British and France before 1917, as well as the airmen and doughboys who came across in the regular service, tell a different story.

A spirit of revenge was rare among Americans at the front. Often their diaries reveal a laconic and detached mood (one might be reading Ernest Hemingway). One such American was the first to capture a German after the United States entered the war. James W. Harle, Jr., an ambulance driver, began to care for the men hit by German shells in the spring of 1915. A few weeks before President Wilson declared war, Harle's *chef* and two other comrades were killed by a

German bombing plane. On April 22, 1917 Harle was on *poste* duty and saw the enemy aviators come out of the sky. Harle wrote in his diary:

> I got behind a small stump for protection. On he came, striking the ground not a hundred feet away from me.
>
> The ground was rough, and his wheels getting into a ditch threw the plane forward, the propeller striking the earth and causing the plane to turn completely over on its back, throwing out the two aviators as if they were giant frogs. I walked toward the overturned plane, meeting the pilot coming toward me; whereupon I announced that they were my prisoners. He replied in better French than mine that he was well aware of the fact, his motor forcing it upon them. I took his picture with his flying-togs on, just as he landed. . . . The pilot told me he had dropped his last two bombs in the lake when he found that he would have to land. These he, no doubt, was saving to drop on us, as was his custom each day. Presently I could hear the French soldiers coming on the run, and I expected to see them carry out their oft-repeated threats as to what they would do if ever a German machine came down there; but nothing of the kind happened, for they seemed interested to hear what we were talking about. This was probably the man who had killed [the *chef*] and two others. In the end, they were marched off to Headquarters.[19]

American aviators adopted a chivalric code that made harsh comments about Germans unseemly. Members of the Lafayette Escadrille frankly admired the professional skill and courtesy of the rival airmen, and these Americans could not easily work up hatred for the culture that produced these "enemy gentlemen." In the midst of a campaign by civilians to suppress German music and literature in America, a leader of the Lafayette Escadrille wrote a public letter from the front denouncing the censorship and defending German culture. Restraint and accommodation were the lessons these fighting men learned in the air. "We could blow the Boche aerodromes to atoms and they could probably do as much for us," an American flyer remarked, "but neither side has started this useless 'strafing.' . . . it only harasses vainly men who need what sleep they get."

Eddie Rickenbacker concluded that it was wrong to shoot back at an attacking Fokker should the German have engine trouble and so be too easy a victim. Indeed, one airman felt that all the revenge in this war belonged to civilians, safe behind the lines. He resigned himself to killing Germans as surrogates for the world's statesmen and editors, whom he longed to see spend some time in the trenches.[20]

In fact, civilians were constantly visiting the trenches to counsel the doughboys and to report home on the progress of the crusade. The visitors were startled to learn that soldiers respected the skill of their adversary across the barbed wire and that denunciations of some German methods were balanced by admiration for Teutonic efficiency. One chaplain claimed that combat soldiers only reluctantly used the word "Hun."[21]

Robert W. Service, in his *Rhymes of a Red Cross Man* (1916), made the most persuasive case for reconciliation with the armed enemy. The Canadian's verse was a best seller in America before the declaration of war, and many doughboys carried memories of his inspirational volume into battle. Service played on the soldier's expectation that he had been sent to kill "only a Boche" and showed fighting men trying to be gleeful or indifferent as they watched their enemy bleed. Neither the farmers off the prairies nor the cockneys from the East End could live with revenge. The wounded Germans in this poetry invariably carry precious charms—lockets, rings, crucifixes—that, when discovered, touch the Anglo-Saxon heart and bring on the revelation: "I guess they're mostly decent, just the same as most of us." The uncorrupted English boys looked forward to a peace where they would embrace the "Un" and while they fought they had but two choices—to be sick with guilt or to try to spare German lives.[22]

But American respect for the enemy did not depend upon talk about fair play and knightly behavior. Some soldiers found the fabled discipline of their enemy admirable—even a model for Americans. Young George Patton spent as much time praising the iron will of Germany as he did commending the Allies. "Germany has the only true idea. . . . To Hell with the people!" he declared as he prepared for war. When Patton's men killed German machine gunners who refused to yield their position by driving a tank over them he praised the doughboys, but then sent them back on the field to set up a monument to the stubborn enemy.

German "ruthlessness" could also be attractive. One doughboy who had fought sleep during a lecture on the Allies' idealism wrote home that his generation had a different fighting faith:

> We shall fight as desperately as the Frenchman . . . but we shall fight differently. There will not be any emotion mixed up in it. We shall be a better match for the Germans to contend with, because we are more like them temperamentally. We shall be cruelly efficient. We'll have no men weeping over ruined Cathedrals. . . . We shall count the days until we can get back to Paris and the cabarets . . . but we shall be good fighters, with scientific methods and American ingenuity without emotion; and we shall be the kind of fighters that Germany needs, her own kind. . . .[23]

Indeed, American soldiers sometimes showed the enemy an ominous cordiality. Just as sympathy for native Americans and Filipinos had been perfectly compatible with bloody "pacification," the vision of the Germans as brothers did not conflict with bayoneting them. Sometimes affection for the enemy was part of a chilling call for his blood. American clerics reminded the doughboy that he could, in good Christian conscience, love the sinner while hating and punishing his sins. Such ministers advised the fighting man to divide his time at the front between kindly thoughts and violent acts: "The Christian soldier in friendship wounds the enemy. In friendship he kills the enemy." The bloodstained warrior of the American Expeditionary Force was never to forget that, in the end, the fellowship with Germans would be renewed:

> We must help in the bayoneting of a normally decent German soldier in order to free him from a tyranny which he at present accepts as his chosen form of government. . . . We must aid in the starvation and emaciation of a German baby in order that he, or at least his more sturdy little playmate, may grow up to inherit a different sort of government from that for which his father died.[24]

No one can measure how often doughboys shed German blood to save Germany, but the great majority of the soldiers' own narratives were not hymns of hate. The doughboys confirmed what a guide book told them in 1917: "the actual Germans in the trenches opposite will not inspire you with many angry feelings." There are, in the earliest testimonies from the Western Front, some extraordinary assertions of comraderie across the lines. "I never took arms out of hatred against Germany or the Germans," Alan Seeger wrote from a French bunker, ". . . the German contribution to civilization is too large, the German ideals too generally in accord with my own to join in the chorus of hate against a people who I frankly admire." Seeger even sent to a New York paper a commendation of a German "*coup d'audace*" that took the life of a corporal in his regiment. "Our men are not coming back hating Germans," a hero from the AEF assured a mass meeting at the 69th Regiment Armory in New York, "No man who has been in the line facing the Germans will bear any malice toward them. I know that if any American infantryman met the Kaiser on the road he would be willing to share his hardtack with him." [25] Certainly not every doughboy felt so, but the American soldier faced his enemy with so much equanimity that by 1918 his commanders worried about fraternization across the lines. And after the armistice, during the occupation, the Army published nearly unanimous praise for their worthy enemy.

There was irony here as well as compassion. The formidable, sincere, and forgiving German was, psychologically, the most satisfying enemy since Appomattox. Yet it was now much harder for the American to use the enemy for self-affirmation. In earlier wars the government had not often bothered about the opinions of the men it had sent to fight; now mail was censored, soldier publications were scrutinized, and officers with troublesome political views were kept at home. The public's appetite for information about exotic enemies was dulled by the patriotic regimen of Teutonic sins. This sort of war—one in which ideas were watched as closely as the stock of shells—became the model for the twentieth century. The inquiring souls in the AEF were at peace with Germans, but they were anachronisms.

One doughboy was so shocked by the mean spirit of the French in their victory that he was moved to assure his family that he had not forgotten the reconciliation preached by Walt Whitman:

> . . . my enemy is dead, a man as divine
> as myself is dead,
> I look where he lies white-faced and
>         still in the coffin—I drew near,
>
> Bend down and touch lightly with my
>         lips the white face in the
>         coffin.[26]

# III

# THE
# ILLUSIVE
# ARSENAL

*America's weapons were as hard to judge as the nation's enemies. An impassioned investigation of the morality of new weapons finally reached two encouraging conclusions. The threat of a holocaust on the modern battlefield was dismissed, and few doubted that the arsenal was benign. The dehumanizing effect of this technology seemed to be a myth, and it appeared, instead, that the arsenal liberated fighting men.*

# 5

# KEEPERS
# OF THE PEACE

Deep satisfaction, even joy in the destructive power of new weapons, has long been commonplace in America. Benjamin Franklin speculated on the positive moral effect of invading airships; Thomas Jefferson believed in the peace-keeping force of new torpedoes; William L. Thornton, another man of patriotism and ingenuity, rejoiced in the prospect of bringing glass-filled grenades and rapid-fire guns to aid French republicans. [1] Robert Fulton was early America's most articulate proponent of a destructive machine to ensure liberty—the submarine *Nautilus*. Fulton's visionary plans, like those of his predecessor David Bushnell, were encouraged by prominent statesmen of the Republic. In 1798 the *Nautilus* was offered to the French to destroy the British Navy's "engines of oppression," but the Directory was skeptical of Fulton's claims and troubled by the morality of a weapon which seemed fit only for "Algerians and pirates." Fulton, spurned, pressed his claims that the liberty-loving people of France and America could find salvation by using his submarine:

> If, at first glance, the means I propose seem revolting, it is only because they are extraordinary; they are anything but inhuman. It is certainly the gentlest and least bloody method that the philosopher can imagine to overturn this system of brigandage and of perpetual war which has always vexed maritime nations; to give at last peace to

the earth, and to restore men to their natural industries, and to a happiness until now unknown.[2]

This millennial dream beckoned to Americans in the nineteenth century as they watched government arsenals produce weapons that surpassed Fulton's imagination. Statesmen and soldiers, munitions makers and peace workers, saw the steel guns that could spray the battlefields with bullets and the long-range cannons that could fire giant shells over the horizon—and they pronounced that ordnance benign. Here I shall look at the Americans' optimism; later I shall take up their rarer but persistent fears about technology in modern war.

Before the Civil War several arguments had been marshaled to show that invention might defeat war itself. Peacetime invention seemed to discourage the impetus to fight. The most spectacular achievements—the railroad and telegraph—promised unity. Many thought that even if peace could not be derived indirectly from inventions, the direct application of science to the battlefield would banish war. As weapons promised more destruction, the urge to use them would diminish. Francis Wayland's textbook of political economy, for example, assured a generation of college students that the new power of ordnance was one of the glories of the age: "The destruction of human life, in this manner, excites less sensibly the ferocity of the human heart. Besides, the more energetic are the means of destruction in war, the less is the loss of life in battle."[3] Here was the faith in the rational, utilitarian deliberation of government and the decisive effectiveness of technology. The antebellum weapons prophets could not imagine the muddled statecraft and stalemated battles of the future.

The extended agony of the Civil War exploded the assumptions of the prophets, but not their self-assurance nor their prestige. Railroads, new guns, airships, mines, and ironclads simply did not prevent or mitigate the years of bloodletting, but American faith in technology endured. Lincoln, himself a patent holder, allowed his office to become a sounding board for the fervid imagination of inventors. Unsolicited letters from crankish mechanics received serious study in the White House. Lincoln frequently gathered his Cabinet together for a "champagne experiment" to test the newest weapons.[4] The South was as hospitable to arms makers as the North. Indeed, Confederate expertise in mine and submarine warfare became the most advanced in the world. Just as Lincoln countenanced morally questionable innovations such as expanding bullets, Jefferson Davis embraced the "infernal machines" of the seas.[5]

The American arsenal was not built by men unmoved by the crape worn by the families of so many of the Blue and Gray; lured by the promise of a decisive weapon, the celebrants of technology thought they were stopping the slaughter. For example, in 1862 Richard J. Gatling lived near the Union terminal in Indianapolis, and he frequently saw the somber farewells between soldiers and their families. Later Gatling met the express trains that brought coffins back to the mothers and wives. He pressed questions on the groups of mourners and found that only a few of the soldiers had died from bullets and that disease was the scourge of war. The inventor immediately saw a way to save the men: "The thought occurred to me that if I could get up a gun with which one man could do the work of a hundred, that it would to a great extent supercede [*sic*] the necessity of large armies." [6]

Though few Americans had personal experience with the efficiency of Gatling's machine gun, time and again they made three points in their discussions of war in the half-century after Appomattox: technology would shorten wars; modern weapons would ensure less bloodshed (even if destruction were increased at certain brief moments); and, finally, the new armed force would discourage belligerence and so strengthen the peace. Virtually no one considered the possibility that war with improved weapons would be longer, bloodier, or less clearly resolved. And it was this optimistic view that guided the American program to keep the peace.

\*     \*     \*

For the peace movement, science—through marvelous inventions—provided signs that moral reform was underway: "Even as the world's work shall yet be done by implements more delicate in design and more efficient in operation, so shall the world's differences be adjusted by the calm deliberation of a judicial body." Science, in this discourse, supplied the devices the peace movement had always wanted: "international consciousness," the "pacific power of touch," and "the mechanics of public opinion." [7] Peace groups borrowed the metaphors of the engineer because they saw him as an ally. In 1893 at the World's Columbian Exposition, for example, the peace movement avoided the baroque style of the white city and used an engineer's functional design to symbolize their dream. A massive "peace plow" was forged to signal the end of war and a whole collection of peace instruments was planned as a lasting monument. Unfortunately, visitors to the Exposition found that the peace display was overshadowed by the more massive (though equally functional) shapes exported by Krupp's arms works. [8]

Munitions had troubled the peace movement for a long time—for were they not also a fruit of the scientific approach? A sentimental renunciation of weapons was always attractive. Peace workers, for example, had welcomed Longfellow's popular verse "The Arsenal at Springfield" in the 1870's. He had written that the "brazen portals" of the arsenal rang with the "endless groan" of war, jarring even the "celestial harmonies" and reminding man of the sacredness of peace. [9] Yet no one in the American peace movement in the late nineteenth century made serious proposals to tear down arsenals and sell off the guns as scrap. And, at the same time, many in the movement began to hope that Longfellow's dark view of modern ordnance ignored its brighter side.

Decisiveness and deterrence were the watchwords of this accommodation with modern weapons. Peace societies frequently applauded the latest arrivals from the arsenals:

> Breech-loading and revolving guns, rifles with telescopic attachments, giving wonderful accuracy and great range, with fearful multiplication of deadly missiles—all these tend to make the battles of the present day short and decisive, and to diminish their comparative mortality. And surely this would seem to be only reasonable, in as much as the greater the capacity of destruction of contending ar-

mies, the less will they be disposed to go to the extreme limit of loss to be suffered or inflicted. [10]

The peace literature of the 1880's and 1890's is filled with observations of the "auspicious omens," "an element of assurance," and a "guarantee" that modern ordnance meant peace. [11] "When the arts of destruction have won their final victory," Josiah Quincy announced, "the wars which call them into activity must of necessity cease."

Despair over the new weapons did not disappear from the peace journals, but the optimists won all the arguments. Peace workers expressed more delight than fear about the American Navy in the 1890's: who could say that the impressive machines *might* not hasten peace? Even *The Peacemaker*—ordinarily skeptical about the security of the armed peace—was impressed by the spectacle of an American battleship visiting foreign ports: "The guns are harmless, the public demonstration expresses the feeling of a common brotherhood and a desire for peace." That "laudable move" was the visit of the *Maine* to Havana harbor in 1898. [12]

\*　　\*　　\*

Such innocence was not parochial. American magazines published many European denials that "improved weapons entailed increased slaughter." [13] Jean de Bloch, a Polish Jew who wrote in Russian, provided an extensive analysis of modern war with a conclusion that pleased everyone in international peace work: war was now "impossible." Bloch showed that the new "mechanism of slaughter" made swift, decisive attacks impossible, and he thought that whichever "victorious" society could outlast a stalemate on the battlefield was doomed to disintegrate from the effort. Wars would cease, Bloch argued, when enlightened nations realized that mobilization was a suicide pact. American peace workers prided themselves on their grasp of such facts. Bloch, America was told, was a thoroughly realistic, "scientific man." The peace movement welcomed the testimony of such experts, sure that facts backed up their millennial predisposition: "The critical student of war becomes the sure prophet of peace." [14]

Expert opinions and facts did not have to be imported, for American engineers had anticipated Bloch's conclusions. Robert H. Thurston of Cornell, for example, had used his considerable influence in the engineering profession to spread the good news about modern ordnance. Thurston had prophesied "glorious distinction" for the mechanical engineer who would make warfare so destructive that the peace and freedom of the seas would be ensured: "This most splendid of revolutions is to be the work, purely of the mechanical engineer. I have no doubt that many among my audience will live to see that forerunner of the millennium." The echo of Robert Fulton's enthusiasm was not accidental: Thurston was Fulton's first serious biographer, and the professor rekindled the faith in weapons technology for a generation of American engineers.[15]

There were practical reasons for this aging optimism to live on into World War I. Puffery had always been the inventor's high card as he played the difficult game for capital and patents, and many inventors cultivated, almost by second nature, a sort of breakthrough ethos—that *their* inventions would sweep away the old strategic problems and create what the military had only dared dream about. Far from being bizarre, that was the way inventors were supposed to act.[16]

Of course any breakthrough in armament, with lives at stake, could be presented in dramatic terms. John Ericsson, the designer of the *Monitor*, was a critic of American attempts to create a modern navy. Ericsson had set in motion the movement for an ironclad navy, but he strenuously opposed the trend toward battleships and other massive armaments; instead he proposed the adoption of small torpedo boats. "Iron clads are doomed," Ericsson proclaimed, for his invention would sweep the seas of the battleships. New ships like his own *Destroyer* would end aggression at sea: "I am doing all in my power to protect the weak, by killing the strong aggressor." Principles and promotion seldom fitted together more harmoniously.[17]

Nikola Tesla, a pioneer genius in electricity, was another inventor who succumbed to the lure of a breakthrough that would end war. For him the attraction of innovation was powerful, even though he had strong doubts about the pacific force of the new weapons. Tesla was an uncritical champion of super-weapons during his early career, but by the turn of the century he seemed ready to give up his faith in the deterrent value of the new ordnance. Modern nations, as he saw it, gave every evidence of matching the "decisive" weapons of their opponents: with forces thus equalized, it was a "profound mistake" to assume that peace would continue. Tesla's dissent was rare among scientists and engineers, and his doubts proved to be a weak restraint on his own participation in arms work. Eventually Tesla tried to break free of the dangerous stalemate by creating completely automatic weapons—thus removing men from the battlefield. Failing in this, Tesla was willing to work on a weapon that would at last end the temptations of battle. (It is to Tesla that we owe the concept of the death ray, a weapon which we may expect to be perfected soon in a Russian or American laboratory, probably with an improved rationalization as well). At the beginning of World War I his unusually strong criticism of war science was nicely balanced by a traditional faith in salvation through technology:

> Modern machinery wrought by science is responsible for this calamity: science will also undo the Frankenstein monster it has created.
>
> The case is desperate, but there is a hope. This hope lies in science, discovery and invention.[18]

But did these inventors really wish to end the monstrous uses of science? It was precisely because many of the architects of the American arsenal were fascinated by the destructive power they unleashed that they continued their work. Often, when the claims about new weapons are read closely, one finds a covert appreciation of destruction which (since it cannot be confessed) is hidden behind denials that inventions are responsible for destruction, or, indeed, that deadly violence *really* occurs. No one can doubt that imaginary—and even real—scenes of destruction are exciting to many. Injunctions against such "lust of the eye" go back to the Old Testament. This amoral excitement was available to weapons makers if they took care not to acknowledge—to others or to themselves—any moral approval of death and devastation. By denying the horrors of the mod-

A Hotchkiss Machine Gun
(Paul Wahl and Donald R. Toppel, *The Gatling Gun*, 1965)

ern battlefield, they could enjoy them without guilt. This dynamic of fascination and denial about destruction in modern war is the emotional bridge between conflicting (and on a logical level, contradictory) appraisals of the new weapons. This dark part of the inventor's vision of war is particularly clear in the career of the most colorful munitions maker of the turn of the century: Hudson Maxim.

Maxim emerged from a backwoods Millerite family in Maine to christen important parts of the American arsenal (the Maxim gun was an improvement over the Gatling gun; "Maximite" was a high-energy smokeless powder). In light of his father's imminent expectation of ascending to Heaven, it was appropriate that Hudson grew up to champion aviation. He ridiculed the claims of his elder brother Hiram, who lived in England and was knighted by Queen Victoria for the weapons Hudson called his own. Hudson was a formidable champion of the Maxim arsenal in America. He had easy access to the Hearst press and his frequent appearances on behalf of preparedness were memorable: he sported a white beard and waved an artificial hand (his left hand had been blown off in the course of the discovery of Maximite).[19]

Maxim's energetic presentation of modern ordnance often seemed written in blood. He spent his time imagining the horrors awaiting unprepared civilians and soldiers should war come to America. His account of the destruction of New York City was lurid (it was adapted into a sensational movie promoting preparedness). In moments of leisure he also liked to make destruction entertaining. *Dynamite Stories* (1916) summed up the mishaps of his generation of ordnance pioneers. The book offered dozens of gruesome incidents—usually involving inadvertent dismemberment—in a droll manner for a mordant taste. Maxim seemed much amused.[20]

Maxim's analysis of ordnance in modern war, however, denied the possibility of most of the bloodshed he delighted in reporting. "The quick-firing gun," he often claimed, "is the greatest life-saving instrument ever invented." Even the reports of millions of casualties in the first months of World War I could not alter his opinion: "Never have they been so scientifically armed, and consequently, never have they, for the numbers engaged, killed so few." In that war, Maxim confessed, "horror obsesses the mind and stumps realization," but he could always find comforting statistics to show that previous wars (or even the accident rates in industry of that time) were worse. In his perspective, the European war placed no guilt on the arms maker. Maxim put the responsibility for the slaughter on the foes of armament—bloodshed was the fruit of unpreparedness. "As nations are bound to fight, it is far more merciful that they should be armed to the teeth." [21]

How could the inventors who had made such destruction possible deny any responsibility for the cataclysm of 1914? One reason they could was that they had had so much practice in living with contradictory emotions about their role in modern war. Thomas Edison, for example, frequently censured war work: "Making things which kill men is against my fibre. I leave that death-dealing work to my friends the Maxim brothers." It is true that Edison, and many inventors, thought armaments were wasteful and unworthy of enlightened societies. Even so, in the 1890's Edison had perfected an electronic torpedo—"a very pretty and destructive toy"—and he seemed eager for more work:

> What I want to see is some foreign nation coming to this country to attack us on our own ground.
> That is what I want to see. . . . Every electrician, when the time comes, will have his plan for making the life of his enemy electrically uncomfortable . . . mowing them down with absolute precision. . . . It would not be necessary to deal out absolute death unless the operator felt like it. He could modify the current gently, so as simply to stun everybody, then walk outside his fort, pick up the stunned generals and others worth keeping. . . .[22]

Several years before the Wrights flew over the sands at Kitty Hawk, Edison proposed an "aerial torpedo boat" that would make bombing possible. "I have no intention of ever devising machines for annihilation," Edison pledged, but it is clear that he had given such devices some thought. After 1914 his objections to war research collapsed. He led the first group of nationally known scientists and inventors to advise the government on defense work. A correctly trained and equipped "machinist army," Edison felt, would defend America with less sacrifice than the old military system had, and he hinted that he had access to unimagined power to fight for the nation: "There are forces available . . . which some of us have run across, which are mightier than anything which has been used as yet." [23]

It was easier to celebrate aerial warfare than the endless exchange of shrapnel and gas across the European trenches. The prophets of flight had long argued that air power would reduce casualties in battle and help ensure peace. As neither stunt exhibitions nor commerce paid the bills of the men who followed the Wrights into the air, their thoughts turned more and more to war and government grants. But they did not give up their benign views as they became falconers.[24] True, the Hague Conference of 1907 had censured aerial warfare as inhumane even before the first bomb was dropped. But in their enthusiasm most aviation pioneers were deaf to that alarm. (Hudson Maxim was only half deaf to it, titillating other inventors with tales of how airplanes might "ravage" unprepared America, but nevertheless insisting that the bombs would save lives.) Henry Woodhouse, editor of the leading journal *Flying*, argued that military aircraft held no terrors. He claimed that bomb-laden planes had saved 20,000 lives and incalculable property during the Italo-Turkish War of 1911–12. Woodhouse's magazine reported that aerial bombardment did little damage, while it created an atmosphere that led to an early peace.[25] In the fall of 1914, *Flying* surveyed the similarly happy results of German bombers over Paris:

> How bomb-dropping aircraft do not terrorize: Crowds in the Place de l'Opéra, Paris, waiting for the German aeroplanes. The moral effect of bomb-dropping from areoplanes in Paris was nil. After the first two days crowds waited for the airmen to appear and were disappointed if they did not come to give their demonstrations.[26]

Yet it was always difficult for the promoters of military aviation to set an emotional distance between bombing and bloodshed. *Flying*—in the same issue that reported the amusing results of bombing—confessed horror at the "organized slaughter" in Europe as well as "breathless interest" in the progress of the airplane in war. That editorial noted how much the drama resembled the new motion pictures—but could the spectator allow himself to enjoy the action? [27]

Many proponents of military aviation learned to enjoy the spectacle of aerial warfare without a sense of guilt. Henry H. Suplee, editor of the influential engineering magazine *Cassirer's*, punctuated his appeals for aircraft to put an end to the horrors of war with gruesome suggestions of what the new technology might accomplish. Suplee relished the "real changes which the engineer has been preparing to surprise the self-confident soldier and sailor." Airplanes might ensure international "order" by poisoning crops and water supplies, dropping explosives, and spreading diseases over enemy land. *Cassirer's*, under Suplee's editorship, offered the engineers a sensational picture of their violent new powers—with assurances that their technology served moral ends.[28] Here is one technical writer's fantasy of how these "birds of hell" might instruct the military establishment:

> The shock of exploding bombs and projectiles seemed like the rumbling of a deadly earthquake. . . . It was an inferno of noise and destruction. Shrieks of agony and fear mingled with the sound of bursting bombs and rumbling explosions.
>
> It was more than human nerve could endure. Men crazed with fear ran wildly from the redoubts fleeing they knew not whither, trying to escape the death that menaced them from the skies. . . . The capital of a great nation, a great army, costly defenses and armament, all at the mercy of a few hundred bird men. War as we had known it was at an end. The world had found a new master.[29]

Many in the American military were skeptical about (and angered by) such attempts to overturn so much of traditional military strategy. But soldiers often shared the assumptions of the civilian prophets: war was becoming less bloody. Wounds from the new small calibre bullets, for example, were frequently judged to be more "humane" than those made of traditional ammunition.[30] Experts did not spend much time on their statistical proofs, nor did they stress qualifications—often they were too interested in publicizing the conventional wisdom: "As the weapons and implements of warfare have increased in destructive power, war has not only become less frequent but battles have become less bloody." In 1911 it seemed obvious to George Patton that modern wars would kill a smaller percentage of soldiers and civilians than earlier battles had. In October 1914 Oliver Wendell Holmes, Jr., America's most prominent survivor of the Civil War, was unimpressed by the scale of bloodshed in Europe. "Except in exceptional circumstances," Holmes wrote, "I think the improved weapons mean smaller losses." [31]

The civilian weapons prophets' dynamic of denial and fascination about destruction was also present in the military's view of modern war. Officers were not taciturn about their weapons, and they spoke of an arsenal which was at once humane and horrible. One commander could extol machine guns as "labor and life-saving machines" while he acknowledged results on the battlefield " *'amounting almost to annihilation.'* " Similarly, Captain E. L. Zalinski, inventor of a famous dynamite gun, enjoyed telling the public that "the *fiendish* possibilities of destruction which the newest weapons of war open lend themselves to the amelioration of human suffering." The military's insistent announcements of hope also expressed their excitement at the prospect of the new battlefields where those claims would be tested in blood.[32]

Many in government found that peace seemed nearer as they contemplated the new possibilities of terror through technology. United States policy on armament was shaped by this abiding (but ambiguous) faith in the humanity of the new weapons. Samuel S. Cox, who as chairman of the House Naval Affairs Committee presided over the revolution in naval weaponry, urged American inventors to get on with their noble and gruesome work:

> At best, it is said that war is human butchery. If our admirals and generals must have war as a profession, if they must deal in blood, let them go to the shambles and learn of the butcher a lesson of skill and humanity. He does not destroy his victim by piecemeal or mangle him in detail. He is more merciful; he understands his business better; with well-directed aim he seeks a vital part; having reached that his work is easy.
>
> Therefore, to lessen human warfare let us cultivate the highest chemistry and make the most deadly armament.[33]

Cox's point of view did not lead to blind acceptance of the military's demands for new ordnance. Indeed, faith that science promised invincible weapons was one argument *against* building a modern Navy. Why spend years to build a fleet that "some whittling or rifling Yankee or some English mechanic" could make obsolete?

Congressmen with faith in such a breakthrough frequently pictured the terrifying destruction that would follow . . . a step, they claimed, to a peaceful world. Those pictures of armed cataclysm were but mirror images of the destruction naval supporters prophesied unless their blueprints for peace were followed. Both sides in the congressional debates over the modern Navy found destruction fascinating to contemplate, and the vote was carried by legislators who were confident that technology lessened the dangers of war.[34]

The American position at the Hague Peace Conference of 1899 nicely expressed the contrasting fascination with modern means of terror and the denial that such weapons would lead to more bloodshed in battle. Americans at the Hague pled the compatibility of those attitudes before a skeptical audience. The United States voted for a minority view that exploding bullets and poison gas might be legitimate weapons. Alfred Thayer Mahan proved ingenious in imagining circumstances in which the use of gas could be humane. And William Crozier argued forcefully that no permanent ban should be placed on the most visionary and drastic offensive weapons. Crozier was particularly insistent that plans for bombing attacks from airships not be ruled out, as such a breakthrough could "partake of the quality possessed by all perfected arms of localizing . . . sufferings [and] . . . to diminish the evils of war." [35] There was dissent in the American delegation on such a permissive approach to arms limitation, but the final votes of the Americans at the Hague reflected the assumption stated at the outset by the Secretary of State: "It is the plain lesson of history that the periods of peace have been longer protracted as the cost and destructiveness of war have increased." [36]

That optimism—and also much of the fascination with destruction—reached well beyond the immediate audience of engineers, officers, and statesmen. Weapons were presented in the same way in the daily newspapers. As Hearst and Pulitzer battled for circulation, they both denied and idealized the implications of modern techniques of destruction. In 1898 American intervention and preparedness sold papers, but very little military news in them suggested that those policies would spill more blood.

The press denied the implications of the technical revolution in land warfare in several ways. The most remarkable was the observation that modern shells killed fewer men. A reader of feature stories on war learned very little about the real effects of shrapnel, but he was often presented with the testimony of experts that great medical advances as well as the "clean wounds" of the new shells made war less dangerous. At its most extreme, the literature consisted of documented stories of men who had walked through the new bullets, and diagrams of new narcotic shells which would heal the wounds they made.[37]

However, for the most part the new weapons were thought of simply as beautiful pieces of machinery completely unconnected with the destruction of human life. The chivalry and excitement described in the musty Civil War volumes was now further refined by breathless, day-to-day reports on the aesthetics of the new guns. There was a connoisseurship in the feature stories before World War I—the "wonderful machine gun," "the beautiful big new Krupp guns thunder forth their music"—that was rarely broken by any reference to the goals of that weaponry.[38]

In the yellow press the contrast between the emphasis on war news and the denial of bloodshed was striking. It was as if acknowledging the effects of war would break the fascination. Ambrose Bierce, a frequent Hearst commentator on military matters, saw that "men's sense of their power to make [war] dreadful is precisely the thing which most encourages them to wage it." His columns—like his short stories—fairly drip with blood. Yet Bierce denied that modern war increased violence: "Of course it is understood that modern long-range cannon, small arms of 'precision' and other 'destructive weapons' have materially reduced the mortality in battle from what it was when men fought hand to hand with sword and spear. . . ."[39]

Similarly, Jack London—Hearst observer at the slaughter of the Russo-Japanese War—seemed overwhelmed by the spectacle, "thrilling gently to the horrors of war," as he confessed. London used a familiar device to cover his excitement, however. "The marvelous and awful machinery of warfare," he wrote, "today defeats its own end. Made pre-eminently to kill, its chief effect is to make killing quite the unusual thing." [40] A reader of those newspapers before World War I found a series of titillating war stories, cleaned up by assertions that machines brought more order and less blood to the battlefield.

A similar denial of the destructive potential of the new war machinery, coupled with an idealization of its power, was clear in the newspaper presentation of the submarine and the airship. The reader was rarely presented with a balanced account of the strengths and weaknesses of either weapon. Instead, mastery or impotence were attributed, alternatively, to these devices. Either they were breakthroughs that transformed war, or they were useless. In one mood the submarine was an "iron coffin"—a hazard to its crew and useless to the fighting fleet.[41] In another, it was a faultless "demon of the seas" and its effectiveness was not questioned. "No navy, however powerful in units or numbers, could hope to escape destruction with these submarine monsters directed against it." [42]

Similarly, the newspapers often wondered if man was capable of effective warfare in the air while at the same time they looked forward to terror from the skies which would—how was never made clear—make the great armies useless.[43] Between such mastery and impotence, there was no realistic picture of the damage likely to be inflicted. By holding up an ideal picture of destructive power while denying the real consequences of the new weapons, the newspapers presented technology as a terrible yet bloodless enforcer of peace: "Behind the images of carnage shines the light of universal peace." [44]

\*      \*      \*

In such a climate of opinion, the American peace movement could not summon up either the will or the facts to oppose armaments. The steady growth of peace societies in the early 1900's provided no check on—and little criticism of—the international arms race.

Hamilton Holt, a prominent peace organizer before World War I, gave a candid assessment of the susceptibility of the new peace recruits to the argument for an armed "preparedness": important peace groups favored increasing armaments, others believed the issue should not be discussed, only one faction entertained the idea of arms limitation.[45]

Holt did not overstate the faith shared by arms makers and peace workers. Eleven leaders of peace societies were also officers of the bellicose Navy League. A prominent engineer, proud of his work in peace societies, saw no conflict in sponsoring the "John Hays Hammond Cup for Accuracy in Bomb Dropping."[46] Emotionally, the weapon fantasies of prominent peace workers were as rich and apparently as satisfying as those of the apologists for warfare. William N. Ashman, vice president of a peace society which opposed armaments, stressed that peace workers were not sentimentalists, but rather were "moved by the sublime and terrible." Ashman tested the point by sharing his private speculations on how modern weapons might advance the peace program:

> Suppose some form of gas shall be produced so poisonous in its effects that in the area over which it shall be spread no creature, man or beast, can inhale it for a moment and live. Suppose, further, that the instrument from which it shall be projected may be handled by a single man. . . . That some such agency will be developed in the near future is certain of accomplishment.[47]

And Edward Atkinson—a tireless opponent of war in the Philippines—found space in his peace tracts to urge American scientists to "improve rifles, guns, or other killing implements, or invent more destructive implements of war than have yet been devised." Perfection in killing seemed an acceptable way to achieve "Eternal Peace." Atkinson's peace pamphlets even described his "singular dream" of ingenious new weapons that could seek out and immobilize the military leaders who allowed men to fight.[48] New weapons thus enticed the practical workers for peace into imaginary scenes of battle.

The lure of military technology remained strong even when peace workers found themselves observing a real war. A clean break with the hopeful view of armaments was rare in the American peace movement after August 1914. Lucia Ames Mead—the most prolific pamphleteer for the American Peace Society before the war—illustrated how difficult it was to discard the traditional accommodation with new weapons. Mead had publicized Bloch's optimistic view of modern ordnance in the decade before 1914. Shocked by the European conflagration, Mead regretted the tolerance which peace workers had shown to arms makers. "In our country," she recalled bitterly, "the militarists blandly supported . . . [peace campaigns] and formed arbitration societies with arbitration and armaments walking abreast arm in arm. . . ." Now the danger of falling into the embrace of arms makers was even greater, Mead warned: Hudson Maxim and the Navy League were pleading for more "siege guns and battleships . . . servile imitation of futile, old-world methods which have brought Europe to the shambles." Yet Mead's peace program for the crisis was far more traditional than she ever admitted. "Scientific experts," she concluded, could ensure America's peaceful defense. She scorned Maxim even while she was fascinated by the "marvelous possibilities" of Nikola Tesla's invulnerable automatic weapons. She attacked the Navy League by pointing to the peaceful world that a gigantic submarine fleet might create.[49] It was as if Robert Fulton's treatise on the promise of a new kind of warfare, which was suddenly reissued in 1914, had never been out of print.

The persistence and power of American optimism about technology constricted debate over modern warfare. Though the choices in Washington were narrowed by the decisions made in the war offices in London, Paris, and Berlin, Americans might have lived in this dangerous world with a more realistic picture of their defenses. This is not to dismiss completely the value of fantasy. Americans were slow to perceive the threat posed by major powers overseas. As latecomers to the international arms race, they may have needed their fantasies about weapons and a logic that said they were harmless. But attention to the possibility of a bloody, prolonged, and inconclusive use of arms would have sharpened the advocacy of all points of view about national preparedness. Peace workers, inventors, soldiers, and political leaders found the power of new weapons exciting. They denied or idealized the violence they foresaw. Living with their hazy memories of the Civil War battlefields and their dreams of the benign weapons of tomorrow, Americans had neither a usable past nor a realistic future.

# "CUNNING
CONTRIVANCES"

Why were the prophesies of more humane war not more effectively challenged? Partly because Americans were distracted by their anxiety about the character of the soldier. Hidden behind his machines, the modern warrior was not a shining example of heroism; in fact, he seemed bewildered and not fully human.

During the Civil War, Nathaniel Hawthorne made a fearful prediction. He despaired for the souls of men on the ironclads. A war dominated by machinery was not ennobling. "How," he asked, "can an admiral condescend to go to sea in an iron pot?" Hawthorne feared that Americans wished to disown the emotions of war—the pain and the aggression: "human strife is to be transferred from the heart and personality of man into cunning contrivances of machinery." The soldier who was emotionally distant from the battle might easily forget his own personality and think of himself as a mere extension of these marvelous inventions. He would become a barbarian, for he would displace his aggression, ignore his pain, and lose his capacity for guilt.[1]

The technology of war disappointed the poet and corrupted the soldier. The disappointment and corruption concerned nineteenth-century Americans more than did the specter of increased bloodshed.

Seasoned campaigners could be as anxious about these issues as citizens like Hawthorne who had never seen a battle. By 1917, the wish to reject technology was no longer heard, for it had become possible to see heroism in the engine room and machine-gun nest. Yet the suspicion that soldiers were being psychologically damaged by the new technology of war was not fully laid to rest.

\*       \*       \*

The notion that machinery was a threat to human character was an invention of the nineteenth century. During the Enlightenment it was conventional to commend even natural beauty by stressing its link to a cosmic mechanism; and man-made machines seemed as benign as the Creator's. It was the romantics and "scientific" socialists who discovered the frightening new world of machines. Out of the factories and laboratories came monsters, dehumanized men who were the result of the scientific method run amok. Mary Shelley's *Frankenstein*, first published in 1818, was the most vivid warning about the laboratory; Karl Marx later added his visions of the "monstrous shape" of the division of labor in the factory, "converting the workman into a living appendage of the machine." [2]

Such monsters, destined to be simplified and turned into creatures of a modern folklore, were really quite complex. Victor Frankenstein's invention had, at first, benign impulses; the monster might have lived a life of virtue had it not been loathed. The beaten industrial proletariat was, for Marx, the repository of morality. Mary Shelley did not clearly indict modern science. Marx was awed by the capitalists' rational exploitation of man by machine, and believed that when the workers rule, the exploitation, not the machine, is to be smashed. The classic nightmares of the machine age were filled with terror, but also with hope.

To this mix of terror and hope American critics of the modern arsenal added nostalgia. The military hero looked different, even unrecognizable behind the steel plate and engine smoke. Hawthorne's friend Herman Melville watched the *Monitor* and *Merrimack* fight, and concluded that the romance of a battle at sea was dead:

> . . . this was battle, and intense—
>     Beyond the strife of fleets heroic;
> Deadlier, closer, calm 'mid the storm;
> No passion; all went by crank,
>         Pivot, and screw,
>     And calculations of caloric.
>
> War yet shall be, and to the end;
>     But war-paint shows the streaks of
>                         weather;
> War yet shall be, but warriors
> Are now but operatives; War's made
>         Less grand than Peace,
>     And a singe runs through lace and
>                         feather.[3]

The longing for warfare untainted by the industrial age appeared many times in the half-century that followed. And this criticism of the arsenal grew more strident. In the Hearst press during the Spanish-American War, Ambrose Bierce denounced the "ingenious scoundrels known as military inventors" for perfecting devices that hid men away from the direct line of fire. He longed for less machinery so "that ships will again fight in their shirt sleeves and the gallant defenders of our seacoast cities come up out of their hole to be shot at like human beings." [4] Indeed, in 1898 many writers for both Hearst and Pulitzer tried to show that the victory over Spain had been won by men detached from their new weapons. The heroes in those newspapers were oblivious to what went on below decks and, like Admiral Dewey, they faced the Spaniards with "heroic contempt" of the enemy's weapons. [5]

Edward M. House banished technology from his picture of military heroism with similar bravado in his *Philip Dru: Administrator* (1912). Colonel House, who clearly identified with Dru, imagined himself to be the savior of a technologically advanced society fallen into civil strife. House's novel gives an insider's view of war consultations in Washington—with Dru, the vital advisor, intervening to preside over the crucial battle. There is no chance Dru will be

Interior View of the Turret of a Sea-Going Monitor
*(Battles and Leaders of the Civil War*, 1887)

strafed by an airship. In this society all advanced war technology is prohibited—it is not used, even as the society fights for survival. With modern ordnance abolished, the hero is able to get a good view of the action: "In that hell storm of lead and steel Dru sat upon his horse unmoved. With bared head and eyes aflame, with face flushed and exultant, he looked the embodiment of the terrible God of War." [6] But House had rehearsed for the wrong role. In World War I he was President Wilson's advisor; science could not then be read out of the script.

\*　　\*　　\*

The anachronistic sentiments of men of letters were more than amusing: they were persistent and respectable objections to the growth of the modern Army and Navy. The European officer corps lent prestige to the prejudice against technology. The great colonial powers used such weapons as the machine gun in distant lands, but took little account of them in their plans for "civilized" warfare in Europe. (In the first years of World War I, many officers charged on horseback through breaks in the barbed wire, looking much like House's God of War—until the rapid-fire guns cut them down.)

The American armed forces nourished a prejudice against new machines as it prepared to fight. The influential *Army and Navy Journal* was often more nostalgic than Hawthorne, Melville, or Bierce. Under the fifty-four-year editorship of William Conant Church, the *Journal* served as a forum for officers who were uneasy about the use of science. Old-fashioned "pluck and skill," Church insisted, could not be improved on by machinists. As late as 1900, the *Journal* entered a touching (though futile) protest against the submarine—a "sneaking sort of business . . . compared to the good old square yard-arm to yard-arm style" of combat.[7]

Love of the old Navy lived on most dramatically in the chief prophet of the new fleet: Admiral Mahan. No one can read his autobiography without sensing that his heart belonged with the Navy he had spent his life persuading the nation to abandon. Mahan continually personalized the great wooden sailing ships, and, indeed, he attributed the survival of naval tradition to the rapport between officers and their beloved weapons: "the beauty of the ships themselves, quick as a docile and intelligent animal to respond to the master's call, inspired affection and intensified professional enthusiasm . . . their mute yet exact response . . . the testimony of a good conscience." Steel and iron seemed to break this bond and destroy the "poetry" of war ships. There might be a "vulgar appeal to physical comfort" in modern vessels, but "Does any one know any verse of real poetry, any strong, thrilling idea, suitably voiced, concerning a steamer?"

"Poetry" and the test of "conscience" at sea concerned Mahan just as deeply as the dazzling attractions of trade, industrial production, or national defense that sold the program to America. And Mahan rejected naval technology which would carry out that program when machines conflicted too openly with his romantic sense of the proper character of the fleet. Mahan—who bragged that he knew no calculus—downgraded technical training at the Naval Academy. In 1906 he called for a halt in the development of long-range guns on battleships because he feared they would have a bad effect on the commanders. Heroism—as Mahan's histories had shown—required close-in fighting. Guns that removed this possibility were a danger to the character—and poetry—of combat at sea. [8]

This form of romanticism was easy to pick up. Peace advocates, for example, were quick to note that the "cold calculation of mathematics" in modern military life had replaced the glory and courage that had made the soldiers' work attractive. For the peace movement, the weapons that made war less likely made it more enervating. [9]

In all of this rhetoric about America's first modern naval battles there was worry about the intrusiveness of the machine. Technology was perceived as something that stood between the sailor and his enemy; it made man lose control, shielded him from danger, and so compromised the heroism of his fight.

Many engineers and technicians objected to all slights against the machine (a machinist journal of the 1890's even objected to such a pejorative reference as "political machine"). Engineering journals made technology the hero of the victory against Spain. Looking at the "steel cells" that housed the new breed of gunners and machinists, they saw the same dirt and confused activity that so shocked Melville, but the technical writers drew different conclusions about those scenes—they saw a "new naval hero," victorious because he was an expert. The Spaniards had provided a moral lesson for Americans: "They had despised the mechanical arts and sciences and by these arts and sciences they fell." [10]

A lot more was at stake than the argument about true heroism that comes up in the arid disputes which follow most wars. Modern fleets and ground forces raised difficult questions about the freedom, discipline, and glory of fighting men. And these questions were new.

Before the Civil War, no one had objected to the image of the Army or the Navy as a "machine." The severe discipline on eigh-

teenth-century war ships and the formations of massed battalions on land made that way of thinking particularly appropriate.[11] Ironically, objections to the metaphor arose only after new machines and more complex organization freed soldiers from the old "mechanical" roles. Better guns, for example, drove armies out of the "machine-like" linear formations and encouraged independent tactical maneuvering. The very military reformers who preached the need for technical training claimed that these skills would free the Army of its image as a "machine." In the American military, the first fruits of science fed an appetite for freedom.[12]

Many claimed that dependence on machines would make military men more flamboyant. The early aviation literature, for example, suggested that discipline belonged on the ground (one prophet of 1913 saw America's air ace in the future war against Germany as an "inveterate mischief maker" and practical joker in battle). And, submarine service was frequently commended as an opportunity for men to fight like Indians.[13] In ground warfare, as well, an American officer saw training as a way to make "an organization, not a machine, but a sentient, vitalized creature . . . viciously effective in battle." That officer, the first commander of an American machine-gun regiment in battle, stressed that the new weapons did not convert his men into "cold-blooded men of science . . . the machine-gun man will belong to a different cult. He must be hot-blooded and dashing. . . . He is not to reason on abstruse theorems nor approximate difficult ranges; his part is to dash into the hell of musketry, the storm of battle, and rule that storm." [14] The new "calculations of caloric" were apparently going to be of the hero's blood pressure, not of the energy of the machines that brought victory.

It was not military men alone who insisted that soldiers were liberated by the weapons and organization of modern combat. After the Spanish-American War President Charles W. Eliot of Harvard told scientists to be proud of their contribution to individual liberty on the battlefield:

> Is it not a wonderful thing that the invention of more and more destructive weapons, like the long-range magazine rifle and the ma-

> chine gun, which has made impossible close formations, and forced
> every modern army to imitate what used to be called Indian warfare,
> should bring out so strikingly as this recent war has done, the im-
> mense superiority of the disciplined freeman to the trained automa-
> ton? [15]

There was, in many views, a happy trade-off: as technology per-
formed man's work, it conferred new power and freedom for the
worker. John Wesley Powell, in his presidential speech to the American Association for the Advancement of Science, announced that
"man transfers despotism from himself to his inventions." [16] Bring
more machines into battle, cultivate the necessary technical skills,
and fears of intrusive and manipulative technology will evaporate
. . . or so it seemed to many close observers of the impact of machines on society.

Soldiers could be heroes of technology if only they worked as well
as their machines. One architect of the American arsenal longed for
fighting men as good as their weapons. "There is a curious likeness
between men and mechanism," Admiral Bradley A. Fiske told the
United States Naval Institute, but because machines could regener-
ate and progress with indefatigable energy for new tasks, the admiral
pronounced these metal forms "less lifeless" than the fragile human
body: "In strength to do, and in delicacy to perceive, mechanism
surpasses anything to which man can dare to aspire." [17]

Though hardly complimentary to mankind, Fiske displayed the
faith in man's ability to control technology that Hawthorne had
ridiculed. The admiral was only one step away from what Hawthorne imagined would be the fighting man's ultimate self-deception:
that he might feel no aggression or pain in a war to be waged by machinery. Thomas A. Edison dreamed of this. When he reluctantly
began arms work for the Army and Navy he took comfort in his
belief that "the new soldier will not be a soldier, but a machinist; he
will not shed his blood, but will perspire in the factory of death at the
battle line." [18] This language magically transformed armies into
angerless teams of puzzle solvers; quiet men who watched as the
machines, alone, roared.

The Prow—Joseph Pennell, 1918
(*Joseph Pennell's Pictures of War Work in America,* 1918)

Nikola Tesla promised these brave new wars. He believed that a radical application of technology could displace human aggressiveness onto machines. This was possible because personality was simply a machine. "I have," Tesla announced, "by every thought and every act of mine, demonstrated . . . to my absolute satisfaction, that I am an automaton." he found this self-concept "elevating and inspiring" and it suggested a way to end human participation in war: we should perfect a "telautomaton"—

> produce a machine capable of acting as though it were part of a human being—no mere mechanical contrivance, comprising levers, screws, wheels, clutches, and nothing more, but a machine em-

bodying a higher principle, which will enable it to perform its duties
as though it had intelligence, experience, reason, judgment, a mind!

It remained only for men to identify personally with the future
armies of telautomatons and satisfy their martial impulses. "Machines will meet in a contest without bloodshed," Tesla wrote, "the
nations being simply interested, ambitious, spectators." *This* was the
ultimate, sanguine acceptance of the machine in war and the mechanical metaphor for the soldier.[19]

\* \* \*

Some students of war thought this had already happened, but they
were not pleased. They shared Hawthorne's nightmare of Americans
so beguiled by their weapons that they would forget about pain and
aggression. Frederic Remington found that the sailors in the "demon
folds" of the modern fleet were bewitched by this machinery.
Officers had become "so perverted, so dehumanized," that they
seemed oblivious to the battle:

> —grave, serious persons of superhuman intelligence—men who
> have succumbed to modern science, which is modern life. . . . I
> believe they fairly worship this throbbing mass of mysterious iron; I
> believe they love this bewildering power which they control. Its
> problems entrance them but it simply stuns me. . . .
>
> Don't waste your sympathy on these men below decks—they will
> not thank you; they will not even understand you.[20]

The modern warriors' detachment was frightening. They seemed
unaware of their own feelings and heedless of the blood the machines shed. Critics of technological warfare foresaw doom for these
soldiers. Unlike the prophets of weapons as keepers of the peace, the
anxious observers of war did not close their eyes to the carnage of
modern battles. Here was fascination without denial—as in Mark
Twain's vision of the soldier's fate amidst electric fences, Gatling
guns, and high explosives. The "Boss's" report of the final battle in *A
Connecticut Yankee in King Arthur's Court* (1889) is one of the few
passages in America's nineteenth-century literature which suggests

that war is hell. He and his few men had surrounded their position with fences, and shot an electric current through them:

> Land, what a sight! We were enclosed in three walls of dead men! All the other fences were pretty nearly filled with the living, who were stealthily working their way forward through the wires. . . . I shot the current through all the fences and struck the whole host dead in their tracks! *There* was a groan you could *hear*! It voiced the death pang of eleven thousand men. It swelled out on the night with awful pathos.

And earlier, when the Boss had set off the first explosives, he explained:

> Of course we could not *count* the dead, because they did not exist as individuals, but merely as homogeneous protoplasm, with alloys of iron and buttons. [21]

Ignorant armies created this carnage. Twain's soldiers are dead, but not just physically. The knights who charge are "automata" and the hard core of technocrats whom the Yankee produced from his "man factories" are easily persuaded to kill. Metal and flesh melt together in the final battle, but when the soldiers had had life they were no better than machines.

Science, in Twain's fantasy, turns out to be much like Merlin's black magic, beguiling and dooming. Twain knew at first hand the spell that technology cast. He completed his story of the downfall of an imaginary world bewitched by a mechanic while at the same time his own real fortunes were being drained away into a marvelous but unworkable printing device. In condemning the Boss, he was indicting himself. And, like most great satirists, Twain was never wholly free of the sins he ridiculed. In a notebook he recorded his glee at firing a machine gun at the Colt factory in Hartford. That was where the Connecticut Yankee had worked, and in King Arthur's Court the Boss's exaltation over the power and efficiency of modern weapons was an echo of Twain's own excitement. The piles of corpses in the *Connecticut Yankee* did not end Twain's affection for messianic inventors. In the 1890's he was drawn to the New York laboratory of

Nikola Tesla, and dreamed of promoting the "destructive terror" he found there. [22]

Consistency was not the forte of the Americans who worried about weapons. They endorsed the arsenal that they feared might corrupt and kill the soldier.

Captain James Chester, a prominent Army tactician, found his orderly view of war changing to a cataclysmic vision when he saw fighting men giving themselves over to the new technology and organization of combat. There are passages in his writings when he seems to think of soldiers as nothing more than pieces of machinery:

> First and foremost [officers] must learn to know "the man behind the gun." It is a wonderful piece of mechanism, with a most mysterious motive power concealed within. Such a machine and such a motor is worthy of patient and protracted study, and no two are alike. Every man constitutes a separate problem to be studied and solved before the officer can control as well as command his company.

Chester took his concept of military instruction from conditioning techniques he had seen attempted in Army prisons. In modern war, he stressed, individualism (even skills like marksmanship) would be worthless: "The soldier in the ranks might as well be blindfolded in battle." The soldier's new job was to accept the unreasoning discipline that would force him to stay at his post while "monsters, vomiting musketry upon each other in the dark" decided the issue. [23]

This sounded like a nightmare, and in fact Chester came to think that a war of machines degraded the men who waged it. Was it moral, he asked, to eliminate close contact with mutilation and death? That efficient tactician, much like the Civil War commanders who had pursued scorched earth campaigns in the South, felt that terror and punishment were useful checks on the human impulse to prolong war. Chester believed that if "monsters" or "greasy mechanics" now engineered destruction beyond the vision of fighting men, then human savagery would be unleashed. He dared hope that men would not let their battles be fought "by means of machinery, cunning devices, infernal machines." Perhaps American officers were too busy readying big guns and drilling their men, as many of Chester's earlier articles had advised, to share his concern. In his last publications, he saw himself as a "superannuated soldier." He was estranged from the optimists in his profession and resigned to the prospect that man's stumbling attempts to deal with the new technology would make the next war more barbaric.[24]

That sense of doom is even stronger in the excited rhetoric of America's leading defender of war in the abstract—Homer Lea. This frustrated soldier of fortune fits the common caricature of the nineteenth-century militarist. He thought that armed struggle was biologically necessary and aesthetically pleasing. Lea displayed those views in sensational accounts of imminent enemy invasions, adding pleas for America to ready its defenses. His potpourri of emotional and prudential appeals was popular before World War I, and Lea had to be taken seriously by preparedness and peace workers.

And yet the alarm Lea sounded was never really clear. He seemed too excited by destruction in battle—"the kindly singing bullets"—to be committed to saving America from war. Lea's response to the largely imaginary battles he wrote about is remarkable because he recognized that the "physical vigor" he idealized was not easily expressed in modern combat. The Army had become a "sober, gigantic machine," capable of only a "dumb heroism." Ultimately, Lea felt trapped as he watched war pass "from the brutish valor of the individual," which he rather liked, to "the calm, angerless domain of science," which he knew he had to accept. Lea called for a "psychological readjustment of the militant spirit" to take account of the intrusion of technology on the battlefield," but in the end his attitudes were in conflict. He treasured the autonomy still left to the soldier and was hostile to suggestions that the fighting man "is only the willless creature of some inanimate instruments." Yet, on another level, he seemed pleased with the manipulation and violence of modern war. He praised the "annihilation of personality" of military discipline then current. He gloried in the mechanical "monsters" that were soon to meet in battle. He stood in awe of the modern technology which—he was glad to see—ensured that humans would continue to fight:

> Man has pilfered what . . . gods once possessed. He has looted Olympus. He whispers across oceans. His voice is heard in its depths, his cries overheard. Yet he is unconscious of the limitations of his theory.
>
> To reduce distance is to increase the convergence of international interests. To diminish space, geographical and political, is to merge small states into greater unity. This passage is war. This unification conflict. Mankind, like metals, is welded together by fire and by blows.[25]

Twain, Chester, and Lea were Cassandras, and yet in another way they resembled the Americans who thought new weapons would keep the nation safe in battle. Few prophets could hide their fascination with the destruction of the people who did not take their advice. In imaginary wars citizens who do not heed the warnings about the new weapons are punished, usually for their own good and always in a melodramatic way. War thus seemed a vivid chastisement.

It was a compelling but dangerous point of view. Those warnings have special resonance in a culture so deeply touched by the Christian vision of Crucifixion and Apocalypse. Countless doughboys quickly judged—after 1917—that the battlefield of France had a holy glow. Even an old sinner like Jack London welcomed the war as a "Pentecostal cleansing." [26] Cast in those terms, the warnings about the weapons of war were undermined, the prophesies of sacrifice and doom became reasons to go to war.

# IV

# THE UNCERTAIN TRUMPET

*The myths of the arsenal flourished in a society that knew war almost exclusively through reveries and anticipations. Early in the century, few men could speak from experience about battle. Few advocates of preparedness after 1914 focused on the military crisis at hand. The more ethereal the war, the more attractive it seemed. But close students of war brooded even as they called the nation to arms. The real battlefield nurtured both cynics and mystics. By 1917 America's fighting faith was a complex creed that brought citizen soldiers together and then let them march in opposite directions.*

# 7

# THEODORE ROOSEVELT: ROUGH RIDER AND GADFLY

Theodore Roosevelt was both the great dramatist and the great critic of war for his generation. No political leader looked more the soldier or posed so often with guns. No American was better able to hold an audience spellbound with talk of the lofty ideals of war. Yet Roosevelt did what few former soldiers could do: he went beyond celebration and probed the meaning of America's wars. He gave Americans the help they needed to look seriously at war.

Roosevelt made his countrymen focus on the battlefield, a considerable accomplishment in an era when military adventures affected few citizens. The regular Army of less than 30,000 had usually not been noticed as they made their advances against Indians. The conquest of Cuba and the naval victory at Manila in 1898 were fast work. Though American troops were sent abroad frequently before 1917, only in the Philippines did the exotic sites of battle stay on the front pages for more than a few weeks. But Roosevelt let no one forget about the actual fighting. His histories of the West, his memoirs of Cuba, and his stump speeches for preparedness reminded civilians that they lived comfortably because soldiers had shed blood.

More than that, Theodore Roosevelt was a symbol of the martial virtues at a time when those values threatened to become diffuse and bewildering. One sometimes feels that at the turn of the century all civilians thought they were in the Army. To critics of laissez-faire such as Edward Bellamy and Herbert Croly, the Army offered a model of community, discipline, and equality for those making an equal contribution to the state. Politicians ennobled their calling with analogues of war: a *campaign* started from *headquarters* with a *war chest*; if the precinct *captains* did their jobs, there would be *spoils*. It was a rare profession or pastime that was not urged to emulate fighting men—in an "industrial army" or as "captains of industry" or even through "football strategy." The president of the City College of New York raised hopes for the military model high indeed in 1907 when he argued that American students could be saved from a "wallow in ease" if the nation's schools would now "keep the hard discipline that is found in the camp, and on the march." William James issued the most famous declaration of how the martial life might inspire commercial society in his "Moral Equivalent of War" essay of 1910, a Spartan vision of lost youth planting seedlings in the wilderness or shipping out to brave the North Atlantic for cod.[1] Those analogues, taken in so many different directions, led to much confusion. What would this ersatz military life be like? At least Roosevelt made his vision of the "strenuous life" clear; one knew what he stood for.

Roosevelt also gave substance to the calls for military preparedness. Until the end of the nineteenth century expert warnings about American weakness were ignored in Washington, while in public debate the nation's strategic problems were often the concerns of cranks. Not a decade passed without warnings of an invasion and plans to beat back the enemy. A "Great Red Dragon" of Oriental peoples was often sighted near the California beaches, ready to land and march eastward. Boys and girls grew up on this fare—F. Scott Fitzgerald's Amory Blaine dreamed of stopping the horde in Minneapolis—but the young soldiers were as likely to be confused as inspired. The watchmen who wrote the tracts had very special ideas about preparedness: the lowering of railroad rates, more money for the Merchant Marine, even sexual abstinence. Roosevelt made the case for preparedness hard to ignore or to ridicule.[2]

Finally, Roosevelt alone spoke candidly and openly about the attraction of war. Other Americans prayed for war and reveled in calamitous battles, but discreetly. The connoisseurs of war, such as the circle around Henry and Brooks Adams, the eccentric generals filled with racial pride, or the literary aesthetes of the *fin de siècle*, were cultists and did not often seek to enlighten outsiders.[3] Roosevelt, however, was the exception. While parlor militarists argued among themselves, he moved the American people. Roosevelt thus defined the many virtues and goals that his generation saw on the battlefield.

But he was not always the grinning Rough Rider with a simple and forthright program to keep the nation strong. In the 1890's Brooks Adams warned him that he was not so fortunate to live at a time when warriors "could still fight, and believe in themselves and their country." [4] Indeed, his close look at war often gave ambiguity to the moral lessons he preached. At turns impulsive and reflective, he could not raise hopes without also expressing fear.

*　　*　　*

Roosevelt first gained national attention after his personal and professional tragedies in the 1880's. His promising political career was stymied by New York party regulars; his wife and his mother died on the same day. Roosevelt retreated to his ranch in the Dakota Territory to gather his life together. As a correspondent from the Badlands he won his first national audience with hunting narratives and histories of the West.

One of the most striking photographs of the young Roosevelt captures him on his return from his new ranch life. The studio portrait is an announcement of his Western initiation: he stands in his prized buckskin suit, which is edged with long fringes from neck to ankle. He thrusts out a hunting rifle amidst the studio's version of the forest primeval. Roosevelt's look of determination is somewhat mocked by the scene. His gun is cradled by the fringe. His firm stance has accidentally buckled the grass mat.[5]

As Roosevelt's studio portrait suggests, he worked hard to live up to his conception of the frontiersman—and his identification could be extreme. Roosevelt admitted to Henry Cabot Lodge that he was apt to speak belligerently of war, *"qua* cowboy." [6] "I suppose I should be ashamed to say that I take the Western view of the Indian," he told a New York audience, "I don't go so far as to think that the only good Indians are the dead Indians, but I believe nine out of every ten are, and I shouldn't like to inquire too closely into the case of the tenth." [7]

This light touch in discussing the deaths of other people was not limited to one race. His Western friends' testimonies of homicide always seemed enormously amusing to Roosevelt in later life. His rough humor was well exercised during his presidency, when a Texas town sought to mark him as one of its own by placing a statue in the main square. At the unveiling of the befringed, buckskinned Roosevelt, excitement grew out of hand. Guns were drawn and a brawl started. The President surveyed the scene and confessed to Lodge that "I think there is something delightful beyond words in the idea of this sudden erection of a statue of me in hunting costume, at the cost of a riot in which one man was killed and nine wounded. . . ." [8]

Overplaying an impulsive, Western role was only one of Roosevelt's moods, however. His second thoughts were expressed in his historical writings. Here he saw a tragic West of weakness and barbarism that could not be "blinked," and which the historian might see "if the standpoint of observation was only close enough." A history of the heroic old West could not ignore the many who "spurned at restraint and fretted under it . . . their feats of terrible prowess are interspersed with deeds of the foulest and most wanton aggression, the darkest treachery, the most revolting cruelty . . . we see but little . . . pity for a gallant and vanquished foe." [9]

Roosevelt's celebration of the conquest of the West was a troubled one. He professed contempt for the Indian (and the defenders of the red race), but he named his home after an Algonquin chief, collected Navajo art, and contributed to a reverent and exhaustive study of native American culture. At times in his saga of the West he could see only a thin line between civilization and savagery, and he conceded that the frontiersman "wrested his land by force from its rightful Indian lords." [10] Roosevelt's celebration of national expansion must be set against his own definition of Manifest Destiny as a "piratical way of looking at neighboring territory" that had "immense popularity among all statesmen of easy international morality." His pride in the conquerors of the Southwest was at variance with his judgment that "the conduct of the American frontiersmen all through [the Mexican War] can be justified on no possible pleas of international morality or law." The historian who dressed in buckskin did not let Americans delude themselves; Roosevelt let it be known that the winning of the West entailed not only bloodshed, but recklessness and cruelty. [11]

\*   \*   \*

It was Roosevelt's fortune that at mid-career he found adventures that brought together his impulsive and reflective moods. The Rough Rider thirsting for a desperate fight was also the prudent statesman, counseling military preparedness. Roosevelt was, by turns, rash and thoughtful; at all times he was conspicuous before the American audience.

When Roosevelt first took up the preparedness banner, he saw only one side: prudential calculation, efficiency, skill, and discipline. *The Naval War of 1812* was written quite consciously to promote the reorganization of American forces in the 1880's, when the bravado of the volunteer tradition seemed the greatest obstacle to American planning. Accordingly, Roosevelt praised regulars and pointed out how many of the militia "ran like sheep whenever brought into the field." He discounted all differences in character between belligerents and showed how their fate was determined by their preparation: "In the engagements between regular cruisers, not a single [victory] was gained by superiority in courage." [12] Roosevelt stuck to that theme in his addresses to Eastern audiences on preparedness in the 1890's.

The emphasis on the control necessary for preparedness was never as prominent in Roosevelt's Western writings. Here another side of the preparedness standard became more important: daring, voluntarism, and courage. Those were the values Roosevelt celebrated in the Western military campaigns. To be sure, some of that energy had been carried to extreme: "The Western people grew up with warlike tradition and habits of thought . . . without any of the love for order and for acting in concert with their fellows which characterize those who have seen service in regular armies." But Roosevelt could never hide his admiration for the less conventional Western military ways. The day after he sent these strictures back to an Eastern publisher, he confided to Lodge that he saw "some good fighting stuff among these harum-scarum roughriders out here." Roosevelt said that he intended "to grasp at every opportunity" to enlist them for a national emergency (and he grasped for national emergencies, too). Looking back on his Western experience with preparedness, Roosevelt regretted that he was not able to test a nation like England with his men. "Of course the cowboys were all eager for war, they did not much care with whom . . . they were fond of adventure, and, to tell the truth, they were by no means averse to the prospect of plunder." [13]

Roosevelt's prudent appeals and reckless asides run through all of his writing on the military before the Spanish-American War. In public, for example, he stressed the value of a large navy; no American, he was sure, wanted to leave the coastal cities unprotected. In private, he played loose with the fate of the metropolis: "Frankly . . . the burning of New York and a few other seacoast cities would be a good object lesson on the need of an adequate system of coast defenses. . . ." He was indifferent to the prospect of a bombardment of the coast during the crisis with England over Venezuela in 1895 if it would allow America to move against Canada. As late as the spring of 1898, when he was Assistant Secretary of the Navy, he confided to Mahan that calls for protection would go unheeded if the Spanish fleet approached: "Take the worst—a bombardment of New York. It would amount to absolutely nothing, as affecting the course of a war or damaging permanently the prosperity of the country." [14]

The First Volunteer Cavalry Regiment institutionalized Roosevelt's fantasies of wild fights within a system of ordered protection. The "grim hunters" and "wild rough riders" could be made to fit into a regular Army operation. Roosevelt boasted that he "spent their blood like water" when strategy demanded. The triumph near San Juan Hill seemed to be the culmination of all his preparation—"the great day of my life." [15] The meaning of this battle, however, was not so apparent.

Roosevelt's adventures in Cuba captured as many critics as Spaniards. *The Rough Riders* has been read as a simple, straightforward celebration of the military life—"Is it any wonder that I loved my regiment?" [16] Students of imperialism have found the exuberance and confidence that prefigures his presidential policies. But a close reading of *The Rough Riders* makes either understanding difficult to share.

The issues of the war are raised only once, and then enigmatically. To begin the narrative, Roosevelt chose Bret Harte's verses on the war drum; the beats remind recruits of their martial heritage, but they also signal death for the brave. The closing appeal is no more cheerful:

> 'But when won the coming battle,
>     What of profit springs therefrom?
> What if conquest, subjugation,
>     Even greater ills become?'
>         But the drum
>         Answered, 'Come!
>             'You must do
>             the sum to prove it,' said the Yankee-
>             answering drum.

Harte's drum sounds like a dirge for the adventure in Cuba. Close to war—as when close to the West—Roosevelt brooded over the conquest he celebrated.

*The Rough Riders* does not sustain that serious mood, however. Roosevelt chose a very strange narrative technique to commemorate the heroism of his regiment. His descriptions frequently mock his announced themes. Thus he celebrates the unity of classes, sections, and races in this regiment at the beginning of the book, but by the end he has documented their most precarious cooperation: "My men were children of the dragon's blood, and if they had no outland foe to fight and no outlet for their vigorous and daring energy, there was always the chance of their fighting one another." [17] Indeed, Roosevelt's picture of the war often makes it unclear how the Rough Riders fought anyone. The interminable battle for passage to Cuba is won against other American troops—and it is a short victory in any case, as the Rough Riders' ship departing is mistaken for the Spanish navy arriving, and Roosevelt's men are ordered back to port. Horses will not fit on board and are left in Tampa, so the Rough Riders never ride. The first attempt to land in Cuba leads to drownings of men and loss of equipment, and the first encounter with the Spanish enemy proves futile, as they cannot be distinguished from the Cubans. Roosevelt further tells us that his sword slipped between his legs and had to be abandoned.

The military campaign runs no more smoothly. The Rough Riders' first fight is controlled by the enemy; the regiment suffers terribly as inadequate equipment and planning give away their position; and Roosevelt admits that they lose more men than the Spaniards do in the eventual conquests. He confesses that he is mistaken for the enemy by his own men, deserted by his comrades during one charge, and actually has to draw his gun to maintain the discipline of some regular soldiers.

The cease-fire brings assignment to idleness in a fever zone and Roosevelt enters into an acrimonious correspondence with Washington to save his men. The journey home becomes the last battle. This time their transport *is* an enemy: a drunken and mutinous American crew has to be subdued by the volunteers to gain passage. Even when victorious and safely encamped on Long Island, the Rough Riders do not often present a heroic picture: "The lithe college athletes had lost their spring; the tall, gaunt hunters and cowpunchers lounged listlessly in their dog tents" and later, Roosevelt writes, "most of the men gave vent to their feelings by improvised dances . . . forming part of the howling, grunting rings that went bounding around the great fires they had kindled." [18]

*The Rough Riders* thus often seems an unintentional monument to literary realism in the 1890's. Like some self-conscious realists, however, Roosevelt does not want to pull down the romantic conception of heroism. He continually tries to portray the courage of his men with reverence and simplicity. In fact, he attempts to refute the picture of complexity and accident that realists emphasized. Stephen Crane, in particular, haunts Roosevelt's narrative. Crane's early report that the Rough Riders' first fight was a "gallant blunder" caused by their loud talking and disorientation tarnished the reputation of the regiment. Roosevelt set out to expose the "minute inaccuracy" by writing his memoirs. Ironically, his candid remarks about the surprise and confusion in the American war effort underscored Crane's point.

Indeed, Roosevelt's eye for the battlefield was much too sharp to fit his own purposes. His battle reports have so many details of deaths, wounds, and needless suffering that the reader loses sight of his "grinning Rough Riders" and has trouble enjoying the "grim game" of war. *The Rough Riders* trades on the grotesque at the expense of the heroic:

> We found all our dead and all the badly wounded. Around one of the latter the big, hideous land crabs had gathered in a gruesome ring, waiting for life to be extinct. One of our men and most of the Spanish dead had been found by the vultures before we got to them; and their bodies were mangled, the eyes and wounds being torn. [19]

Before World War I those words would be hurled back at Roosevelt. Angry pacifists quoted sections from *The Rough Riders* to show that real war was far from a glorious adventure. [20]

War might be confused; suffering grotesque; and heroes mute—Roosevelt's realism never weakened his celebration of his military life. Indeed, the accident and pain heightened his appreciation of the adventure. (Roosevelt later claimed that "I have always been unhappy, most unhappy, that I was not severely wounded in Cuba

. . . in some . . . striking and disfiguring way.") He found personal consolation in American disorganization: "unlimited opportunity for the display of 'individual initiative,' and . . . no danger whatever either of suffering from unhealthy suppression of personal will, or of finding . . . faculties of self-help numbed by becoming a cog in a gigantic and smooth-running machine." [21] We are a long way now from the calls for efficiency and planning that Roosevelt had made so often in his early work for preparedness. Risk and daring at first hand seemed more appealing than when studied in the early nineteenth-century militia. *The Rough Riders*, though a case study in military confusion, contains no appeals for better planning. Roosevelt did not accept the lesson of his own book: that modern war was too complex to be fought by the spirited but disorganized soldiers he idealized.

Roosevelt did renew his campaign for preparedness, and he used the bungling of the Cuban campaign to support his case. But he endorsed the rebuilding of the Army and Navy on his own terms. He had little patience for the true believers in technology and efficiency. The American fighting man had disproved the thesis that "mechanical devices will be of so terrible a character as to nullify the courage which has always in the past been the prime factor in winning battles." Roosevelt seemed proud that "we did not win through any special ingenuity," and he was forever wary of movements for more efficiency in the armed forces. [22] His perception of the modern organization and equipment of war was shaped by his fond memories of the chaotic mode of fighting. Roosevelt's Secretary of War, Elihu Root, spoke like many Army reformers when he treated soldiers as members of a great "machine." Provoked by the disarray of the Cuban adventure, Root called for more extensive offices for training and planning, narrower responsibilities, and closer control of men in the field. [23] This Roosevelt translated as getting "active, living knowledge" behind policy to abolish the inertia and "soft places" in Washington. Roosevelt explained to Congress that "nowadays the most valuable fighting man and the one most difficult to perfect is the rifleman who is also a skillful and daring rider." [24] Similarly, Roosevelt found that "a curious feature of the changed conditions of modern warfare" was the greater need for the "individual initiative" that hunting developed. This plea for "the widest scope to individual initiative under the present conditions of actual warfare" even led him to cite the breakdown in the chain of command in Cuba as a "blessing." Roosevelt lived with a desperate hope that the new shape of war would leave him a place. During the rest of his life he offered to raise new regiments.[25]

\*  \*  \*

As the memories of campaigning in Cuba faded, the fruits of war seemed less sweet. It was the uniform, the bivouac, and the sound of guns that excited Roosevelt. The political consequences of war were secondary and usually, in the long run, a disappointment. As President he was an apologist for imperialism who found the responsibility of colonial rule enervating. He blessed the European nations as they "snatched" more of Asia and Africa "from the forces of darkness," but he concluded that America's civilizing mission in Cuba and the Philippines brought few rewards and great dangers. "At the moment," he confessed in 1906, "I am so angry with the infernal little Cuban republic that I would like to wipe its people off the face of the earth." Nor were the pacified Philippines a comfort; he feared that they had become America's "heel of Achilles." [26]

Roosevelt also came to fear the international arms race that he had blessed during his presidency. He had prepared America to play a powerful role in the world, but he welcomed the appearance of her modern enemies as well. The man who had longed for the Kaiser to "strike savagely at the point where danger threatens" and lectured anti-imperialists on the beneficence of Japan's military preparations lived to fear those powers. And Roosevelt was not sanguine about how Americans would fare in the dangerous new world. He warned his countrymen not to fall away from the strenuous life, but he sensed that spartan habits might not be enough to keep them safe. The Moroccan Crisis, which occurred toward the end of his presidency, raised the specter of a "world conflagration" that might be a "calamity for civilization." [27]

Just beneath all the calls for national strength, in the last decade of his life, lay the fear of personal weakness. Roosevelt had revealed that wistful mood in the verses he chose to begin *The Strenuous Life*:

> —you and I are old;
> Old age hath yet his honor and his toil;
> Death closes all; but something ere the end,
> Some work of noble note, may yet be done,—

After his presidency, on expeditions to Africa and Brazil, he brooded. As a young hunter in the West he had observed, with great feeling, that wild animals reflected the heroic character of the men who pursued them. The heads in the trophy room ennobled the hunter. But in the tropics Roosevelt stopped treating the animals as foils. The wilderness was no longer a stage where a man could prove himself with a gun. As he explored the River of Doubt in Brazil in 1914, he shunned simple lessons save one—nature "is entirely ruthless, no less so as regards types than as regards individuals, and entirely indifferent to good or evil, and works out her ends or no ends with utter disregard of pain and woe." [28] Roosevelt's insight was better prophesy than he knew.

*  *  *

Roosevelt kept watch on the European war for Americans. At first he took an Olympian view. The holocaust was exciting and instructive, but did not make him a partisan.

In the fall of 1914 he explained how each nation acted from a sense of necessity and honor; no nation, he stressed, could be charged with guilt. The sacrifice of the fighting nations was sublime. Clearly, he envied their intense experience. At times, he seemed even to wish that more nations could participate:

> The storm that is raging in Europe at this moment is terrible and evil; but it is also grand and noble. Untried men who live at ease will do well to remember that there is a certain sublimity even in Milton's defeated archangel, but none whatever in the spirits who kept neutral, who remained at peace, and dared side neither with evil nor with heaven.

War taught the values of strenuousness that the western nations had forgotten in peace: "manhood . . . purged in the ordeal of this dreadful fiery furnace"; a *Titanic* scene of "elemental disaster" where true character stood revealed.[29]

Roosevelt paid little attention to the victims of the cataclysm. As the Belgians stood up to the Germans, he praised their "proof of virile strength"; but he was skeptical of atrocity reports, and his expression of regret at the devastation of Flemish cities was *pro forma*. Luxemburg and Belgium offered "instructive commentary" on the perils of unpreparedness, but they did not prompt public laments. Indeed, in the early months of the war Roosevelt even urged the Germans to act with "unsparing rigor" against the allies of the *franc tireurs* who hindered the military campaign.[30]

He came to regret that gratuitous advice, and he may, as he later claimed, have been trying to preserve his credibility by hewing to the Administration's neutral line. But his public bows to Germany were so frequent in the first weeks of the war there seems no reason to doubt that on some level he wished to pay the Prussians his respects. German "efficiency" was awesome to Roosevelt, and "it is impossible," he confessed, "not to feel a thrill of admiration for the stern courage and lofty disinterestedness which this great crisis laid bare in the souls of the [German] people." Rather than drawing back in horror from German actions, he glimpsed a worthy enemy, one so admirably defiant that he empathized with their struggle: "The Germans are not merely brothers; they are largely ourselves." [31]

Much of Roosevelt's agitation through the war years focused on American refusal to match the German commitment. He found, for example, that the ruthless self-interest of German foreign policy was preferable to the faith of Secretary of State Bryan and President Wilson in neutrality and arbitration. Later, even after Roosevelt came to see Germany as a murderous outlaw, he could not stop using that nation as a model to instruct the American audience: "I believe that this country has more to learn from Germany than from any other nation—and this in regards fealty to nonutilitarian ideals, no less than as regards the essentials of social and industrial efficiency. . . ." [32]

Whatever Roosevelt's evaluations of the European antagonists, while he watched their struggles he rehearsed his own action. He dreamed of the war brought to America. He gave frequent counsel to the "strong men" who "will gladly acquiesce in the absolute destruction" of major American cities rather than pay tribute to an invader. He rehearsed New York's imaginary surrender to Germany as many times as he had contemplated the city's capitulation in 1898, and he told one visitor that a German invasion would teach Americans a useful lesson.[33]

Even so, by the beginning of 1915 Roosevelt had decided that he must fight the Central Powers. Germany had become—at least in part—an insidious force that had to be stopped by American might. The motives behind that shift away from neutrality were complex. In part Roosevelt acted on a view of *Realpolitik*—that a victorious Germany might next turn on America. The toll of neutral civilians killed by German submarines surely affected him. But Roosevelt found the most compelling reasons to fight by looking at Americans at home—not at the war overseas. Intervention was not a preemptive strike or an overdue punishment as much as a possible salvation for the Americans watching the war.

"Preparedness" was the cry Roosevelt took up to challenge his fellow citizens. Once again, though, his warnings were uncertain. His emotional calls for immediate action often overshadowed the programs that were prudent. As the war became more personal and emotional he found himself ignored by the war effort he sought to lead.

In his attack on the "yellow" national leadership and "the foes of our own household," Roosevelt's argument proved to be double-edged. He preached "100 per cent Americanism," yet denigrated the government and the Army. Democrats, especially, saw his aspersions as disloyalty. The lower house of Delaware came within one vote of calling for his arrest, and the mayor of a Texas town thought that the first shot of the war should be aimed at the Rough Rider. Wilson's Cabinet seriously considered banning Roosevelt's preparedness appeals from the mails. More painfully, Roosevelt's partisan thrusts handed Wilson a weapon. Critics of American policy, the President said, trampled on "the peace and dignity of the United States." [34]

Roosevelt's notion of preparedness also proved to be a snare that kept him away from the battlefields. He was unable to meet his own call for "efficiency." Following the German model, Roosevelt endorsed scientific planning for both the military and civilian war efforts, especially through training camps—those "huge factories" and "laboratories of Americanism." [35] As efficiency suggested sacrifice and a vigorous life in the open, it fit nicely into the strenuous life. Understandably, however, not many scientific plans took account of the Bull Moose. Roosevelt begged the Administration for permission to take a regiment into the trenches (a scheme Europeans favored), but Secretary of War Baker blocked the adventure by emphasizing the "stern, steady and relentless" nature of modern war. Spirited volunteers did not fit into the Administration's picture of an efficiently organized campaign. Roosevelt's pleas for a uniform hastened the creation of a conscription policy that excluded such eager recruits. Preparedness had turned on its leader. [36]

As months of planning passed without Americans entering combat, Roosevelt's resentment at the official version of preparedness transcended that personal issue. There was a way to break away from the ethos of efficiency that thwarted so many enthusiastic patriots. Planning could be called timidity. Reliance on science could be made to seem disloyal. Efficiency might be revealed as an insidious German concept.

In the summer of 1917 Roosevelt lent his name to a play that put the "mechanical" image of the Germans in a strong light. *Efficiency, A Play in One Act* was far from subtle, even by wartime standards. The power-mad Kaiser was shown to rely on his master scientist to bring victory. The scientist's sinister plans seem to be foretold by his shrunken body, gothic wardrobe, and "portfolio containing reports and statistical matter." "Number 241" is the fruit of his research: it is a half-human, half-mechanical automaton that is presented to the Kaiser as the prototype of the invincible German Army. The Kaiser's euphoria turns to horror as the new soldier attacks him. The curtain falls as the mechanical hands tighten around the Hohenzollern throat. "Efficiency!" the Kaiser gasps.

Roosevelt was enthusiastic about the work. The play revealed Germany as an "inhuman machine" that had unleashed "materialistic science" on the Allies. He was only sorry that room could not be found to depict the "efficient ally" of the "brutal German militarist"—which included all who had turned from the fight in America.[37]

Roosevelt's view of national policy became so abusive that he was unable to believe in America's idealism or material aid in the first year after the declaration of war. A crusade for democracy seemed to him shameful hypocrisy. The Fourteen Points were mere distractions. America's deeds were no more impressive than her words. Roosevelt found it "ludicrous—and humiliating" to think of America as the greatest factor in the war; he put his country's contribution on a par with Portugal's. He wrote in the spring of 1918:

> If in this mighty battle our allies win, it will be due to no real aid of ours; and if they should fail, black infamy would be our portion because of the delay and the folly and the weakness and the cold, time-serving timidity of our Government, to which this failure would be primarily due. If those responsible for our failure, if those responsible for the refusal to prepare during the two and a half years in which we were vouchsafed such warning as never [a] nation previously received, if those responsible for the sluggish feebleness with which we have acted since we helplessly drifted into the war—if these men now repented of the cruel wrong they have done this Nation and mankind, we could afford to wrap their past folly and evil-doing in the kindly mantle of oblivion. But they boast of their foolishness, they excuse and justify it, they announce that they feel pride and delight in contemplating it. Therefore, it is for us, the people, to bow our heads on this our penitential day; for we are laggards in the battle, we have let others fight in our quarrel, we have let others pay with their shattered bodies. . . .[38]

Roosevelt had begun to think of himself as "an elderly male Cassandra has-been." [39] In part, he brought it on himself. His abusive language had made enemies. Carrying on as a Rough Rider had made his offers to serve seem impractical. He was so willing for the nation to suffer that his calls to safeguard the country seemed hollow. He could not shout for 100 per cent Americanism and then brand the government disloyal. But fundamentally, Roosevelt did not lose credibility through his own faults. Before 1917 his exaggerations had not been offensive and his dark thoughts and inconsistencies had been overlooked. It was not Roosevelt, but his audience that had changed. Americans now lived with real war and they had testimonies from the front and information from a war government to set against Roosevelt's view. Perhaps a nation at peace or oblivious to its army must have a Roosevelt. However, America at war thought it could dispense with his melodrama and inconsistencies.

Yet Roosevelt's mercurial moods were not unique. The most fervid champions of intervention in Europe and the first Americans to fight for the Allies were often just as unsure about their enemy and just as transfixed by the awesome forces on the modern battlefield as he was. In the name of loyalty they made scathing criticisms of American pretentions. Calling for national protection, they extolled self-sacrifice. Like Roosevelt, the vanguard at the front and the leaders of preparedness brooded as they called Americans to join the fight.

# 8

# THE AMERICAN VANGUARD ON THE WESTERN FRONT

Roosevelt spoke to the last generation which had reason to feel that war was kind. The old campaigns had been reduced to stirring yarns; the modern arsenal was seen as life-saving and labor-saving machinery. The heritage of anger, fear, and guilt in American wars was inaccessible to the young soldiers who would now carry on the fight.

Yet innocence alone did not send Americans to France. Realists and scoffers had fed the national taste for self-sacrifice in war as surely as the soft-minded optimists had. The nineteenth-century veterans willing to talk about the gore of battle had been made reverent by the discipline and destruction. Soldiers who had realized the predicament of their enemy continued to fight him, sometimes with increased determination. Weapons prophets with the darkest vision advised fighting men to stand up to the crushing power of the new warfare. The martial spirit, then, grew from ignorance and insight, pleasant dreams and terror. And by 1917 this double vision of war tempted Americans to welcome adventure on the Western Front.

Before the American Expeditionary Force landed, there were thousands of volunteers who would not wait. From the winter of 1914, the American vanguard was a source of inspiration at home. Preparedness leaders agreed with Roosevelt that the testimonies of sacrifice for the Allies "have been helping this nation to save its soul." [1] The volunteer soldiers, nurses, and ambulance drivers—as well as the reporters in the trenches—produced two kinds of inspirational literature. First, there were commemorative volumes: the letters of dead soldiers and reports of the good works of hospital volunteers. Typically, they were lavishly printed, slim editions that ended with appeals for money and more volunteers. The next testimonies from Europe used more direct means to arouse passions. Those thicker, cheaper books took Americans into the trenches and field hospitals, just a few months behind the reporters. The authors stressed the need for America to prepare for war, adding lurid engravings and photos of the destruction to show what might happen if the nation did not awaken.

Today, those scores of earnest, excited volumes have been forgotten. Our picture of the war has been formed by the more articulate and sadder reflections of the 1920's and 1930's. The inspirational literature could not outlive the cause it served. There is, however, good reason to reconsider those earlier views. The first Americans at the Western Front thought seriously about the war they promoted. Roosevelt was wrong to see the American vanguard as soul-savers: those writers wrestled with the same divided feelings about modern warfare that afflicted him. Some of the men and women who rushed to France presaged the disillusionment with the American crusade that characterized the more familiar literature of the postwar decades.

\*     \*     \*

Judged by the books they produced, Americans did not go to war because they hated Germans, nor did their commitment rest on patriotism toward their homeland. If any of them thought they were safeguarding the United States, they failed to mention it. Many disclaimed a patriotic impulse, and some broke off careers in the American armed forces to fight abroad. One volunteer for France was a deserter from the United States Navy. [2]

Articulated political ideas of any kind were rare in the first American writings about the war. There is very little talk about freedom or democracy—no doubt troublesome topics for men fighting on the side of the Czar. One member of the Lafayette Escadrille counted, at most, two colleagues "who enlisted from a sincere desire to be of service" even to the French! The first American to fly for the Allies explained: "It mattered little to me which of the warring nations I would join, and finally I chose to throw in my lot with the army possessing the largest number of aeroplanes." [3] More typically, the decision to serve was presented as a spontaneous—even a capricious—act. Men said, simply, "I decided that I might do lots of worse things than to see a little of the biggest scrap the world has ever known." Volunteers often struck this apolitical and light-hearted tone even after American intervention. On April 7, 1917, E. E. Cummings wrote that he could get through only one paragraph of Wilson's war message, "being taken with a dangerous fit of laughter." Two weeks later, Cummings chose to drive an ambulance at the front, appreciative of "the amazing vulgarity of the whole deal." [4]

That enigmatic mood was very strong among the early volunteers. To be sure, some did refer to the principle of Belgian neutrality, the honor of French self-defense, and the moral imperative of defending civilization west of the Rhine. What is striking is that those who did spoke so little about them after they heard the sound of guns. The elaboration of the Allies' interest into a crusade occurred almost entirely on the home front. Close to battle, we see men and women who can act, but not explain their allegiances; they face danger, but with an emotional life that is determinedly unserious.

A false jovial note was sounded, for example, by an American general on an inspection tour to prepare for the first wave of doughboys. As he typed a note to a close friend, the general had trouble celebrating his adventure, for he had not always felt like a hero. He had

> been bombed from planes, lived within the sound of the constant roar of so many guns I am afraid to number them, have heard the air hum with big shells going over . . . [yet] am well and hard as nails, and the whole thing seems as natural as driving the car down Pennsylvania Ave. Only I was scared quite genuinely sometimes, especially when the big shells came along, but hope I hid [here the

general scrawled "it" in the margin with an apology for this slip] and guess I did because no one pointed a finger at me. It is the greatest game in the whole experience of man, if he lives through it, and the best if he doesn't. I wish you were with me.[5]

Many of the first American volunteers protested their high spirits too much. One camion driver with the French, for example, made a confession using a verb form that might be called anxious present:

There is no more glamour about it all any more, no glory. The things I have seen in days to come will make me shudder when I have time to think. . . . The best of it out here is that we do not have time to think, but feel somehow a sense of duty that sends us along well enough in content, and we live more or less on the day-to-day excitement. . . . Mostly it is laughter and joke about the things that happen, no matter how serious they may be, and sing a bit at night.[6]

John Dos Passos, an ambulance driver for the French at the time, spoke of his "snailshell of hysterical laughter," but many American writers never saw what the blithe spirits hid.[7] Newspaper readers could easily get the impression that the war was a grand outing. The Hearst and Pulitzer papers, in particular, gave an image of the battle-field far different from *All Quiet on the Western Front:* there was slight attention to the mud, blood, and despair in the trenches. The dispatches often followed a pattern. Much time was spent describing the writer's difficulties getting to the front and his amazement at how little seemed to be going on there. Perhaps from boredom, the visi-tors asked that guns be fired and even began to lift and rearrange shells. An exploration of the intricacies of trench construction followed, "I am something of a connoisseur when it comes to trenches," a reporter for the New York *World* admitted. Popular journalists seldom found soldiers with anything to say, and the cheery, matter-of-fact tone of the dispatches gave little sense of the pathos of trench life. Indeed, during the first year of the war, reports from the front often ended with impromptu (yet oddly similar) ban-quets—lobster and fine liqueurs served in a "sylvan grotto"; caviar and chocolates served on the Eastern Front—in any case, "as good as any I had in first class Paris restaurants" and "the equal of anything you could buy in London." In *Golden Lads*, a book especially endorsed by Theodore Roosevelt, the banquet scene follows a carefree analysis of the Belgian and French soldiers. Those fighting men show "a dash of fun" when wounded and are "happy in their death." [8]

In a way, the very different reports on the first years give common testimony that all *was* quiet on the Western Front: the fighting men are mute. Whether we meet the men who return from over the top with shattered nerves, the polite *poilu* at the trench banquets, or "the joyous wounded" behind the lines, they choose not to tell us what they think they are doing. The "silence of the soldier" is acknowledged by both sentimentalist and realist—the "futility, the emptiness of words in the face of unspeakable experiences." [9]

American volunteers noted—and sometimes consciously adopted —that style of refusing to speak about either the aims of the war or their own response to the violence. Americans rejected the idea of the serious and articulate soldier. One seminary student in training camp, for example, claimed that he and his comrades had come for the adventure—they would rather talk baseball than ideals: "We have little imagination and less idealism. I've heard none of us seriously speak of dying for love of America, I doubt if any of us care very much about dying for posterity or liberty, or anything else. . . . I don't believe we care very much if France is torn to bits." [10]

Indeed, the American vanguard was transfixed, and often pleased, by the shells that crashed around them. "The sight was superb and the excitement intense" a volunteer wrote of a German bombing raid: "One had a delicious feeling of danger. . . ." [11]

An admirer of artillery fire in the American ambulance service spoke of "what interest we felt when a fragment of shell, smoking hot, fell almost at our feet, and what envy of the man who gathered in this first memorable 'souvenir'!" Malcolm Cowley joined such shrapnel hunts and he found the "*spectatorial* attitude" central to the volunteer's life at the front. Richard Harding Davis, the dean of American war reporters, claimed that this enjoyment of shelling never wore off. And one seasoned American volunteer expressed similar feelings (the same day he was killed examining the target area): "It's a pleasure to shoot a place up and then be able to go and see the damage you have done." [12]

The American vanguard was neither as amused nor as tough as it sometimes claimed to be—frequently the insouciance was short-lived. When finished with their bravado letters back home and the staged trench banquets, these soldiers tell us a good deal about the terror and despair of the Western Front. They refused to join those stoical and contented veterans of nineteenth-century battlefields who dominated American literature on war before 1914. One Californian in the British Army learned that denial no longer worked. That volunteer wanted to believe that the shrapnel barrages that kept him crouching in the mud

> threaten no danger to the mind, because a very few seconds after you are scared out of a year's growth by a shell arriving in the next ravine, or turned sick by the sight of some uncleared remains of a late battlefield, you have forgotten about it, and while the item un-doubtedly has left a permanent *subjective* impression, it's [sic] effect on the *objective* mind of you and on your good health and spirits is *nil.* . . . Out of sight, out of mind—is the rule of the soldier on ac-tive service.

He was proven wrong. Several weeks later "shell shock and severe nerve strain" forced him from his post. [13]

In December 1917 instructors at Camp Custer in Battle Creek, Michigan, spent a half an hour a day reading aloud to their men from two best-selling narratives of Americans at the front. Target practice and bayonet drills were not thought to have the galvanizing effect on recruits of *Over the Top* and *Kitchener's Mob*. The camp commander was not interested in the inspirational themes of those books. Rather, he thought the American testimonies about the trenches made the war seem like such a nightmare that the recruits would be "guarded against panic" when they landed in France and discovered that the real war was not quite so bad.[14]

It would have been understandable, however, if the recruits had panicked in Battle Creek. The books they were force-fed tended to subvert the Allies' cause, for they frankly reported the terror of modern war. In *Kitchener's Mob*, for example, an American volunteer embraced life in the English trenches, as "on those trench-mortaring days, when I watched boys playing with death with right good zest, heard them shouting and laughing as they tumbled over one another in their eagerness to escape it." Yet on reflection, the American author confessed that combat made cynics of his comrades and he had a "glimmering realization of the tremendous sadness, the awful futility of war." *'Over the Top' by an American Soldier Who Went*—the most popular narrative written before United States' intervention—stressed the satisfactions of fighting for the Allies. Yet the author depicted a war of unrelenting mud, cold, suffering, and death. The Allies were shown sharpening their trench weapons and killing prisoners. American enthusiasm for the high-minded war that President Wilson proposed cannot be credited to such books. They described such great suffering and destruction that they suggest, and sometimes admit, "the utter damnable wickedness and butchery of this war." [15]

Indeed, in World War I, disillusionment began with the men and women who heard the first shots. The volunteers did not have to wait for the novelists of the 1920's to learn that reality betrayed the rhetoric of the crusade. Dos Passos and Hemingway rarely sounded more bitter than a favorite drinking song of the Lafayette Escadrille:

> Cut off from the land that bore us,
> Betrayed by the land that we find,
> The good men have gone before us,
> And only the dull left behind.
>
> So stand to your glasses steady,
> The world is a web of lies,

Then here's to the dead already;
And hurrah for the next man who dies.[16]

Since August 1914 the regular Army had been contemptuous of
the Administration's caution and idealism. Leonard Wood, publicly,
and John J. Pershing, in private, excoriated the President, and regular soldiers felt trapped by what they felt were government lies. On
the punitive expedition into Mexico in 1916 there was an anonymous poem in the men's knapsacks that anticipated Dos Passos's acid
portrait of America's unknown soldier:

Nothing much in front of us but the baking
    sun;
Less 'n nothing back of us—I mean Washington.
Out in front—Carranza's men, no one safe at
    night;
Right behind us government, still too proud
    to fight. . . .

Take their murdered bodies up, calk them
    from the sun.
We let them die, but, now oh, my plot in
    Arlington!
Dead march, cart 'em across the bridge, a
    flag atop of each
And ship one to the White House, so a man
    may make a speech.[17]

Yale University Press brought that despair to the world beyond the
bivouac. *A Book of Verse of the Great War*, prepared just before the
United States declared war, was a bitter reply to the jingoes. Select-
ing from British, French, and American poets, the editor excluded
all harsh judgments of Germany and emphasized verse from the
trenches that encouraged a "renewal of the fellowship of the universal community of mankind." He gave space to the ethereal fighting
faith of patriots like Rupert Brooke, but aside from a few odes to the
poppies of Flanders, the stunned and cynical soldier-poets predomi-

nated. Martian landscapes nurture only the guns ("Misshapen monsters squat with wide black maws/Gulping smoke and belching flame"); soldiers, strung helplessly on the barbed wire, beg for death. These are ignorant armies. There are no heroes left alive, the survivors are sustained by cynicism; the dead never understood the cause they fought for. The American Oliver Tilford Dargan sums up the epitaph the Yale Press provided for the armies of 1914:

> For "honor" lift we dripping hands.
>> For "home" we loose the storm of steel
>> Til over earth Thy homeless reel.
> For "country!"—Thine are all the lands.
>> We pray, but Thou hast seen our dead
>> Who knew not why they bled.[18]

The cruelest blow dealt by the cynics in uniform was Ellen N. LaMotte's *The Backwash of War, The Human Wreckage of the Battlefield as Witnessed by an American Hospital Nurse* (1916). Had Ambrose Bierce lived to write the history of an ambulance unit, he could not have improved on her vignettes of mutilated soldiers begging for death and medics mindlessly and vainly trying to keep them alive. LaMotte's book was banned in Britain, France, and America after 1917, and this time the censors were correct in detecting subversion. *The Backwash of War* made a savage indictment of male behavior. Unlike the earlier realists who took pride in the soldier's endurance and discipline, she saw a battlefield where men's emotional life was uncontrolled: the men were licentious and untrustworthy in camps and paralyzed by self-pity when wounded. LaMotte saw how easily Germans used prostitutes to learn military secrets and she found the Allies' idealism ironic:

> They are vile themselves, these Germans. The curious thing is, how well they understand how to bait a trap for their enemies. In spite of having nothing in common with them, how well they understand the nature of those who are fighting in the name of Justice, of Liberty and Civilization.[19]

LaMotte did not consistently villify the Allies' crusade, however. She acknowledged an heroic and noble side of combat and suggested that the war might be part of the upward evolution of humanity. This mixture of the orthodox with the taboo strongly marked the disillusionment before 1917. Americans were talking at cross-purposes: chanting against war as they fought, using the poet's view of the battlefield inferno to illustrate international fellowship, showing the butchery of the trenches as they encouraged more men to sail. Angry veterans in the 1920's strove to be more consistent, but they were not always successful.

\*      \*      \*

It is not surprising that Americans were hesitant or inconsistent about the benefits of the war by 1917. The scale of military operations and the determination of the men who fueled the war machine seemed awesome. Yet each spring as the Americans watched the campaign renewed, they saw the common wisdom about modern war mocked—the new military technology did not make war either decisive or humane. After the German drive through Flanders in the first month of battle, the forces on the Western Front were caught up in a futile exchange of lives across a maze of trenches that stretched from the North Sea to Switzerland. The promise of decisive machines to break the impasse was not fulfilled—machine guns, airplanes, subs, and tanks all proved inadequate during the first years of the war. The lure of a "breakthrough" never disappeared from strategists' thinking, however. Americans watched infantry attacks that frequently penetrated less than a mile and exacted as many as 60,000 casualties in a day. To make sense of this sacrifice many Americans at the front abandoned political or moral catagories and began to think of their place in the mechanical process of marshaling force.

At first there was shock at the way regimentation and technical skills were used in the war. Arthur Sweetser registered the startling discovery described in countless news features and soldiers' letters.

> Where, I wondered, were the glories of war, the heroic charges, the cavalry dashing through a rain of smoke and iron, the batteries close

behind, messengers, aides-de-camp, and orderlies dashing about; where indeed was the bird's-eye battle-scene which I had visualized from paintings and war books? Few such delusions were held by those poor devils crouching resignedly in the trenches across the river while death flared down on them from above, and little heroism or grandeur of soul was shown by the men floundering around on the road before me.

Modern battle is the cold, calculating work of science, largely shorn of the human element. Men mechanically load and unload artillery, firing in cold blood without enthusiasm, even without knowledge of results. . . . I watched this long-distance slaughter for a long, long time. [20]

The deadening impact of modern war could, for a time, be denied. There were always Americans who doubted what they saw, sure that a more romantic version was the truth. One ambulance driver, for example, saw battlefields he could not reconcile with his idealism about the war. Henry Syndor Harrison recorded his darkest observations (and so rather subverted the commemorative volume, *Friends of France*) and then refused to take what he saw too seriously:

. . . it will not do, I am aware, to overemphasize the purely mechanical side of modern war, the deadly impersonality which often seems to characterize it, the terrible meaninglessness of its deaths at times. Ours, as I have said, was too much the hospital view. That the personal equation survives everywhere, and the personal dedication, it is quite superfluous to say. Individual exaltation, fear and the victory over fear, conscious consecration to an idea and ideal, all the subtle promptings and stark behavior by which the common man chooses and avows that there are ways of dying which transcend all life: this, we know, must have been the experience of hundreds of thousands of the young soldiers of France. And all this, beyond doubt, will one day be duly recorded, in tales to stir the blood and set the heart afire.

Harrison died in action, still anticipating (he tells us in the posthumously published *When I Come Back*) the discovery of "spiritual ranges" the soldiers reached. [21]

The "unknown hero" loomed large in the vanguard's celebration of the war. He was the man, now lost amidst the machines and bound by the iron discipline of the trenches, who would eventually tell the ennobling story of combat and defend his independence in modern society. But the most flamboyant heroes of the vanguard did not have to keep those virtues concealed. Ironically, it was the fighting men most dependent on machinery—the aviators and drivers—who sought to appear the furthest removed from the calculating work of long-distance slaughter.

They cultivated the role of "knight" and claimed brotherhood with other outsiders in the industrial age. The Lafayette Escadrille and the American First Ambulance Section both placed an enraged Indian— in full war cry—on each machine.[22]

Some of these aviators and drivers dismissed the fears that man was corrupted by his technology. The machine was so much a part of their self-image that it could not threaten them. Aviators and drivers affectionately decorated the sides of their machines with personal symbols and super-graphic initials. No interpretation of the equation between man and machine can be cruder than that found in a favorite song of the Lafayette Escadrille—"The Dying Aviator":

> Two valve springs you'll find in my stomach,
> Three spark plugs are safe in my lung,
> The prop is in splinters inside me,
> To my fingers the joy stick has clung.
>
> Take the cylinders out of my kidneys,
> The connecting rods out of my brain;
> From the small of my back get the crankshaft,
> And assemble the engine again.[23]

In 1917, amid the rubble on the Western Front, William Rose Benét saw something more frightening than the mere personal identification with the cunning contrivances of the war:

> The Beasts are back,
> And men, in their spreading shadow,
> Inhale the odor of their nauseous breath.

> Inebriate with it they fashion other gods
> Than the gods of day-dream.
> Of iron and steel are little images
> Made of the Beast.
> And men rush forth and fling themselves for
> ⠀⠀⠀ritual
> Before these gods, before the limbering
> ⠀⠀⠀Beast,—
> And some make long obeisance.[24]

The homage Benét feared is written into a great many of the volunteers' explanations of the test of endurance they found on the Western Front. Those trenches became the setting for a ritual—a purification of character frequently compared to the exacting preparation of the metal for weapons: to "knock what is false out . . . and weld and temper the fine part that is left." [25] Submerging the "self" in the energy and machinery of battle might yield the calm mystics knew: one's life seemed expendable, one's resistance unthinkable. Thus Alan Seeger regarded his fallen comrades as "empty cartridge cases" and claimed to view his own death with equanimity—he sought to become an "instrument of destiny." Soldiers proud to have such a small sense of "self" often contemplated their lives as tools or weapons in the struggle. One volunteer was eager to get back in the Somme offensive in the winter of 1917—up to that time the battle had caused more than 600,000 Allied casualties:

> . . . our power, our final power, is still unknown, but the next campaign should solve the enigma. . . . I am confident because I have seen and know the feeling of the men. It is as if a great river must be bridged by building a causeway of human bodies to allow those that come after to cross in safety. It has been half-built already, thousands of men have thrown themselves in and formed a strong foundation, but it is still far below the water level. The bridge must be built, and we are ready and waiting for the order to advance." [26]

Men become instruments and gain heroic stature through sacrifice—this was a theme of the literature of the American vanguard.

Optimists at the front testified that men could identify with the new weapons and regain freedom behind the throttle of a plane or the wheel of an ambulance. Pessimists like Seeger were resigned to the manipulation and even to death, mesmerized by the forces at work on the modern battlefield. Behind those two responses lay the assumption that the increased power of weapons had a purgative effect. Americans at the front were unsure of their political aims and their feelings about the enemy. But standing up to the fire and discipline of combat—that was presented as an inspiring experience by nearly all. After Albert Beveridge's tour of the trenches he confessed he was uneasy when deprived of the "tang of the unusual and perilous." "Can it be," he asked, "that the fuse which explodes the destroying shell also tears apart those gold and silken meshes with which convention and the ordinary wrap, mummy-like, the intellect and aspirations of man?" Many Americans under fire answered "Yes." The volunteers took pride in writing home about the "battlefield with its sprawling dead, its pity, its marvelous forgetfulness of self."

By the spring of 1917 they were urging Americans to meet that severe spiritual test—even looking for "stigmata" among the new wave of recruits:

> . . . its [*sic*] so easy to find excuses for not climbing to Calvary; sacrifice was always too noble to be sensible. I would like to see the country . . . become splendidly irrational even at this eleventh hour in the game; it would redeem her in the world's eyes. She doesn't know what she's losing. From these carcase-strewn fields of khaki there's a cleansing wind blowing for the nations that have died. [27]

The ordeal in France tested the faith of some volunteers and created a faith in others. The doubters were the most significant. Responding in contradictory ways to the spectacle of battle, they confessed the same ambivalence about war that the nineteenth-century veterans had so often felt. If the questioning volunteers of 1914–1917 were pompous and confused, they had the saving virtue of responding directly to their battles; even their laughter can be taken seriously. The soldiers who found a faith ready-made in World War I were not impressive disciples. No volunteer added a thing to Wilson's moral vision of the crusade. Alan Seeger alone seems to have thought through the implication of a selfless, mystical surrender to the destructive power of the new arsenal. Most of the volunteers took their apocalyptic vision from Christian texts, of course, and yet they managed, quite remarkably, to reduce its eschatology to stale formulas.

By 1917, on the home front, the Wilson administration had built a fighting faith with more eloquence and care.

# 9

# MANAGERS,
# MUCKRAKERS, MARTYRS

Theodore Roosevelt is but one piece of the puzzle of the preparedness movement. The rhetoric of preparedness was constantly at cross-purposes with the announced aims of the movement. Alarmed at America's precarious strategic position, the watchmen did not offer ways to meet the dangers posed every day by the European navies. Though the tracts urging preparedness preached patriotism, they often denigrated the nation's military heritage. And while committed to defending American shores, preparedness advocates often relished the prospect of an invasion.

Preparedness was inconsistent because it allowed members to march to several drummers. Patient citizens heard three different kinds of alarms sounded about national security between 1914 and 1917. Social planners both inside and outside the Wilson administration felt that the crisis could be managed and made to serve liberal ends; they spoke calmly as they defined America's duty. Louder and less reflective critics called citizens to arms with the melodramatic appeals of muckraking journalism. Still more desperate sentinels praised self-mortification, and for them the war was the Americans' precious opportunity for martyrdom. Each of these appeals called the nation to a different war, a war only tenuously connected to the real dangers of the European conflagration, but sharply defined by the

critics' anxiety about the peacetime nation. When the Wilson administration finally embraced many of the preparedness appeals, it
also absorbed some of their inconsistencies.

\*      \*      \*

Predictably, scientists first sounded the call to arms and were eager to
manage the war. Nearly every enterprise had recently been evange-
lized by disciples of "scientific management" promising efficiency as
well as uplift to those who would embrace scientific methods. Increasingly, in the pulp press and opinion polls, the researcher was
taken out of his laboratory and placed in a pantheon of heroes.
Josephus Daniels, Wilson's Secretary of the Navy, announced that
men of science now held the key to peace and war. "The glitter and
the pomp of brilliant uniforms are gone forever," the Secretary
judged, "one chemist, one electrician, might be greater in the warfare of the future than Napoleon, at his best, was in the warfare of
the past. One scientist very probably may do more for the United
States than any Admiral or General could do." Appropriately, in
1915 Daniels turned to inventors, scientists, and engineers for advice
on preparedness. His Naval Consulting Board did not engage in
saber rattling, nor did it call for mass sacrifice; it approached national
defense calmly, seeking a "shield of science" for America by converting the nation into "a vast storage battery charged with war forces." [1]

Just behind the scientists in the preparedness movement stood Progressives and officers, united by a common lament: to them the federal government was drifting and parsimonious. The professional
military had been reined in by spartan budgets for a generation. The
prizes thrown their way during the conversion to a steel navy and the
campaigns of 1898 only made their normal allocations seem more
unjust. In the half-century before 1917, the military journals complained constantly about the lack of money and status granted to
men in uniform. The military warned that it was unready and, at
times, conceded the harshest charges of its critics: fighting men were
misfits, cut off from the rewards of American society. [2] Administrative
reform of the armed forces was not always the sort of attention the

military welcomed, but after 1899 Secretary Root's staff system and War College provided the military with the first effective platform from which it could seek more government support. That new bureaucracy harassed the Wilson administration with the statistical proof of American weakness in modern war.

At the same time that officers found the real armed forces so feeble, political reformers took inspiration from the ideal of military organization. For the core of Progressives that looked to Herbert Croly for theory and to Theodore Roosevelt for action, war was the analogue of their reform ideas and a short-cut to Progressive goals. The attempts by anti-war Progressives such as Jane Addams to find "a moral substitute for war" suggest how central the military model had become.[3] The preparedness movement united critics who were worried about social drift. The political reformers, no less than the officers, feared that Americans were too caught up in pleasure-seeking and political inertia to set a strong national policy.[4]

When the crisis came in 1914 the managerial rationalists, both in and out of uniform, had a great deal to say about how America could be safeguarded. They rushed to the public with plans for universal military training, industrial efficiency, and a build-up of armaments. Yet the outpouring of ideas never quite hid the fact that these men and women were unlikely guardians of American security.

The managers of preparedness were led by technical experts of a marked cosmopolitan temperament. Inventors, following in a tradition that went back to Robert Fulton, were accustomed to selling military devices to the highest bidder on the international market. Many of the men who were brought to Washington to aid Secretary Daniels had supplied America's military rivals earlier in their careers.[5] Altruism unsuited them for superpatriotism when self-interest did not. Many men of science took the ideals of peaceful internationalism quite seriously. Just as the inventor-heroes in nineteenth-century dime novels refused to let their marvelous weapons serve the narrow purposes of the American Army, the real heroes of technology such as Thomas Edison and Wilbur Wright agonized before offering their skills to the government. At the Massachusetts Institute of Technology in the decade before 1917, those pacific ideals seem to have dampened interest in military research. "Science is more important than the preservation of any one country's independence," *Scientific American* had warned at the outset of the European war.[6] With that habit of mind, it was difficult to sound an alarm about Germany, and, indeed, Germany was more often a model than a threat in the preparedness literature. Teutonic science and efficiency were continually held up for emulation. In 1916, for example, the Navy League published an appreciative article on the German armed forces suggesting that criticism of such actions as the destruction of Louvain was too harsh.[7]

The preparedness movement was led by Americans more interested in polishing the fire engines than finding the blaze. One can read a great deal about civilian training camps, industrial armies, and universal military service without sensing that there was a world war in progress that threatened American security. The architects of the programs did not stress their military applications—such training, Theodore Roosevelt admitted, "would not be of prime military consequence"; rather, the programs would be "of prime consequence to us socially and industrially."[8] Efficiency, training, and specialization were ends in themselves for the managerial reformers. The Army, Navy and defense industries were to be showcases of such virtues. The planners were often not interested in calls to combat that took men away from their lessons in industrial efficiency. *Scientific American* preached preparedness even as it called for military exemptions for all scientists and skilled workers.[9]

That failure to connect preparation to an imminent risk of life led to surreal deliberations in Washington. Twelve days before Wilson called the nation to take up arms, Secretary of War Baker presided over the Munitions Standards Board, and he gave this instruction: "I think it important at the outset to say that what you are now asked to do has no immediate and direct relation to the present acute international controversy. . . ." The Board minutes then record fifty-three pages of testimony about ammunition and guns, broken by the reminder of one engineer that the gathering "has no relation to the possible emergency that may present itself to us shortly." [10] The Board may have been seasoning the historical record so they could not be accused of an unseemly rush to war, but if that was on their minds, we would expect other self-serving statements, which we do not find. The members of the Munitions Standards Board seem victims, not practitioners, of disingenuity.

The managers of preparedness continually looked above any definite threat in the actual war. As Herbert Croly conceded in July 1916, "We have to take the risk of preparing first and of deciding later just what we are preparing for." [11] That approach did not yield imaginative countermeasures against submarine attacks, sanctions that might dissuade the Central Powers from violating American interests, or ways to insulate the American economy from hostile competitors. The military dangers that fascinated the advocates of preparedness were more dramatic, more distant, and, as they put it, more lurid.

The invasion of the United States was the most seriously studied military problem in the Progressive era. Beginning in 1912, the War College churned out estimates of the days and weeks it would take various nations to conquer the East and West coasts. That danger was heightened by the European war, planners claimed, because the belligerents might turn eastward to recoup their losses in this "undefended treasure land." These studies were a wonderland of military contingencies: the American Navy was assumed to be completely impotent and the logistic feats expected of the enemy have not yet been equaled in any twentieth-century war. At the military preparedness hearings in 1916, the Chief of Staff told Congress to expect 72,000 Austrians, or 160,000 Frenchmen, or 387,000 Germans to come off the ships in the first wave of an invasion. [12] From those predictions, it followed that Americans must support long-range plans to meet this challenge—massive naval programs and training for the Army that could have yielded security no sooner than the 1920's. There was no official consideration of ways to send an expeditionary force to Europe. "Preparedness did not get the United States ready to intervene in World War I," an historian of the movement has seen, "—but then it was never designed to." [13]

\*      \*      \*

While plans to protect the nation were almost always long-range, campaigns to awaken the public were pressed immediately. Filling in the order forms and organizational charts for the armed forces of the 1920's was slow work, but preparedness advocates quickly reached for the muckrake to show the voters the shame of the camps and arsenals. In the rush to reveal the "adulteration" of the nation's armed might, the critics reduced American military history to a series of shams and needless sacrifices. [14] Like Roosevelt, these critics were unimpressed by Americans' fighting record. The military histories popular in the preparedness movement were censorious. Leonard Wood, for example, divided the nineteenth century into the "years of inefficiency" and a later "period of dry rot." Commonly, the conduct of the Revolutionary War was "an unanswerable condemnation of the American military system," and the campaign against Spain was dismissed as "a pitiful exhibition of incompetency and unreadiness in every department." [15]

That military history—as the critics admitted—did not read like the pious stories of American battles in school texts. There was a demystification of the goals of these blundering campaigns as well. Selfish economic benefits and the belligerent use of power at the expense of weak neighbors now seemed to be the motives behind American expansion. Such "realism" about the growth of the nation united such disparate critics as Herbert Croly and Homer Lea in the decade before 1914. The crisis in Europe led to many more examinations of the legend of American disinterestedness and pacificism. Jennings C. Wise, a political scientist at Virginia Military Institute, provided the most articulate attack on American innocence about national interests in his *Empire and Armament, the Evolution of American Imperialism and the Problem of National Defense* (1915). Wise dedicated the book to Leonard Wood and began with citations from Charles Beard—throughout making a radical view of American history serve conservative purposes. Economic self-interest lay at the heart of American nationalism, Wise revealed; the popular view that statesmen "have created an empire without knowing it" was dangerously naïve. American self-righteousness and belligerency could cause a confrontation abroad, and in the twentieth century the nation's blundering military force was not sufficient protection. Wise wanted the nation to confess its greed for power and wealth, and then rely on a strong arsenal—not self-righteousness—to pursue these goals.[16]

Oswald Garrison Villard was not alone in viewing the patriots' self-flagellation for preparedness as an unusual spectacle:

> . . . no writer who favors greater preparedness seems to have any faith whatever in our present navy. If I were a naval officer, I should be deeply humiliated by the fact that every one of the dozens upon dozens of articles . . . run down the navy and . . . have no doubts whatever as to what will happen to our fleet in any possible action. To them, forsooth, any battle spells defeat, overwhelming, disastrous, complete defeat.[17]

Many of the critics who dramatized the weakness of American defenses left themselves open to that attack: there was something hostile, even taunting, in their view of their society. In their invasion fantasies they saw the poor, the rich, or the immigrants eager to surrender American cities to the enemy—even the "gentle readers" who meant well, one writer predicted, would not have the courage to fight effectively. Among the citizens who could defend themselves, there was a "curious intoxication of destruction." America was to be torn apart in the coming war. The amoral delight in the power of new weapons, so common in Americans' imaginary wars, remained strong as the prophets contemplated the destruction of American cities. It is understandable that one preparedness film was banned from export because of the unflattering picture it gave of the Republic.[18]

Often, the muckrakers of the preparedness movement sought to shock Americans not with fantasies of war at home, but instead with reports of German atrocities in Belgium and on the high seas: stories of crucified soldiers and screaming women in life boats. Germans, in this view, practiced gratuitous terror: there were no mitigating precedents for that kind of warfare and no rational plan to the violence. The muckrakers' short memories of the Civil War and the pacification of the Philippines are less remarkable than the fact that they publicized such a horrifying view of battle at all.[19] None of the atrocity publicists appreciated the counter-argument that much of their material suggested: If the European war was an orgy of violence, unrestrained by the rules of civilization, why should not Americans be *more* content with their isolation? If the war had turned barbarous, why should Americans rush to join it?

*       *       *

One reason that muckrakers did not see the pacific implications of atrocity stories was that some of them valued martyrdom more than national defense. "It would be better for us, rather than the securing of our own soil against attack or invasion, that an American flag should wave over American troops in Flanders," Irvin S. Cobb wrote after returning from the trenches. The most energetic workers for American intervention professed to envy all the victims of the European war. Congressman James Beck, for example, inspected Verdun and found the fortress at once Calvary and Gethsemane. The half-million *poilus* and Germans who had fallen there seemed proof that miracles of heroism were possible in that decadent, commercial age. Similarly, one of the leading purveyors of Belgian atrocity stories felt that "their lot, with all its pain, is choicer than ours." The Belgians, crushed, had "felt greatly" and restored their patriotism, while Americans drifted and were out of touch with elemental experiences.[20]

In the impassioned debate over intervention it is not hard, in the year before that intervention, to find clergymen who thought that Flanders Field was Gethsemane and urged men to the front in the name of a Christ who "is willing to risk a world catastrophe." But the conviction that "we needed a cross" is more pervasive in the preparedness campaign in a secular form—where leisure and money-making are sins and America is a god that demands sacrifice.[21]

The spiritual dangers of peace were crucial to many in the preparedness movement. Looked at in that way, intervention designed to protect American material interests seemed an unworthy goal. Robert Bacon, who directed the American volunteer ambulance service in France and was president of the National Security League, confessed the shame and anger so many felt as his countrymen stayed safe at home:

> . . . we Americans must pay our share in some way, and our inordinate and unconscionable prosperity, and disregard of our obligations and willingness to go on in the old way . . . makes me sick, and I want to wear a hair shirt. . . . The world—*our* world—is not lucky enough to be snuffed out as was Pompeii. We have got to go through a long sickening decadence. Theodore [Roosevelt] is right— I have always known he was about the only one who understands, but he has more courage than I. . . .[22]

The taste for bloody sacrifice was not confined to watchmen on the right. Progressive journalist Lincoln Colcord spent the war lecturing his mentor, Colonel House, on the dangers of an imperialistic peace and then, as an associate editor of the *Nation* after the armistice, defended the Soviet government. Before the first doughboy reached Europe, however, Colcord displayed the same apocalyptic vision of the spectacle that some of his political opponents relished. His book of verse, *Vision of War,* did not express conventional sentiments. Colcord was not angry at Germany and he wasted no sympathy on the Allies—he suggested that friends of the Belgians remember their behavior in the Congo, and anglophiles the blood that had flowed when the English had planted the Union Jack in Africa and Asia. Though Colcord's first career was in civil engineering, he did not have the professional's appreciation of a battle well fought; in fact he delighted in the inefficiency of the European armies and ridiculed the technology brought to the battlefield. Colcord described the suffering in the trenches, but he belittled it; he was no more reverent of death than of the efficiency or ideals of the war:

> I do not see where men are anywhere living
>     forever—

> so we can reckon death out of the
> question;

There was nothing to lose in a bloody campaign earnestly fought, and everything to gain. Colcord commended the war to Americans because it promised personal and political liberation. Amidst the paradoxes of Colcord's verse, we see a man who has found fulfillment of a simple Progressive faith:

> Only the intricate web of convention, the
> artificial fabric is disturbed by
> war;
>
> . . . . . . . . . . . . . . . . . . . . . . . . . . . . . . . . . . . . . . . . . . . . . . . . . . . . . . .
>
> 'O, I tell you, in this campaign there are
> no defeats.'
> 'O, I tell you, the retreating and advanc-
> ing armies are equally triumphant!'
>
> . . . . . . . . . . . . . . . . . . . . . . . . . . . . . . . . . . . . . . . . . . . . . . . . . . . . . . .
>
> War offers a freer field for rich and
> poor to suffer and pay alike;
> And only out of war shall come eventual
> universal equity.
>
> . . . . . . . . . . . . . . . . . . . . . . . . . . . . . . . . . . . . . . . . . . . . . . . . . . . . . . .
>
> 'I hope, for the sake of your dreams, that
> you may have many revolutions;
> I hope, for the sake of your spirit, that
> you may have many desperate wars.' [23]

The appeals of the preparedness movement were at cross-purposes with many of the actions needed to defend the nation. The watchmen alerted Americans to danger, but their remedies were always insufficient, and sometimes contradictory. The prudent and emotionally cool plans of the managers promised efficiency, but did not tap the public's hatred of the enemy or love of a good fight. The muckrakers played on American anger and shame, but, like the managers, they did not offer plans or ideals to guide the nation through the pressing dangers posed by Germany. The promoters of martyrdom had ideals and fervor of a sort, but the idea of purgation did not take into account the need for long-range planning or, indeed, the desirability of survival.

From any of those three points of view, the citizen learned that his personal courage was inadequate to defend the nation. The managerial rationalists emphasized that the patriot was helpless without technical training and the right machines. The muckrakers reminded the volunteer that he had never fought effectively. The promoters of martyrdom suggested that even technical efficiency was not enough, that the patriot's blood must be shed to expiate his sin of holding back from the fight. Until the President called on the Congress to declare war, the American people had heard only an uncertain trumpet.

*       *       *

Woodrow Wilson was at turns the maddening target and the ardent ally of the preparedness movement. In the first year of the war, he seemed too stunned to listen to the watchmen. Wilson's metaphor for the war was that it was a consuming inferno, beyond American control or comprehension: "The world is on fire," he said repeatedly, "and there is tinder everywhere." "Blind recklessness" characterized the European struggle, the President told Americans, and the war's "origin and objects never have been disclosed." [24] Americans who wanted immediate action, definite plans, adventure, or vengeance were incensed by Wilson's discussion of the war. There was something too abstract and indirect in his view of the challenge: one's pulse did not quicken while listening to this professor. After his conversion to preparedness in the second year of the war, he seemed lackadaisical to his critics. Wilson suggested that details of preparedness plans "do not make any difference" and that his mind was "to let" on competing programs to safeguard the nation (Secretary of War Garrison was so frustrated by the President's flexibility that he resigned). If Wilson groped, however, it was toward a brilliant answer to the preparedness movement. The President gave to the

American people both the sense of control over the war popular with the managers of preparedness and the excitement of joining in a cataclysmic struggle that had been cultivated by the muckrakers and martyrs. Though he still enraged many critics, Wilson created for the nation the war they had longed to fight.

The President moved toward intervention as he began to point out order and ideals in the use of arms; he came to see a structure in the war that he had not glimpsed at first. Preparedness was attractive to him because he saw the opportunity to discipline Americans in peacetime. Using the language of the managers, he spoke of the "spiritual efficiency" of preparedness, an alternative to "a great military machine whose only use is for war." The President, in 1916, looked beyond the immediate military threat from Europe and posed an alternative to an arms build-up:

> We ought to have in this country a great system of industrial and vocational education . . . in which a very large percentage of the youth of this country will be given training in the skillful use and application of the principles of science and manufacture and business . . . [to] make . . . men . . . industrially efficient and immediately serviceable for national defense. The point about such a system will be that its emphasis will lie on the industrial and civil side of life, and that, like all the rest of America, the use of force will only be in the background and as the last resort.[25]

Wilson allowed himself to believe that fighting men could be models of passionless self-discipline. In the first Mexican intervention, for example, it was the soldiers' "self-control" that most impressed him; he planned Army training camps free of "military ardor"; and in Europe, Wilson expected Americans to fight "without rancor . . . without passion."[26]

Wilson transformed his nightmare of violence in Europe into what Randolph Bourne called "a cosmically efficacious and well bred war." In a world he had once described as mad and on fire, Wilson challenged Americans to intervene, observing "with proud punctilio" the rules of fair play—and he also asked men to serve without hating the German people. In a war among belligerents whom Wilson had first thought were largely indifferent to political principles and American rights, he identified the cause of democracy and national honor with one coalition.

However, Wilson did not disown the despair he had sown about the conflict. He expressed it in a way that answered the impulse for martyrdom that his critics had cultivated in their agitation for intervention. We find that despair in his speech for the declaration of war as a counterpoint to the ideals and the restraints—that is the "tragical character of the step" the President acknowledged as he called the Congress "into the most terrible and disastrous of all wars." Wilson further explained in June 1917 that he stood resigned to a war of national chastisement. He chose to make that statement to a group of Americans he could be sure would understand—the Confederate veterans:

> We have prospered with a sort of heedless and irresponsible prosperity. Now we are going to lay all our wealth, if necessary, and spend all our blood, if need be. . . . I am thankful for the privilege of self-sacrifice, which is the only privilege that lends dignity to the human spirit.[27]

The first Southern President after Appomattox thus told Americans to emulate the men who had served the Lost Cause. Wilson, the only man who could prepare the nation to defend itself, welcomed the new chance for martyrdom.

# V

# A SEPARATE PEACE

*Wilson called the nation to a war that would uplift humanity and chasten Americans, a war at once gallant and terrible. During mobilization, however, the nobility of the war seemed irrelevant to many who answered the call. Doughboys and planners lived by a more personal fighting faith, one that often provided peace of mind on the battlefield and values for the postwar world. In the 1920's it was not easy to share the memory of this war. The young writers of that era spent less time condemning the crusade than studying the detachment of Americans at war.*

# 10

# WARTIME
# PEACE OF MIND

America went to war in 1917 surrounded by mirrors. Billboards, walls, and fences across the land were adorned with posters in which the mobilized nation could see itself. Some reflected anger and anxiety; one could not look calmly on as Huns menaced Belgian women or as New York City exploded beneath the enemy's air fleet. Yet many of the posters were not really alarming. They gave a calm, often lyrical view of Americans in wartime. Those posters show a war too good to be true. Families work in their gardens, eat sensibly, turn down the thermostat to 68 degrees. Money is collected for the government and books are sent to soldiers. Women are glorified as healers and industrial workers; men are preoccupied with weapons that are as glamorous as Pierce-Arrow automobiles.

Of course, the fear and suffering of the war were real. Families kept an anxious watch for letters marked "somewhere in France." In the offenses of 1918, especially between the Marne and Meuse rivers, the doughboys learned of the deadly effectiveness of barbed wire, machine guns, and shrapnel. And yet the calm and uplifting posters, not the alarming ones, best reflect the mood of Americans caught up in the war. That outlook was eloquently expressed by the high diction of Wilsonians: American policy was "sacred," the broken bodies were the "sacrifice." And even those Americans who gagged on such words and stripped the war of Wilson's ideals sounded just as pleased by the opportunity to serve.

Americans in 1918 were as eager to talk about the personal satisfactions and general beneficence of the war as their ancestors had been to recall an ennobling Civil War. Now mobilization satisfied the longings for recognition and power. For many citizens World War I, on the home front as well as in the trenches, brought peace of mind. The Civil War generation insisted that their ordeal had been a blessing as they made peace; Americans of 1918 counted their blessings as they made war.

\*       \*       \*

In the summer of 1917 the Administration waged a psychological campaign to inspire civilians and soldiers. Wilson's call to arms was echoed and enforced by Cabinet members and the energetic Committee on Public Information. Indeed, in the first months after the declaration of war the Administration contributed little beyond words to the war effort. An expeditionary force had not been decided on in the spring of 1917, and few doughboys reached Europe that summer. Colonel House agreed with the President that an injection of Yanks into the trenches ("the most effective immediate help we could give the French and English," House called it) must be held back. To the horror of Europeans, strategists in Washington seemed in no hurry to act and preferred a high casualty rate or outright German victories to an unseemly rush of Americans to the front. Worried about how doughboys would fare with the remnants of the armies of 1914, the Administration took time to inculcate the correct morale.[1]

The managers of the war were never comfortable with calls for retribution against the Central Powers. George Creel at the Committee on Public Information damped hatred of the "Huns" at the same time he stoked up support for the Allies. In striking this balance, the CPI was often denounced as a hotbed of disloyalty. Creel refused to distribute atrocity stories and General Pershing went further, attacking the genre in his official bulletin of the American Expeditionary Force.[2]

In indirect ways the President sometimes abetted those enthusiasts who longed for German blood, but in general, Wilson skillfully kept the ideals of this campaign before the public. On the one hand there was his protest of friendship for the German people and pleas to the doughboys to fight without rancor. On the other, there was his Flag Day Address and the stern call for "Force, Force to the utmost, Force without stint or limit," which gave some comfort to the enthusiasts. By the time that force was ready, however, vengeful Americans were disappointed. The essence of the ennobling war for Wilson was restraint (the annotated edition of the President's war address blamed Clausewitz—not Sherman or Sheridan—for leading Germans astray). Wilson was shocked to learn that the Air Service contemplated the strategic bombing of Germany—terror and disruption through "promiscuous bombing" had no place in his conception of war. Americans fought in a dream, not a nightmare:

> Speaking with perfect frankness in the name of the people of the United States I have uttered as the objects of this great war ideals, and nothing but ideals, and the war has been won by that inspiration. . . . men in khaki coming across the sea in the spirit of crusaders . . . reckless of danger not only, but reckless because they seemed to see something that made that danger worth while. Men have testified to me in Europe that our men were possessed by something that they could only call religious fervor. They were not like any of the other soldiers. They had vision; they had dream, and they were fighting in dream; and fighting in dream they turned the whole tide of battle, and it never came back.[3]

True to American tradition since Appomattox, the President fixed the nation's vision above the battle. Here was a war without hatred of the enemy or guilt about the bloodshed—a war that could only be described in the language of dreams.

Wilson did not wish to be awakened. He declined to make a short trip from Paris to see the famous battlefields. "It was as if some camper had left a careless fire, and was loath to view the blackened stumps of a once verdant wood," Laurence Stallings recalled.[4]

\*     \*     \*

Were the men who fought those battles ever so tranquil? There is much proof that they were. Consider the surprising testimony of the Commissioner of Training Camp Activities. Raymond B. Fosdick went to the Western Front in the summer of 1918 and in his candid letters to his family he described the war the President had missed. Fosdick saw the gassed and mangled doughboys; this battlefield was "the work of devils." But Fosdick found no anxiety at the front.

> I have yet to discover [he wrote home] in myself or in any of the men I have talked to any feeling of fear or even nervousness. To a stranger it is all immensely exhilarating—a gigantic, thrilling game. The thicker they come the more thrilling it is. Officers tell me that when the order comes to go over the top the men respond with an almost unbelievable joy—and I know just what they mean. It's the sheer thrill of the game. I saw one of our divisions going into action the other afternoon in a place where the fighting has been fiercest. The men decorated their helmets with red poppies from the fields and they swept by like plumed knights, cheering and singing. I could have wept not to be going with them.[5]

It is true that on the Western Front happiness was encouraged systematically. The AEF newspaper, *The Stars and Stripes*, taught soldiers to be cheerful. The journalists in uniform gathered upbeat war news and prompted doughboys to write happy letters home. Indeed, the paper was so infatuated with letter-writing campaigns that it frequently buried news of considerable interest to the soldiers. One had to read closely to see that all leaves were canceled in the spring of 1918, so thorough was the coverage of a scheme to make sure every mother received greetings. On November 15 of that year, illustrations of the "Father's Christmas Letter Plan" sprawled across the front page, leaving only one column to break the news of the Armistice. *The Stars and Stripes* was so intent on keeping morale high that it lost sight of what the morale was for.

This is not to say that soldiers were passive victims of a public relations campaign. Some doughboys, like their predecessors in the
vanguard, knew a mystical calm as they contemplated their awesome
weapons. One soldier assured his family that he had no worries: "If
we allowed ourselves to think too much we would make poor cogs in
this big machine, and Dad that is all we are. It is a war of machines
and machinery and officers and privates are mere cogs." Some
doughboys seized this analogy with braggadocio—they were "living
bayonets" proud to be used up in the struggle. That identification
with weapons turned the whole genre of attacks on technology on its
head. Death through one's own machines, which, since Marx's early
writings, had seemed the absurd extreme of alienation, now restored
to the warriors a comfortable sense of themselves.

If we may judge by poems from the trenches printed in *The Stars
and Stripes*, the soldier's weapon was much like his lover— "mlle.
Soixante-Quinze." "Banal writers tell you science has taken the romance
from fighting," one veteran reflected, "in truth, it has multiplied it a
hundredfold and given war a fresh and burning magnificence." [6]

Most doughboys who published their reflections immediately after
the war (and the lifting of military censorship) wrote of happy days.
Fighting men were quick to acknowledge the camaraderie of their
unit, the restorative effect of life in the open, and the excitement of
the adventure—and many recruits felt that twentieth-century civilization made those pleasures rare. Wounded men were as likely to
share such sentiments as luckier soldiers. Unit histories display a
pride and buoyance about life in uniform whether the outfit was
decorated, held back from the front, or reprimanded for incompe-
tence. [7]

This is what most journalists had reported throughout the battles of
1917 and 1918. Patriotic newsmen assured readers that it had been a
war without drawbacks: the soldiers had learned discipline and piety
as they passed from innocent camp amusements to duty in comfortable trenches and battles without terror. The YMCA, with its net-
work of "huts" at the front, was particularly energetic in extolling the
good spirits of the men it served: "I say to you that the most buoyant,

U.S. Navy Recruiting Poster—R. Fayerweather Babcock, 1918

happy, hopeful, confident, crowd of men in the wide world is the American Army in France." Few of those accounts of the doughboys lack a visit to hospital wards for portraits of the laughter and high spirits.[8]

A generation of World War I writers was later to find these reports saccharine and a little sickening. In fact, the sentimental feature stories bear comparison to the literature of disillusionment, for the good cheer in the reports mocked the crusade. Here the war had no political meaning and the soldiers do not seem to be about any serious business. Indeed, there is more reason to think the soldiers were happily oblivious to the ideals of the war than to believe they were fooled by political rhetoric. William L. Langer, the first person to write the history of a combat unit and, perhaps, the man best trained to observe the political conscience of the AEF, could "hardly remember a single instance of serious discussion of American policy or of larger war issues." YMCA surveys in the field revealed that as many as 90 per cent of the doughboys could offer no principled reason for wearing their uniforms. A 1917 guidebook for the soldiers made the point bluntly: "America, according to the remarks of President Wilson, is entering this war in defense of her honor to keep democracy alive. You haven't the slightest interest in democracy." The Council of National Defense was so disturbed by the fighting man's lack of interest that the board insisted a copy of Wilson's declaration-of-war speech be placed in the knapsack of every soldier and sailor.[9]

\* \* \*

Uninterested and grinning warriors were not what some patriots at home demanded. Those enthusiasts thought the soldier must be angry and that the Administration should frankly promote revenge. The journalist Mark Sullivan counseled:

> War, after all, when you get down to its essence, is sticking a bayonet into another man's stomach—and pulling it out and sticking it in again. It is the second thrust that is important; *that* can only be inspired by high anger. It is not a thing that a man can do except in emotion. It is against every moral instinct. It is contrary to all habit of our ordered lives. It cannot be done in cold blood.[10]

In the summer of 1917 there were agitated Americans not inspired by the series of four-minute talks on ideals and annotated copies of the President's speeches arranged by the Committee on Public Information. Those citizens were enthusiasts for a far-reaching violence. National groups, long embittered by the tortuous path to intervention, now sought a license to hunt internal enemies. In cities and states the patriotic symbols from Washington were quickly marshaled to settle old grudges. The war could easily serve as a convenience for the men who drafted spider-web spy charts showing Teutonic subversion and the Connecticut Yankees who did not want their legislatures slowed down by the representatives immigrants might elect. Such enthusiasts also spread inflammatory tales about the external enemy: they built American rage by circulating stories of atrocities of the "Huns."

The Reverend Newell Dwight Hillis was the most accomplished purveyor of atrocity stories in America, and his techniques reveal much about the enthusiast's approach to the war. Hillis had carried on the pastorate of Henry Ward Beecher—and also Beecher's penchant for melodramatic language and hasty publication. Like Roosevelt, Hillis admired German efficiency and discipline; long after Germany had crushed Belgium the minister praised the Kaiser and was skeptical about atrocity reports. But Hillis paid penance after America intervened: he gave more than 400 speeches across the nation to advertise Liberty Loans and tell about an extraordinary variety of German crimes. After laying out the record of the enemy's legal duplicity, bloodthirstiness, and sexual excesses, Hillis asked Americans to consider carefully the nature of Germans. The atrocities were not aberrant or deranged acts, but rather signs that German society was functioning properly in its own terms. At times he compared the enemy to Indians and wild beasts who lacked a moral sense; in a more damaging (though inconsistent) image, he cast Germans as the corrupters of science—the atrocity was "the German notion of scientific efficiency." [11] That understanding of cultural differences had a profound impact in America, Hillis claimed, and he foresaw a war aim quite different from the Fourteen Points:

> A singular revulsion of sentiment as to what must be done with the
> German army after the war, is now sweeping over the civilized
> world. Men who once were pacificists, men of chivalry and kind-
> ness, men whose life has been devoted to philanthropy and reform,
> scholars and statesmen, whose very atmosphere is compassion and
> magnanimity towards the poor and weak, are now . . . talking
> about the duty of simply exterminating the German people.[12]

The enthusiasts were temperamentally unsuited to carrying out
their violent plans. Neither Hillis's language nor his bearing suggested that he could stick a bayonet into a Hun. The Reverend Samuel C. Benson, who had declared that "death is not important.
Death is not an enemy; not on the Western front," fainted when he
saw the reality of the trenches: "The piles of dead and wounded
men, bleeding, groaning masses of human pulp, rotting flesh and
decaying bones. . . ."[13] Doughboys who were shown how to kill
prisoners in a popular handbook might naturally have become suspicious of the author's nerve after he admitted he could not bring himself to lay down his life for his buddies. "Personally I know that I
wouldn't have the courage to do it, but many of you have."[14]

So too on the home front, some enthusiasts seemed uneasy with
their own reign of terror. Emerson Hough's *The Web* is the *summa*
of the intense nativism of the war years, and yet while looking at
(and gloating over) the vigilantes' victories, Hough was in some ways
appalled at the society his band of super-patriots had goaded into violence. The net his American Protective League cast for traitors came
in too full. Hough was vexed by the many hapless Red Cross workers
accused of sprinkling powdered glass on bandages and food, and of
poisoning water. The APL, as Hough looked back, now appeared to
have wasted its time chasing after innocents. "It is we Americans
who are the most hysterical people in the world," he fretted, and he
was so discouraged by the instability of the patriots that he feared, in
1919, that America had lost the war.[15]

Those propagandists did not have the stomach to carry out their
plans, but some of the men they encouraged to fight were well satisfied. A few soldiers gloried in the bloodshed, celebrated the killing

of prisoners, and looked forward to punishing the German people.

The connoisseurs of violence were irascible men—they posed as enemies of the conventional sentimentality about the crusade. They criticized the American humanitarian agencies at the front as often as they vilified the Germans.[16] Too, these boasts of aggression were usually aimed to shock the guardians of idealism—women. (Sensational stories are almost always found in letters to wives and mothers, not to other men.) One doughboy, for example, continually wrote his mother to contrast her genteel household with his savage behavior in every battle: ". . . a little baby of our own and its mother for us to worship. I suppose that sounds weak—but just the same, mother dear, we kill all the better for just those thoughts." Now such passages suggest that the soldier felt aggression toward someone besides the enemy. Willa Cather, who respected those men, gives an analysis in *One of Ours* (1922) that psychohistorians are not likely to improve upon: the "crackle of excitement" that ran through these violent men was the erotic energy they could not direct toward their wives and mothers.[17]

We know from close studies of combat in World War I that much of the enthusiasts' writing about bayonet charges and hand-to-hand fights was greatly exaggerated.[18] The fantasy element never restricted the circulation of these stories, but a more forthright statement of the enthusiasts' view might well have made their confessions of bloodletting embarrassing to patriots. If delight in killing was a healthy response to combat stress, the fighting man might be an unreliable servant of his government.

The letters of George Patton from the front reveal a man inebriated by combat and detached from any political cause. Patton's enthusiasm for World War I was undimmed by his observation of the slaughter of the armies of 1914 and his own serious combat wounds: "The more one sees of war the better it is." In the vignettes of the battlefield that Patton composed for his wife his aggression was directed against both friend and foe. He seems as proud of the work of his tanks as, for example, he is of his work with a shovel that he used in an attempt to kill a recalcitrant doughboy. That was not the war planned in Washington.[19]

*        *        *

For many of the civilians who called the soldiers to the trenches, the Administration's picture of a comprehensible, restrained, and ennobling war was not spoiled by the loud talk about bloodletting and the mute testimony at home of veterans' empty sleeves, wards filled with shell-shocked men, and rows of white crosses. To many Progressives in 1918 "the cleansing influence of the war" seemed to herald an age of reform guided by military ideals: "Why not continue on into the years of peace this close, vast, wholesome organism of service, of fellowship, of creative power?" Later, betrayed by both the Allies and the Senate, and rejected by the electorate, liberals did not abandon hope in the analogue of war. In the 1920's the memory of social planning grew golden, and in the next decade the legend was put to use. The Depression revived memories of selfless administrators organizing citizens to fight dark forces. Franklin Delano Roosevelt constantly invoked the wartime mood, used mobilization as a model of his domestic program (as in the Civilian Conservation Corps), and won the allegiance of many liberals who had become nostalgic for the vigorous government of 1917–18.[20]

In the 1920's a parade of professional groups saluted the war. Scientists used the war to vindicate science, and science to justify the war. The astronomer George E. Hale and the physicist Robert Millikan welcomed the new prestige and power of military projects, and other scientists were not slow to point out that the failure of mere inventors to achieve a breakthrough in weaponry was proof that government should turn away from the "wizards" and listen to the men with academic degrees. To the "scientific observer" the wartime laboratory and the progress of society measured by scientific methods "far outbalance the total losses in life and health occasioned by the struggle." The leading American scientific journals lacked any tragic sense of the war; rather, they seized the opportunity to convince the nation that scientific methods promised the social control and military power that would keep the peace.[21]

Engineers were just as ready as scientists to praise the war for furthering their work. Frank A. Scott, chairman of the National Defense Division of the American Society of Mechanical Engineers, chided the military for not relying more on the judgment of his profession, but celebrated the boon to technology in war. The Army's client-professionals provided a friendly forum for such views throughout the 1920's. The Army Ordnance Association also provided a social life that mixed business with pleasure—as with one of their well-advertised excursions to the Aberdeen Proving Ground for "Aviation Night—Firing Will Be Interesting and Spectacular—DO NOT MISS IT."[22]

There were other men of science who had to look more closely at less pleasant effects of the war—the physicians in the AEF who treated cases of "shell shock." The register of the shell shocked was nearly as long as the death list. Doughboys whose courage was unquestionable suddenly had "staring eyes, violent tremors, a look of terror and blue, cold extremities." Hearing such reports, the American press made a pessimistic prognosis. Doughboys would be coming back with damaged brains and permanent disabilities. It was left to the medical officers of the AEF to show that their patients were not pariahs. Those doctors waged a campaign on two fronts—in their treatment centers and in the American press—to return the cripples to service and to remove the stigma of their breakdown.

The psychiatrists in the AEF and their allies at home, The National Committee for Mental Hygiene, brought extraordinary dedication to the shell shocked. Even the professionals who had been hardened to the pathos of state hospital wards and immigration examination centers found the trembling doughboys most affecting: "These monstrous maladies devour our sons. . . . Pierced by the iron shards of a perverted science, they can be rescued only by science undefiled. . . . Awake! Arise! Multiply research! Forge the weapons which alone shall save the lives of those who fight our battles!"[23]

In the campaign for the shell shocked the doctors were not only trying to aid their patients. Dr. Thomas W. Salmon, a director of psychiatry for the AEF and a formidable champion of the shell shocked after the war, saw the opportunity for his profession immediately. "The soldiers have a hold on the hearts of the people which no other mental cases ever had," he wrote a friend from France. "Do all that you can to capitalize this in their behalf. . . . Don't let anybody be satisfied with classifying these cases at the ports of arrival and sending as many as possible to their homes. . . ." Mental hospitals for veterans and "a psychiatric ward into every general hospital" were Salmon's dream—a cause he pleaded for successfully to the American Legion and finally lost only in President Harding's office.

The more Salmon spoke about mental health programs the less he chose to talk about the battlefield where men had broken down. Salmon discussed the personal weaknesses of soldiers, but not the war they endured. He forbade mention of "shell shock" in his hospital at Savenay, succeeded in having the term barred in cabled news from France, and constantly rebuked American editors who continued to use the forbidden words.

Salmon had good reasons to censor the news. There was no direct connection between bombardment and "shell shock," and some soldiers with the syndrome had not been under fire. But in abolishing the misleading term Salmon did not give his patients or the public a way to understand how real conditions on the battlefield affected the mental health of soldiers. "Shell shock," he explained to one editor, "simply confirms in their belief a lot of our most difficult patients who are determined to see in their nervous condition the effects of some external cause rather than the operation of unhealthful mental reaction or abnormal suggestibility." Abolishing the "external cause" of course, meant ceasing to talk about the war in therapy. And, indeed, at the Savenay hospital Salmon guarded the doughboys against "rehearsing painful experiences in the war. . . . check these unhealthy trends of thought," he insisted.

That may have been a good thing for Salmon's patients, as it prevented the deepening of hysterical reactions through autosuggestion. But it was not as salutary for the healthy. The same waters of Lethe that Salmon prescribed to trembling doughboys, he dispensed to all—and took himself. Salmon had ridden in an ambulance at the front to see what his patients had faced. But he did not use his impressions of battle to help the public understand veterans or to help soldiers talk about what they had seen. Freud in the 1920's drew on the war to explore darker theories about man and to reevaluate what a therapist might accomplish. Salmon, with the best of motives, tried to build hospitals and boost his profession. He might have done more had he not, like so many of his time, assumed that peace of mind was to be gained by standing above the battle. War, Salmon explained to a neuropsychiatrist in the Surgeon General's office,

> is not clarified in the least by thinking about it and herein war differs from every other human experience. Thinking is about the most foolish thing a man can do when he is close up to a war. The only proper thing to do is to try on several sets of formulas and, without being too fussy, take the one which most nearly fits your level of intelligence, experience, religion and general outlook on life. Thereafter, the set that you select should be used so exclusively that you would as soon think of dressing in some other color than khaki as to use another. [24]

\* \* \*

The slaughter in Europe did little to diminish the sanguine mood of American munitions makers. Simon Lake, a major contributor to submarine work, spoke with the assurance of Robert Fulton throughout the war. When confronted by the rolls of U-boat victims, Lake said that more lives would have been lost if no submarine had put to sea. "It is my firm conviction," he added, "that it is the destiny of the submarine to put an end forever to the possibility of warfare upon the high seas." [25]

Neither were promoters of aviation hesitant to put forth the airplane as the solution to the bloodshed in Europe. "Every twenty-four hours lost in the enactment of the aviation program means the loss, perhaps, of tens of thousands of lives ultimately" the head of the

Aircraft Production Board announced. American pilots seem never to have entertained the idea that their dogfights and primitive bombing runs were peripheral to the fate of the hundreds of thousands of soldiers below. And both the aerial bureaucrats and aces promoted themselves as peacemakers with great success. Yielding to the lure of a breakthrough in the war, there were many Congressmen willing, as one admitted, to "buy a pig in a poke and take a chance on it." The way had been prepared for men such as "Billy" Mitchell, who broadcast cheerful folklore about an "air power" that could cut short any war by finding "vital centers of the opposing country directly, completely destroying and paralyzing them." [26]

Poison gas warfare had its defenders as well. Specialists in that new ordnance reviewed battle casualties and boasted that they had achieved the most humane weapon of the war. The conclusion of a chief of the Chemical Warfare Service reaffirmed the faith of every nineteenth-century arms booster: "The death rate has constantly decreased as methods of warfare have progressed in efficiency as the result of the application of scientific discoveries." [27]

By the early 1920's the faith that would sustain weapons work was reaffirmed: technology made war briefer, more humane, and less frequent. Rear Admiral Bradley A. Fiske, as proud of his patents as his ribbons, imagined that harnessing the force of the atom in a bomb would be a great sign of the progress of civilization. Thomas A. Edison predicted that the development of such a weapon would make war "unthinkable, and therefore impossible." [28]

In the 1920's, however, the illusion of an arsenal that would contain or abolish war was challenged. The Washington Armament Conference of 1921–22 was not graced, as the pre-war meetings at the Hague had been, by benign judgments on the new ordnance. Colonel House, excited by the new generation of heroes such as Charles Lindbergh, was haunted by the thought of the women and children that the machines might someday kill from the air. And the young men destined to control those weapons were candid about their nightmares. *The Macon Daily Telegraph*'s columnist from Warm Springs, Franklin Delano Roosevelt, ridiculed the notion of a technical breakthrough that would ensure peace and suggested that modern warfare might soon revert to the barbarism of the Dark Ages. John Foster Dulles returned from Versailles appalled at the way the industrial nations clung to their arsenals: "It will be quite fitting if the next war, like a cleansing flood, wipes them away." [29]

# 11

# THE
# WAR OF THE DÉGAGÉ

There was a deeper sort of despair after the Armistice. The "disillu-sioned" writers did not often react directly to the wasteland they had seen (or heard about) in France; rather they were haunted by the unwillingness of their society to listen to what the stunned veterans had to say about war. The emotional distance from battle that Amer-icans had kept since the Civil War became the central concern of the young writers of the 1920's. These novelists and poets provided the most complex working out of American ambivalence about modern war: they addressed what their predecessors had felt.

Not yet a year after the Armistice, Ernest Hemingway's Corporal Krebs learned "that to be listened to at all he had to lie." The lies denigrated his days in uniform and then they eradicated them:

> All of the times that had been able to make him feel cool and clear inside himself when he thought of them; the times so long back when he had done the one thing, the only thing for a man to do, easily and naturally, when he might have done something else, now lost their cool, valuable quality and then were lost themselves.
>
> . . . when he occasionally met another man who had really been a soldier and they talked a few minutes in the dressing room at a dance he fell into the easy pose of the old soldier among other sol-

diers: that he had been badly, sickeningly frightened all the time. In this way he lost everything.[1]

Hemingway and America's other serious novelists of the war began a search for the words that might bring the survivors together. Was there a language that would express what the veterans knew, and that the home front could hear? In the end words failed Krebs, as they failed so many doughboys in novels of homecoming after Versailles. Refugees from the Western Front blundered dumbly on, half-human, unable to share what they had endured. Those broken men found their separate peace in a private ritual of withdrawal. America's best writers denied themselves the powerful and simple responses that control the European novel of disillusionment: revulsion at the blood and anger at the absurdity of the war. America's novelists and poets were anti-war (sometimes by declaration, always at least by implication), and yet they were not lost in a rage about the bloodshed they had seen. Surveying the battlefield, those writers were transfixed, suspended between awe and fright.

\* \* \*

There was no bull market for war books in the 1920's. Volumes such as 'Over the Top' and *Rhymes of a Red Cross Man* dropped from best-seller lists, and in the ten years after Versailles no stories of the war took their place. What publishers called "the taboo on war literature" silenced both bitter and fond talk of war. Revisionist scholarship on the origins of the cataclysm was well under way, but those publications did not draw a wide audience until the 1930's. The publishing house of Doubleday secured lavish praise from General Pershing and Secretary Baker for Thomas G. Frothingham's *American Reinforcement in the World War*, then Doubleday canvassed thousands of administrators and officers who had carried on the mobilization. In all, 28 orders came in (a figure that makes the six-month sale of 63 copies of Dos Passos's obscurely published first novel seem respectable).

This was not a war to be shared. The Library of Congress asked the public for soldiers' letters to build an archive, but the response filled only one small box. Five years after the Armistice, Hollywood had not made a film about the war. To one critic, it seemed that the soldiers had been defeated by the crowds that greeted them, "they laid down a restraining barrage of soft-nosed chocolates and high-explosive cigarettes on the Hoboken docks and withdrew in disorder to the bomb-proof depths of their inner selves. And as the hobnailed feet clattered down the gangplanks, the cry arose, 'The War is over. The next duty of every patriot is to forget it.' " [2]

Laurence Stallings shows us a doughboy so furious at the deaf ears at his old school that he contemplates "tearing down the flagstaff on the campus and removing the silly field gun, and masking all the statues of soldiers." Many novelists of the 1920's strove for the literary equivalent of that vandalism. Those writers led readers onto the killing ground and almost gleefully threw away the last props of sentiment and boasts of self-control that survived on the battlefields of Bierce and De Forest. Women, for example, are no longer the pitiful victims of man's aggression—they are harpies calling for blood. Dos Passos's YMCA girls want Huns mutilated; the mother in Thomas Boyd's *Through the Wheat* offers to send her son a capsule of cyanide of potassium—the poison is to be his comforter. Women, we are made to feel, would be better off without such men, who "played dirty in and out of action and ate up the war." Those doughboys endure too much and freely confess their dumb fright and hysterical laughter as shells churn up the bodies of fallen comrades. [3]

The best American writers, however, were not choked by blood. Despite our alleged national appetite for violence, bloodshed plays a comparatively small part in the American vision of war. The bodies of fighting men pile up much higher in the works of Remarque, Barbusse, and Chapman than in those of Dos Passos, Hemingway, or Faulkner. [4] The simplest reason is that the Americans had seen less of battle. William Faulkner, for example, had little military experience. He stuffed himself with bananas to meet the weight limit for service, paraded around Oxford, Mississippi, in his Canadian uniform when the trick worked, and improvised a war record for gullible biographers. His foibles did not affect the power of his writing, but as an over-eager spectator he was bound to have a different angle of vision than the young novelists of Britain, France, and Germany who fought for years while thousands of men around them died.

Unlike Europeans, American writers could appreciate that hell had exits. The novelists and poets of this country were volunteers who returned with the burden of explaining a war that had touched few lives at home. It is not surprising that American writers chose to study men hurled back from the action into an uncomprehending society. Escape, not blood, was the motif of serious fiction, and it was the achievement of the best writers to make the escape as harrowing as the battle.

No one really leaves the war behind when he flees the front. The healthy are most easily trapped—as in E. E. Cummings's pilgrimage to the "enormous room" or Dos Passos's portraits of doughboys who are chased by MPs or caught, as if on flypaper, by "a sticky juice" of government lies. But the cripples are in a more desperate, but futile, hurry—as with Hemingway's *blessés* who flee to Switzerland, Spain, and Michigan. The broken Donald Mahon in Faulkner's *Soldiers' Pay* is put on a train not able to understand that he is rushing to his homecoming and funeral. The aviator Bayard Sartoris careens down the roads of Yoknapatawpha County gathering more scars for a few months before returning to the sky to find the death he had missed in France. The 1920's furnish a chronicle of withdrawal in which the trapped and damaged soldier wins the victory to "feel cool and clear inside himself" or dies in the last battle to make himself heard.

*      *      *

With John Dos Passos's novels of 1920–22 the compromises made by realists since the Civil War were broken. Previously, the fighting man had been allowed to confess his confusion, cry out in pain, and even remain silent when overwhelmed by violence; but no writer had presented his ordeal as illusory or empty. The wars made sense and the pain was redemptive—even Crane's Henry Fleming dimly realized this. Yet Dos Passos's lost soldiers cannot recover from their confusion and fright and they rage against the authorities who insist that there is rational order and emotional uplift at the front. The dazed Martin Howe in *One Man's Initiation—1917* (1920) learns that there is no red badge of courage for him. He feels caught in a nightmare imposed by society:

> "It surely is different than you'd pictured it, isn't it, now?"
>
> They sat looking at each other while the big drops from the leaky roof smacked on the table or splashed cold in their faces.
>
> "What do you think of all this, anyway?" said the wet man suddenly, lowering his voice stealthily.
>
> "I don't know. I never did expect it to be what we were taught to believe. . . . Things aren't."
>
> "But you can't have guessed that it was like this . . . like Alice in Wonderland, like an ill-intentioned Drury Lane pantomime, like all the dusty futility of Barnum and Bailey's Circus."
>
> "No, I thought it would be hair-raising," said Martin.
>
> "Think, man, think of all the oceans of lies through all the ages that must have been necessary to make this possible! Think of this new particular vintage of lies that has been so industriously pumped out of the press and the pulpit. Doesn't it stagger you?"
>
> Martin nodded.
>
> "Why, lies are like a sticky juice overspreading the world, a living, growing flypaper to catch and gum the wings of every human soul. . . . And the little helpless buzzings of honest, liberal, kindly people, aren't they like the thin little noise flies make when they're caught?" [5]

Dos Passos mocks the initiation theme again in his finest war novel, *Three Soldiers* (1921). John Andrews, the central character, looks to the Army for rejuvenation and finds instead slavery to a civilization that is "nothing but a vast edifice of sham, and," he concludes, "the war, instead of its crumbling, was its fullest and most ultimate expression." With Andrews and Howe we have new war heroes—men who refused to feel and act as their culture dictated. Dos Passos suggests that their defiance was self-destructive and a little mad, but also admirable: "Every man who stood up courageously to die loosened the grip of the nightmare." [6]

The war is too big for Dos Passos's doughboy victims to grasp— "hurried into the jaws of it" or thrown "under the wheels," they cannot tell us what has set this monster on them. In the *USA* trilogy, the words that make sense of World War I are pulled apart and garbled, hung like funny signs through the text. Dos Passos's veterans speak not quite loudly enough to be heard, or the survivors slur their words in their more serious effort to eat bouillabaisse. [7] Dos Passos, however, was neither ignorant nor inarticulate about why he rushed to the front. And his own initiation was more complex than the shattering discoveries of the doughboys in his books.

As a young man, Dos Passos had felt it was his destiny to wear a uniform. He wanted to go to the Naval Academy, and when he settled on Harvard he quarreled with pacifists and endorsed the Plattsburgh military camps for civilians. He could not make up his mind on the question of American belligerency in 1916, but he was quite sure he wanted a place at the front. He was turned down by Herbert Hoover's relief agency in Belgium and prevented by his family from making an early start with the Norton-Harjes volunteers, but he finally joined that ambulance unit in the spring of 1917. [8]

Dos Passos, like some other Harvard poets, had nothing like a conventional martial spirit. E. E. Cummings mocked the very cause he joined; Robert Hillyer threatened Congress in *The Masses* as he volunteered; and Dos Passos, similarly, struck a precarious balance between his intense desire "to see a little of the war personally" and his expectation that this was a "senseless agony of destruction." [9] Though he hoped American intervention might cut short the butchery, he had no patience with optimists. *The Masses* was for him "the word," and the Wilson administration the enemy: "My only refuge from the deepest depression is in dreaming of vengeful guillotines." [10] Dos Passos's initiation and disillusionment were well planned. "I'm sure that by the time I get back from the war," he wrote a close friend in June 1917, "you'll disown me entirely, I'll be so red, radical and revolutionary." [11]

Dos Passos was not disappointed, for the war matched and encouraged his fantasies of violence. He now carried buckets full of amputated hands and limbs behind the lines, and, near Verdun, he seethed at the mindless defense of an absurd cause: "None of the poor devils whose mangled dirty bodies I take to the hospital in my ambulance really give a damn about any of the aims of this ridiculous affair—They fight because they are too cowardly & too unimaginative not to see which way they ought to turn their guns—"

But Dos Passos protested too much and his anger lapsed too often to run very deep. His correspondence reveals a man addicted to danger and discipline, transfixed by a spectacle that fed his art. The war, for Dos Passos, did not taste of ashes, it was bittersweet: we find him savoring it in the same letter in which he longed for doughboys who would shoot their leaders:

> Apart from the utter bitterness I feel about the whole thing, I've been enjoying my work immensely. . . . All the time—ever since our section of twenty Fiat cars climbed down the long hill into the shot-to-hell valley back of this wood that most of our work is in, we've been under intermittent bombardment. . . .
>
> It's queer how much happier I am here in the midst of it than in America, where the air was stinking with lies & hypocritical patriotic gibber—

In his diary, three days later, Dos Passos continues:

> But, gosh, I want to be able to express, later—all of this—all the tragedy and hideous excitement of it. I have seen so very little. I must experience more of it, & more—The grey crooked fingers of the dead, the dark look of dirty mangled bodies, their groans & joltings in the ambulances, the vast tomtom of the guns, the ripping tear shells make when they explode, the song of shells outgoing, like vast woodcocks—their contented whirr as they near their mark—the twang of fragments like a harp broken in the air—& the rattle of stones & mud on your helmet— [12]

Dos Passos's anti-war rhetoric was sincere, too, and eventually his skepticism deprived him of the satisfactions of the front. He taunted and tested the censors in his correspondence and finally they drummed him out of his ambulance unit. Safe in the United States, he then used his family's influence to clear his record, found a doctor to fake a physical examination, and enlisted in the Army. It was the third time he had volunteered to serve the Allies at the front. He did not see action then, but he did contemplate the manuscripts that were to be the opening salvo against the war in the 1920's. Dos Passos's army diary, it must be said, confesses a contentment that he did not often allow his fictional characters. As the Armistice was signed, Dos Passos was an acting sergeant in charge of a mess hall, enjoying the camaraderie and making his men "submit cowedly to my shoutings. . . . I have more hopes of the U.S.A. since I've been in their damned Army than I ever had before—" [13]

\* \* \*

Not all of the soldier-novelists succeeded, like Dos Passos and Faulkner, in keeping their personal attraction to the war out of their work. An excitement and reconciliation with the war is a controlling theme of much of the literature so loosely called "disillusioned."

In the 1920's Ernest Hemingway ran a horror show of war that began with "On the Quai at Smyrna" and ended with the retreat from Caporetto in A *Farewell to Arms*. Hemingway used a harsh light in his close-ups that seemed to reveal a war that was morally empty and physically disgusting—as in the stills he placed throughout *In Our Time*:

> While the bombardment was knocking the trench to pieces at Fossalta, he lay very flat and sweated and prayed oh Jesus Christ get me out of here. Dear Jesus please get me out. Christ please please please Christ. If you'll only keep me from getting killed I'll do anything you say. I believe in you and I'll tell every one in the world that you are the only one that matters. Please please dear Jesus. The shelling moved further up the line. We went to work on the trench and in the morning the sun came up and the day was hot and

muggy and cheerful and quiet. The next night back at Mestre he did not tell the girl he went upstairs with at the Villa Rossa about Jesus. And he never told anybody.[14]

Often, silence and laconic notes of battle are all we get from Hemingway's fighting men. They spin off quizzical reasons for enlisting in the first place, and refuse to talk about the ordeal. These men are curiously detached from the concrete and immediate world that they tell us about ("It did not have anything to do with me. It seemed no more dangerous to me myself than war in the movies," Frederick Henry thought). And Hemingway's soldiers have grown sick of the words that make sense of their campaigns:

> I was always embarrassed by the words sacred, glorious, and sacrifice and the expression in vain. We had heard them, sometimes standing in the rain almost out of earshot, so that only the shouted words came through, and had read them, on proclamations that were slapped up by billposters over other proclamations, now for a long time, and I had seen nothing sacred, and the things that were glorious had no glory and the sacrifices were like the stockyards at Chicago if nothing was done with the meat except to bury it.[15]

Yet in the 1920's the war did make sense to Hemingway, and he did not wish to disparage the sacrifice. Though he ran a horror show, he had a sporting enthusiasm for the violence. Hemingway spent happy, early days of the war rushing to fresh bomb craters, and later, when shrapnel finally ripped his own body, he retained a singular allegiance to the "great sport" of the campaign. "It does give you an awfully satisfactory feeling to be wounded," he wrote to his family, ". . . and how much better to . . . go out in a blaze of light, than to have your body worn out and old illusions shattered."[16]

Hemingway's fighting men, also, were not used up by the war. As Edmund Wilson noted in the first American review of his work, he "has no anti-militarist parti pris which will lead him to suppress from his record the exhilaration of the men." The soldiers in the vignettes from *In Our Time*, for example, construct an obstacle course for their enemy and are delighted when they have "potted" the Germans who leap across the "topping" battlefield steeplechase.[17] Hemingway's veterans flee to bull rings and trout streams to carry on the exacting contests they have played on the battlefield. The ritual makes those contests restorative and thus the ex-soldiers transcend the anger they bring away from their absurd battles. Frederick Henry, for example, has been maimed and sent back to the front, driven into retreat and then threatened by the Italians he serves—but his escape into the icy current of the Tagliamento is a baptism that wipes away those horrors:

> Anger was washed away in the river along with any obligation. . . . I had taken off the stars, but that was for convenience. It was no point of honor. I was not against them. I was through. I wished them all the luck. There were the good ones, and the brave ones, and the calm ones and the sensible ones, and they deserved it.[18]

Similarly, both collections of Hemingway's stories of the war years take us, finally, to a river and unembittered escape. In "Big Two-Hearted River" he draws out each moment of a veteran's spiritual retreat to study a ritual of renewal. Nick arrives in a burnt-over land and must fight to "choke" his mind from working. He walks away from the charred town and forest and fixes his mind on the vibrant life of the river, breaking the outing down into a series of reverent acts. This water, as surely as the Tagliamento, is a river of life: Nick learns to use the current and avoid the dark swamps. Hemingway's imagery is deliberately transparent—Nick can find in the ashes the means to master nature—he takes grasshoppers blackened by the fire to catch the trout that struggle in the current.[19]

To be sure, the fish may be defiled by Nick's touch; he will have to fish the swamp someday—and the world of all of Hemingway's veterans is dark and painful. But war, for Hemingway, does not make that so. His soldiers do not use the war as devil or alibi. Instead, they view combat as an alternative to the contests of peacetime, one that offers reconciliation with a tragic human condition lasting longer than any battle.

\* \* \*

In peacetime Hemingway's veterans finally manage to live within the private emotional world they had created during the campaigns. Two soldier poets, Harry Crosby and E. E. Cummings, did so by making peace and war equally rapturous.

In 1929 Harry Crosby published a lengthy poem in a tooled leather volume that measured 2 × 2½ centimeters—about the size of his thumb. His writing was explosive and he knew that the effect would be greatest if placed in the smallest possible space. That American in Paris fascinated the most brilliant expatriates of his generation. T. S. Eliot, Ezra Pound, Stuart Gilbert, and D. H. Lawrence wrote the notes for his four slim volumes of collected verse. Crosby's *roué* diary, filled with lyrical notes on his journey through literature, drink, drugs, and sex, forms a centerpiece for some of the best memoirs of the 1920's. Always in a hurry to die (the diary explores exotic methods of self-destruction) Crosby's suicide pact with a lover was well-timed for literary effect. The New York tabloids reported the hero's death in 1929 with Crosby's own staccato of excitement.

Crosby began the war with a different enthusiasm. He qualified for the volunteer unit that Theodore Roosevelt had longed to take to Europe, and he rushed over to France to help the wounded before America entered the war. His early letters from the field are filled with pious homilies about the crusade, and the trauma of service under fire never killed the sentimentalist in him. Crosby drove an ambulance across the bare hills near Verdun. He saw the debris of the greatest concentration of firepower history had ever seen. From Verdun in 1917 he wrote his mother to confess that "general ghastliness pervaded the whole ungodly, awful scenery. Death's hand is written over it all," but then he added: "in spite of it all this foreboding evil scenery embodies a certain fascination, a sort of lure that acts as a magnet."

Four days after he wrote home of his fascination, the battle reached the young American. He was trapped in a line of vehicles as German artillery found their range. There was a direct hit on his ambulance: Crosby's wounded were killed, the chassis and motor were blown to pieces, but he was miraculously spared. Crosby had nightmares about that shelling for the rest of his life, but neither his trauma nor another year of war carrying the wounded over the battlefields of eastern France made him bitter. His harrowing moments under fire did not stop his enthusiastic letters home. His affection for the war was permanent; the battle remained an alluring spectacle no matter how estranged he became from the society that had sent him to fight.

After the Armistice he accepted the *Croix de Guerre* with glee ("Oh Boy!!!!!!" he entered in his diary). In the early 1920's he returned to France for a holiday tour of the battlefields and edited an anthology of great poetry that gave generous space to the verse that ratified the crusade. After his terrible shelling and in the midst of the private hell of his diaries, Crosby commended Kipling, Sassoon, Brooke, and Seeger—as well as the stirring martial call of "In Flanders Fields." [20] During the summer of 1925 Crosby brought his wife to live in a deserted gun emplacement in France and dedicated his life to his own poetry.

Crosby kept a picture of the war dead on his study door, and in *Red Skeletons* (1927) he spoke of his nightmare about the "wintersodden slain." He was haunted by the men who had fallen beside him, and yet his are not bitter verses. The war had become exquisite moments of pain. Crosby thought of the ordeal as "Crucifixion" and he was just as earnest in his use of his religious language as the enthusiasts of 1918 had been. *"Tout est dangereux et tout est nécessaire—"* Crosby chanted, but not as a stoic. He was obsessed by the war and cherished it as much as he did his gin bottles, opium pipes, and "fire princesses" of his last years around Paris. Amidst his revels, he recorded "the very impressive" unveiling of a statue of Alan Seeger; Crosby marked Armistice Day as the most significant moment of the year; and he bribed his way to the top of a huge crane for a better view of the funeral procession of Marshal Foch.

Arming himself again and making an act of love consummate in death was the last, logical step in Crosby's martial life. The sun was all important in Crosby's inner war. It was the explosive source of energy that he invoked both to charge his erotic dreams and to fuel his fantasies of death. The battlefields of France had meant "the first stray thrusts of Sun into the Soul" and as a worshipper of the sun in the 1920's he returned to the war. Just as his sexual imagery is frequently martial, his furious thanatopsis casts him as a mad warrior, daring to destroy everything the sun has created and, finally, he wrote "I lay Siege to the Sun." As an old soldier, Crosby was not bitter; as a sensualist, he stayed in uniform.[21]

Harry Crosby in the 1920's.
(*Courtesy of Morris Library, University of Southern Illinois at Carbondale*)

\*     \*     \*

E. E. Cummings was obsessed by the men of the war who had gone quietly to their deaths as well as the mad old soldiers, like Crosby, who ranted and clung to life. He meditated on the corpses, those "vivid noiseless boys" who had heard "death's clever enormous voice." He scorned the society that had sent men to die and wanted the soldier's story untold.[22] It is true, however, that Cummings's heroes were the incoherent and the half-dead.

Cummings's war poetry was published in the 1920's with a page stained purple, an orange cover specked with gold—as if to defy the camouflage of the Western Front. *The Enormous Room* (1922) was his most sustained effort to expose the war. Here he told how he spent most of the war blissfully trapped with men nearly as mute and forgotten as the dead soldiers. An ambulance driver of suspicious habits, Cummings was imprisoned by the French with other outcasts in the "enormous room" at La Ferté Macé. In his chronicle of that time, he spoke of people in the prison as mannequins and sought to

> lift from their grey box at random certain (to me) more or less as-
> tonishing toys; which may or may not please the reader, but whose
> colours and shapes and textures are a part of that actual Present—
> without future and past—whereof they alone are cognizant who—so
> to speak—have submitted to an amputation of the world.

Those war toys give few hints of their suspicious thoughts or subversive actions; the government seems to have locked them away simply because they were playful—just as Cummings wound up there because he was pleased to say he would bomb Germans but not hate them. Cummings celebrates those "Delectable Mountains" among his cellmates who are childlike or mad enough to mock the conventional nonsense about the war. And Cummings believed those mannequins were dangerous men. In the happy face of the primitive, he saw revolution:

> O *gouvernement français*, I think it was not very clever of you to put
> this terrible doll in La Ferté . . . for when Governments are found

dead there is always a little doll on top of them, pulling and tweaking with his little hands to get back the microscopic knife which sticks firmly in the quiet meat of their hearts.[23]

The shells of men that Cummings parades in *The Enormous Room* are the most subversive characters that turn up in postwar American writing. They do not learn to live with the war in Hemingway's contests and bars, they reject Dos Passos's soap box, they refuse to smash themselves up as Faulkner's veterans must. Cummings's men grin from the corner society allows them and encourage the primitivism that will make a sham civilization collapse.

Behind these mannequins there is, of course, Cummings and his own subversive grin. The poet was not a pawn in the war. He had come freely to France, volunteered for the Lafayette Escadrille when ambulance work became tedious, and after his tour in the enormous room he happily accepted his call into the American Army. Cummings loved to explain his compulsion to seek out camps and battlefields. "I am he who would drink beer and eat shit if he saw somebody else doing it, especially if that somebody were compelled to do it," he wrote his father, ". . . noone [*sic*] shall come out of the valley and the mountain with the same music in his eyes as me." [24] War had become the moral pilgrimage for the artist—as Cummings sought to make clear through all his allusions to Bunyan in *The Enormous Room*. But Christian, this time, gains insights through laughter and is cleansed by filth. It is the mad joy of the toys that saves Le Nouveau—his Christ is, appropriately, a "doll": "a little wooden man hanging all by itself . . . with . . . a ponderous and jocular fragment of drapery." The "unmistakably ecclesiastical" enormous room where Le Nouveau is initiated is ringed by pails of excrement. He jumps from the *douche* that threatens to remove his dirt, takes the "urine-coloured" soup and "liquid slime" coffee and "I felt a renewed interest in living as soon as the deathful swallow descended to my abdomen." Cummings is now ready to join the fellowship of the men whose hidden virtue is signified by the thickness of the caked dirt on their bodies. The hated authorities are immaculate;

the Christ-like prisoner, "Surplice," is the man who carries the pails of excrement.

Cummings's initiation and salvation were complete: "I was happier in La Ferté Macé, with the Delectable Mountains about me, than the very keenest words can pretend to express." [25] Other major writers, no matter what their affection for their life in uniform, come back to speak of loss—the wounds that will not heal, the words they can no longer use. Cummings alone speaks as a man whole and reborn. Serving his country, he has become a confident enemy of its culture.

\*       \*       \*

The doll-like men who inspired Cummings were everywhere after the Armistice—as if to signal the personal detachment of so many after the years of blood. The effigies in literature are more memorable than the fully human characters: Henry Adams posed as a mannequin in his *Education* (which was enormously popular in 1918); T. S. Eliot exhibited the hollow men; and Karel Čapek added the word "robot" to our language. William Faulkner was the most acute student of these phantom men. His homecomings capture the silent incomprehension that he knew stretched back to the men who returned with their mules after Appomattox. Though Faulkner is more shocking than other American novelists of the war in Europe, his nightmare shows us little of the blood. Rather, we have a vision of the terrible detachment of fighting men.

Faulkner wrote of a war that did not unfold. It is that sense of discovery which tied all the other writers of the 1920's to the Civil War realists: we see battle through the eyes of naïve or incredulous initiates; we watch the soldiers get their bearings, lose their illusions, and learn to stand it or run. Only Faulkner refused to provide such a delicate unfolding of feelings. Old women and young blacks may form insights about war—thus Aunt Jenny is contemptuous of the Sartoris campaigns and the family's black recruit declares that "War unloosed de black man's mouf. . . . Give him de right to talk"—but Faulkner's white boys neither learn nor explain. [26] His warriors endure or fight back, but they lack the ability to make sense of it all. John Sartoris has a vocabulary of only two hundred words, and not enough teeth to make himself understood. Bayard, his brother, is no more articulate. Donald Mahon's head has been crushed; we hear nothing from him. Even when Faulkner provides a sheaf of war letters, as in the short story "Victory," the childlike sentences hide everything the soldier endured.

Free of any duty to disclose, Faulkner's soldiers have a more frightening capacity to act than any of the other damaged young men in the literature of the war. His soldiers do not keep diaries or start conversations, they brood silently and when pushed too far they lash back at authority. None of Dos Passos's or Hemingway's rebels seek such a bloody separate peace. John Sartoris stamps on the hand of his corporal and "he could feel the man's bones through his boot"; another soldier sticks his bayonet through the neck of his sergeant-major and "tries to shake the speared body on the bayonet as he would shake a rat on an umbrella rib." [27]

But killing and revenge are not the heart of the horror in Faulkner's work. The greater terror is that dead bodies have come back to remind the living of those battles. Faulkner's soldiers have not gained any new understanding of themselves at the front; they have simply died and come home. "They are dead, all the old pilots, dead on the eleventh of November, 1918," Faulkner judged; "you will not know it," the fighting men are warned, "but you are all dead." [28]

For a time, the ghosts were welcome. At first "uniforms could all walk: they were not only fashionable and romantic, but they were also . . . going too far away and too immediately to tell on you." When uniforms stopped running, those uncomprehending dead have none of the dignity and honor of the decently buried old soldiers in the town—represented by the Confederate near the courthouse who, shading his eyes with his stone hand, keeps watch on the homecoming. "The man that was wounded is dead and this is another person, a grown child," Donald Mahon's friends conclude in *Soldiers' Pay*, "it's his apathy, his detachment that's so terrible." [29] In fact it is the town's lack of interest that hurries such "walking funerals" on. Donald Mahon is a sphinx without a riddle to all his old intimates; they have no curiosity about this relic that has suddenly been shipped home to them. Bayard Sartoris and the other soldiers have no one to listen to them, and so they lose their grip on the little they know. Bayard finds only one man in Yoknapatawpha County who has fought and wants to talk:

> It was a vague, dreamy sort of tale [that Bayard heard], without beginning or end and filled with stumbling references to places wretchedly mispronounced—you got an impression of people, creatures without initiative or background or future, caught timelessly in a maze of solitary conflicting preoccupations, like bumping tops, against an imminent but incomprehensible nightmare.

As the unreality of this shared experience hits Bayard, he comes to the judgment pronounced on him when he was still at the front: "Perhaps he was dead. . . . That would account for it, would explain so much; that he too was dead and this was hell, through which he moved for ever and ever with an illusion of quickness. . . ." [30]

\* \* \*

The novelists and poets of the dégagé bring a half-century of American discourse on war to a logical conclusion. Silent men have again come home from war, just as they had after Appomattox. But this time the veterans are mute because they are half-dead and cut off from the society that sent them to fight, not because they guard the treasured memory of an inexpressible ordeal. That evanescent enemy in American wars, so abstract that he might be crushed one moment and welcomed as a comrade the next, has at last disappeared. A "worthy enemy" has lost the power to validate the warrior's campaign, and for that reason the literature of the war in Europe tells us nothing about Germans. Coming to terms with war now means coming to terms with yourself, with the men who fought at your side, and with the citizens who sent you to fight. Finally, the destructive power that mesmerized the prophets of the modern arsenal has stunned the most sensitive men on the Western Front. After Versailles no one is left to make sense of violence on this new scale. Empty men have come home, unable to share their nightmare, and beyond anger.

# AFTERWORD:
# AMERICA'S HEALING WARS

In the sixty years after the Civil War Americans struggled with a divided vision of armed conflict. It shaped their memories of war as well as their plans for new campaigns. Soldiers sought to reconcile their duty to pursue their enemy with a compulsion to respect him. Students of the arsenal felt both liberated and manipulated by their new weapons. And Americans glimpsed a nightmare on the battlefield that could not be shared with the people on the home front. By the 1920's none of those tensions had been resolved, and some had grown so acute that they prefigured our own.

It is a mistake to believe that we can see all of our anxieties on the anxious faces of Americans at war before Versailles. Though nineteenth-century Americans lived with contradictory feelings about battle, they were more inclined to say, with Walt Whitman, "Do I contradict myself? / Very well then I contradict myself, / (I am large, I contain multitudes.)" For that reason, I do not wish to change the stern faces of the warriors that stare at us from the corners of our parks.

The campaigns after Appomattox, reconstructed by the old soldiers or anticipated in the imaginary battles of prophets, had a healing effect. That curious bullet promoted in the Hearst press before World

War I might be the symbol for that generation's vision of war: just as the shreds of metal plunged into the bodies of the enemy, a capsule of medicine exploded into the flesh, deadening the pain and healing the wound. America lost the ability to imagine such weapons after Versailles. For nineteenth-century Americans the gathering destructive power of their arsenal was benign; we, on the other hand, must think about the unthinkable. Where they closed their eyes to the violence of battle, we imagine bloodletting to be a special curse of our culture. They pronounced their enemy worthy, and still fought him without quarter; we have found enemies whose determination saps our will to fight and whose way of life seems to provide a powerful critique of our own. Soldiers of the last century rarely spoke about their guilt as executioners . . . or as survivors in battle. The literature of our time carries voices of veterans who are ashamed to have lived when other men died—soldiers filled with the animating guilt of men who have shot into the darkness too often and will kill no more.

Those anxieties, like the consolations of earlier wars, are in some ways timeless. Modern warfare has clearly touched on ancient fears, particularly on the Christian fascination with punishment and retribution in the form of calamity. All cultures find ways to pay respect to their enemies. Since the Renaissance, Europeans have produced a rich fantasy literature about the beneficence of weapons. Yet Victorian America was not simply struggling with other peoples' problems. No other nation survived a fratricidal war to find an "alien" enemy on native soil. No nation was to carry the fascination with a protective arsenal further. Because war touched Americans so deeply, they were not always able to talk directly about their dilemmas. The reticence was not innocence. By the 1920's the Americans who built the arsenal and fought the first modern wars had defined most of the problems about armed force that we now grope to resolve in different ways.

To reject the path taken by the children of the Civil War is not to denigrate them. We denigrate Victorian Americans by assuming that they have nothing to teach and by making their confusions our own.

We can broaden our vision of soldiers, weapons, and violence by seeing how other Americans at war narrowed theirs. By placing themselves above the battle, the old campaigners have left it to us to find our way out of it.

# ACKNOWLEDGMENTS AND SOURCES

This has been a project that, I fear, exhausted colleagues sooner than sources. I began this study as a dissertation for Samuel Haber and over the years I have not been able to plumb his fund of good advice; his labor on this project has been extraordinary. Richard Abrams, Henry F. May, and Henry Nash Smith offered extensive suggestions and encouragement about the manuscript at an early stage. More recently, John A. Garraty and Eric L. McKitrick have been invaluable editors. Michael Rogin, Martin Sherwin, and David Lundberg have helped me avoid many mistakes. David Hollinger has shared his considerable editorial skills and knowledge of nineteenth-century attitudes about science. Ronald Walters and Carol H. Leonard have helped in a variety of ways, particularly by drawing my attention to psychological aspects of the literature on peace and war. Hiroko Tsuchiya has been a fine research assistant. Caroline Taylor and Sheldon Meyer of Oxford University Press have done excellent work in shepherding this manuscript into print. Finally, my students at the University of California at Berkeley and those at Columbia University deserve considerable credit—for hearing out (and questioning) many of my ideas about war in American culture.

I am grateful for research grants from the Council for Research in the Social Sciences at Columbia University; the Committee on Research, University of California at Berkeley; and the U.S. Arms Control and Disarmament Agency through the National Academy of Sciences.

Librarians at the following archives have been most helpful in my manuscript research: Library of Congress, Manuscript Division; National Archives; Henry E. Huntington Library; Oberlin College Library; Mark Twain Papers, University of California at Berkeley; Swarthmore College Peace Collection, Friends Historical Library of Swarthmore College; Hoover Institution on War, Revolution, and Peace, Stanford University; Yale University Library; William L. Clements Library, University of Michigan; Robert A. Millikan Library, California Institute of Technology; Nebraska State Historical Society; Special Collections, Columbia University; U.S. Army Military History Research Collection, Carlisle Barracks, Pennsylvania; and the Library of the Peace Palace, the Hague.

✻ ✻ ✻

In the Notes I have tried to supply a rich sampling of the sources that led to my conclusions, but some readers will find a very short list of sources more helpful. I include here titles I wish to rescue from general neglect as well as works, which, though well known, I am indebted to in ways a note cannot show.

It is also true that in considering six decades I have had to limit my sources severely and, to some extent, arbitrarily. Though I think the same pattern of responses to soldiers, weapons, and violence would emerge if different materials were used, serious readers will want to know where to find alternative views.

## GENERAL WORKS ON WAR

The most important single book I read was J. Glenn Gray, *The Warriors: Reflections on Men in Battle* (New York, 1959). Gray's attempt to come to terms with combat in World War II raises questions rarely recognized by military historians. I. F. Clarke, *Voices Prophesying War, 1763–1984* (New York, 1966), is an invaluable guide to the European imaginative literature. Edward Mead Earle ed., *Makers of Modern Strategy: Military Thought from Machiavelli to Hitler* (Princeton, 1952), seems to me still the best general work on military thought. There are two invaluable books on U.S. strategists: Russell F. Weigley, *Towards an American Army: Military Thought from Washington to Marshall* (New York & London, 1962), and Walter Millis, ed., *American Military Thought* (Indianapolis, 1966). John Shy, "The American Military Experience: History and Learning," *Journal of Inter-Disciplinary History* I (Winter 1971) 205–28, brings out some new perspectives that lie outside of my study. The separation between the culture of civilians and that of the military is a major theme of Walter Millis, *Arms and Men: A Study in American Military History* (New York, 1956), and Samuel P. Huntington, *The Soldier and the State: the Theory and Politics of Civil-Military Relations* (Cambridge, Mass., 1957). Every historian of war is indebted to two pioneering cross-cultural studies: John U. Nef, *War and Human Progress: An Essay in the Rise of Industrial Civilization* (Cambridge, Mass., 1950), and Alfred Vagts, *A History of Militarism: Civilian and Military* (rev. ed.; New York, 1959). John Keegan, *The Face of Battle* (New York, 1976), sets forth the limitations of traditional military history and then shows how a gifted historian may overcome them.

Other scholars' problems and methods, though quite different from my own, have helped me think through my approach: Franco Fornari, *The Psychoanalysis of War* (Garden City, N.Y., 1974); Martin J. Sherwin, *A World Destroyed: The Atomic Bomb and the Grand Alliance* (New York, 1975); and Robert Jay Lifton, *Home from the War—Vietnam Veterans: Neither Victims nor Executioners* (New York, 1973).

## NINETEENTH-CENTURY MILITARY MEMOIRS

Edmund Wilson's cranky introduction to his languid—and perceptive—essays in *Patriotic Gore: Studies in the Literature of the American Civil War* (New York, 1962) helps make his the liveliest work on the Civil War; Kenneth Lynn, "The Right to Secede from History," in *Visions of America* (Westport, Conn., 1973), throws some light on Wilson's murky intentions. Daniel Aaron, *The Unwritten War: American Writers and the Civil War* (New York, 1973), appeared too late to influence my conclusions, though I have learned much from the broad range of Aaron's scholarship. Given the choice between Aaron's measured judgments (which are quite compatible with my own) and Wilson's wrongheadedness, I would still recommend *Patriotic Gore* as the better book.

George M. Fredrickson's pioneering effort to achieve an "inner" view of the Civil War seems to me to stand up quite well. Indeed, he is so persuasive that historians must work hard not to tell the story of *The Inner Civil War: Northern Intellectuals and the Crisis of the Union* (New York, 1966) simply with a different cast of characters. Frederick C. Jaher, *Doubters and Dissenters: Cataclysmic Thought in America, 1885–1918* (Cambridge, Mass., 1964), is an important study of war and the American imagination.

The best places to start reading on the Indian wars are George Custer, *My Life on the Plains* (New York, 1874)—even though most of Custer's own colleagues deleted the "f" from the second word of the title—and George Crook, *Autobiography*, ed. Martin F. Schmitt, (Norman, Okla., 1960). The clearest brief narrative of these campaigns is Ralph K. Andrist, *The Long Death: The Last Days of the Plains Indians* (New York, 1964). Don Rickey, Jr., *Forty Miles a Day on Beans and Hay; The Enlisted Soldier Fighting the Indian Wars* (Norman, Okla., 1963), is an impressive research effort with results that parallel my conclusions about the ambivalence of the officers. Stephen E. Ambrose, *Crazy Horse and Custer* (New York, 1975), makes the sort of comparative study that has long been needed. Robert M. Utley, *Frontier Regulars: The United States Army and the Indian, 1866–1890* (New York, 1973), appeared after I reached my conclusions, but broadened my understanding of the Army's predicament in several ways and led me to evidence that I would otherwise have missed. S. L. A. Marshall, *Crimsoned Prairie: The Wars Between the United States Army and the Plains Indian*

*During the Winning of the West* (New York, 1972), is not as concise as Andrist nor as extensively researched as Utley, but his work does put the Indian wars in the perspective of twentieth-century counterinsurgency strategy.

## COMBAT AND PREPAREDNESS: 1898–1917

Three books provide a clear narrative of the war against Spain and the "pacification" of the Philippines: Graham A. Cosmas, *An Army for Empire: the United States Army in the Spanish American War* ([Columbia, Mo.], 1971); Frank Freidel, *The Splendid Little War* (Boston, 1958); John Morgan Gates, *Schoolbooks and Krags: The United States in the Philippines, 1898–1902* (Westport, Conn., 1973). Richard Hofstadter, "Cuba, the Philippines, and Manifest Destiny," in *The Paranoid Style in American Politics and Other Essays* (New York, 1965), is probably the best known article on the war, yet it remains rich in insights and suggestions that no historian has taken further. Gerald F. Linderman, *The Mirror of War: American Society and the Spanish-American War* (Ann Arbor, 1974), is certainly the most sensitive major study of the war. Linderman's use of small-town newspapers is particularly illuminating.

The most balanced appraisal of Theodore Roosevelt is William H. Harbaugh, *The Life and Times of Theodore Roosevelt*, (rev. ed.; New York, 1975). Harbaugh's judicious and graceful treatment is not, however, in all ways superior to the acid portrait offered by Henry F. Pringle, *Theodore Roosevelt: A Biography* (New York, 1931). Two studies with quite different views than my own deserve the attention of all serious students of Roosevelt. David H. Burton, *Theodore Roosevelt: Confident Imperialist* (Philadelphia, 1968), seems to me not to deal adequately with the evidence that casts doubt on his conclusions. Richard T. Fry, "Community Through War: A Study of Theodore Roosevelt's Rise and Fall as a Prophet and Hero in Modern America" (Ph.D. diss., Univ. Minn., 1969), is the most successful attempt to view that mercurial American as a man held in harness by a philosophy.

Debate on American wars in this period seems to me not to have produced a very distinguished polemical literature. Major exceptions are essays written by two anti-imperialists just before they died: William James, "The Moral Equivalent of War," in the valuable anthology edited by Staughton Lynd, *Nonviolence in America: A Documentary History* (Indianapolis, 1966), and William Graham Sumner, "War," in *War and Other Essays* (New Haven, 1911). Overviews of the opponents of intervention and overseas expansion are offered by Robert L. Beisner, *Twelve Against Empire: The Anti-Imperialists, 1898–1900* (New York, 1968); E. Berkeley Tompkins, *Anti-Imperialism in the United States: the Great Debate, 1890–1920* (Philadelphia, 1970); and Roland Marchand, *The American Peace Movement and Social Reform, 1898–1918* (Princeton, 1972).

## WORLD WAR I AND AFTER

As Warren Cohen has shown in *American Revisionists; The Lessons of Intervention in World War I* (New York, 1967), the attention historians have paid to intervention must be called obsessive. Edward M. Coffman, *The War To End All Wars; The American Military Experience in World War I* (New York, 1968), is the best one-volume survey of this vast literature. The impressive works analyzing the decision to intervene may make us forget how many questions about preparedness have been untouched. We have very few regional studies or sophisticated works on the draft, for example. John Patrick Finnegan, *Against the Specter of a Dragon: The Campaign for American Military Preparedness, 1914–1917* (Westport, Conn., 1974), is an important, balanced study. These monographs are well written and approach the war years in fresh ways: Frederick C. Luebke, *Bonds of Loyalty; German Americans and World War I* (DeKalb, Ill., 1974); Joan M. Jensen, *The Price of Vigilance* (Chicago, 1968); George T. Blakey, *Historians on the Homefront; American Propagandists for the Great War* ([Lexington, Ky.], 1970); Bruce Frazer, "Yankees at War: Cohesion and Cooperation on the Connecticut Homefront, 1917–1918" (Ph.D. diss., Columbia Univ., 1975).

Students of World War I, of whatever political persuasion, will find Randolph Bourne's dissenting essays of 1917 and 1918 invaluable. They have been collected in *War and the Intellectuals*, ed. Carl Resek (New York, 1964). Christopher Lasch, *The New Radicalism in America, 1889–1963: The Intellectual as a Social Type* (New York, 1965), seems to me unfair to Bourne, but Lasch makes acute observations about many other dissenters. For an understanding of how the war shook the verities of the older generation, Henry F. May, *The End of American Innocence; A Study of the First Years of Our Own Time, 1912–1917* (New York, 1959), is essential. George Creel has remained a curiously neglected figure. I have discussed his case in my sketch in Supplement V, *Dictionary of American Biography*.

I learned the most from two of the briefest discussions of the combat literature: John Genthe, *American War Narratives, 1917–1918* (New York, 1970), and Charles A. Fenton, "Ambulance Drivers in France and Italy, 1914–1918," *American Quarterly*, III (1951), 326–43; I reached different conclusions than Genthe and Fenton, but I would not have been able to disagree without the bibliographical information they supplied. John D. Davies, *The Legend of Hobey Baker* (Boston, 1966), is an indulgence in Princeton nostalgia that is most successful in evoking the mood of the volunteers from the Ivy League. The three-volume *History of the American Field Service in France, 'Friends of France,' 1914–1917* (Boston & New York, 1920), is a beautiful monument to the men of that class.

Stanley Cooperman, *World War I and the American Novel* (Baltimore, Md., 1967), is the most comprehensive treatment, but Frederick J. Hoffman, *The Twenties; American Writing in the Post-War Decade* (New York, 1962), chap. 2, is also very valuable. There is a brilliant exchange between Archibald MacLeish and Malcolm Cowley on the meaning of the war in the *New Republic*, LXXVI (Sept. 20, Oct. 4, 1933). Paul Fussell, *The Great War and Modern Memory* (New York, 1975), deals only with the British literature, but his judgments of how the war changed modern sensibilities apply to American culture as well. John Ellis, *The Social History of the Ma-*

*chine Gun* (New York, 1975), is particularly good on World War I. Dixon Wecter, *When Johnny Comes Marching Home* (Cambridge, Mass., 1944), remains the broadest survey of the demobilization of the common soldier. One of America's most bizarre soldiers has at last been studied by a careful scholar: Geoffrey Wolff, *Black Sun: The Brief Transit and Violent Eclipse of Harry Crosby* (New York, 1976). We badly need a comparative study of the novels of World War I that respects—yet transcends—the literary tradition of each novelist's country. Judith L. Johnston has made an excellent start: "The Cultural Legacy of World War I: A Comparative Study of Selected War Novels" (Ph.D. diss., Stanford Univ., 1975).

# NOTES

## 1
## THE ENDURING AND THE FORGOTTEN WAR

1. Karl von Clausewitz, *On War*, ed. Anatol Rapoport (Harmondsworth, Eng., Pelican, 1968), pp. 345, 103, 150–51.
2. There are two excellent discussions of the impact of Jomini on American military thought: David Donald's essay in *Lincoln Reconsidered: Essays on the Civil War Era* (New York, 1956), pp. 82–102, esp. 88–90; and Russell F. Weigley, *Towards an American Army: Military Thought from Washington to Marshall* (New York & London, 1962), pp. 55–78. In 1861 Col. S. B. Holabird wrote an important introduction to his translation of Jomini's *Treatise on Grand Military Operations* (New York, 1865).
3. Jomini was critical of the eighteenth-century rationalist approach to war, which, ironically, his writings perpetuated among nineteenth-century strategists. See the essay on Jomini by Crane Brinton, Gordon A. Craig, and Felix Gilbert in E. M. Earle, ed., *Makers of Modern Strategy* (Princeton Univ., 1941). On the chivalric outlook of two of the most influential students of Jomini see D. H. Mahan, *Advanced Guard Out-Posts* . . . (3d ed.; New York, 1864), p. 24; H. W. Halleck, *Elements of Military Art and Science* [completed 1859] (New York, 1862), p. 13 (quoted). Francis Lieber, *Instructions for the Government of Armies of the United States in the Field*, rev. ed., (New York, 1863), pp. 5, 7, 18–19 (quoted).
4. Donald, *Lincoln Reconsidered*, p. 95; Bell Irvin Wiley has made the most extensive survey of the narratives and personal papers of the war.

His two volumes of research are combined in *The Common Soldier in the Civil War* (New York, n.d.). Nearly every chapter is rich in these varied responses.

5. Andrew P. Peabody, *Lessons from Our Late Rebellion* (Boston, 1867), p. 2. Paul H. Buck, *The Road to Reunion, 1865–1900* (Boston, 1937), p. 247. This work is the most valuable single study of the theme of reconciliation in military memoirs.

6. This laconic, never sensational treatment of suffering in war is common in the most popular memoirs, e. g. Geoge B. McClellan, *McClellan's Own Story* (New York, 1887). McClellan wrote vividly about combat only once, in a short paragraph (p. 439) he seems to have composed on his deathbed. John Gibbon, *Personal Recollections of the Civil War* [1885] (New York & London, 1928), pp. 423–24.

7. Robert U. Johnson and Clarence C. Buel, eds., *Battles and Leaders of the Civil War*, 4 vols. (New York, 1887–88), I, 238. The *Century's* circulation jumped from 127,000 to 225,000 during the first six months of the series. Another massive collection, *The Annals of the War*, was brought out by the *Philadelphia Weekly Times* in 1879. *The Annals* had more contentious Northern and Southern contributors, but they avoided the unpleasant details of the fight. Only 2 of the 56 sketches offered any realistic description of bloodshed.

8. Grant contributed essays to the *Century* series that later became part of his *Memoirs* 2 vols., (New York, 1885). Grant's concise style is perhaps best illustrated by his one-sentence description of the destruction of Atlanta (II, 361). Edmund Wilson, *Patriotic Gore* (New York, 1966), p. 152.

9. Horatio C. King, *The Society of the Army of the Potomac: Report of the Seventeenth Annual Re-union at San Francisco, Cal.* (New York, 1886), p. 55. Others recalled the mild and humane feelings of the men in arms: see James A. Beaver, *The Society of the Army of the Potomac, . . . Re-union* (New York, 1888), p. 15; speech by George W. Curtis, pp. 27–42. The presentation of Army life as droll and colorful reached a large audience in articles such as C. F. Williams, "Lights and Shadows of Army Life," *Century*, XXVIII (1884), 803–19. The effect was also achieved by a sort of petty realism—the recollection of such trivial, everyday details of life at the front that the battle-field seemed like a normal environment, and suffering was lost sight of. That is the approach of Assistant Secretary of War Charles A. Dana, *Recollections of the Civil War* (New York, 1902). Here we often learn more of the condition of Dana's tent than what happened near by—at the Bloody Angle or Shenandoah Valley. *Selected Prose of John Wesley Powell*, ed. George Crossette (Boston, 1970), p. 1. Buck, *Road to Reunion*, p. 194.

On Southern reconciliation: Henry W. Grady, quoted by Buck, *Road to Reunion*, p. 194. R. E. Colston, "Gettysburg 20 Years After," *Century*, XXXVI (1888), 792. Southern contributors to the *Century* series in the 1880's avoided shocking or distressing details of battle as consistently as Northern veterans did.

10. Richard Taylor, *Destruction and Reconstruction* [1879] (Waltham, Mass., 1968), pp. 50–51, 74; on total war, see pp. 39, 147, 192–93. Mary Chesnut, *A Diary from Dixie* [1905] (Boston, 1949). On other Southern attempts at realism see *Minutes of the United Confederate Veterans: 10th Meeting* (1900), pp. 58–64; and speech published separately, delivered at 15th Meeting: N. E. Harris, *The Civil War: Its Results and Lessons* (Macon, Ga., 1906).

11. *Ingersollia*, ed. Elmo [pseud.] (Chicago, 1882), p. 84, and *Donnelliana: An Appendix to Caesar's Column*, ed. Everett W. Fish (Chicago, 1892), p. 66.

12. The war as catalyst for economic and technological growth was a strong theme in late nineteenth-century memoirs—e.g. G. M. Dodge, *How We Built the Union Pacific Railway* (Council Bluffs, Iowa, n.d.), p. 73; Dodge, *Romantic Realities, the Story of the Building of the Pacific Roads* (Omaha, 1889), p. 20; this speech to the Army of the Tennessee was followed by similar sentiments by Gen. Sherman, p. 24 (quoted). Oration by G. W. Curtis, *Proceedings of the Society of the Potomac, 19th Reunion* (1888), p. 31. Address by Gov. J. B. Grant, *Journal of the 17th Annual Session, National Encampment, G.A.R.* (1883), p. 196.

13. The most persuasive analysis of the importance of discipline to Northern policy-makers and cultural critics is George M. Fredrickson, *The Inner Civil War: Northern Intellectuals and the Crisis of the Union* (New York, 1968), Parts II and III. *The Papers of Woodrow Wilson* (Princeton Univ., 1966–), ed. Arthur S. Link, I, 665, 619 (1880). To the editor (and to Wilson?) "inestimable" was a questionable part of the draft; I have deleted the editor's question mark. On Wilson's deepest perceptions of the war, see *Papers*, XI, 474–75 (1900).

14. Whitman, *Specimen Days*, in *Leaves of Grass and Selected Prose*, ed. John A. Kouwenhoven (New York, 1950), p. 634–36.

15. Clausewitz, *On War*, pp. 386–87.

16. Sherman, cited in Weigley, *Towards an American Army*, p. 88. See also Lloyd Lewis, *Sherman, Fighting Prophet* (New York, 1958), p. 335. Among fighting men, Sherman was undoubtedly the most articulate (and the sternest) lecturer to the South on the consequences of disobedience to the law of the Union, e.g. see *Memoirs* [1875] (Bloomington, Ill., 1957), II, 227, 249. Sheridan, cited in Harold D. Lasswell, *Propaganda Techniques in the World War* (New York, 1927), p. 83. It is conventional to give Grant some credit (or blame) for the innovation of bringing war to noncombatants. Of course Grant approved the tactics of his field commanders, and he sometimes commented favorably on their marches in his *Memoirs* (e.g. II, 369). But the usual analysis is built almost entirely upon what others said about Grant's intentions—he rarely made any comment on the innovation.

17. Sherman, cited in Lewis, *Sherman*, p. 416. Sheridan, *Personal Memoirs of Philip H. Sheridan*, 2 vols. (New York, 1888), I, 487–88.

18. *McClellan's Own Story*, p. 101; Sheridan, *Memoirs*, I, 487; John M. Schofield, "Notes on 'The Legitimate in War,' " *The Journal of the Military Service Institution of the United States*, II (1881), 6; see also his *Forty-Six Years in the Army* (New York, 1907), pp. 313–14. Francis Lieber's *Instructions*, Parts 18, 19, give the new rules of war for non-combatants.

19. *McClellan's Own Story*, e.g., presents the general speaking both for and against a war on population—with no sense that there is a contradiction (pp. 101, 488). Weigley, *Towards an American Army*, has studied the reluctance of late-nineteenth-century strategists to face the implications of this new kind of war, pp. 94–99. *Spanish Diplomatic Correspondence and Documents: 1896–1900* (Washington, D.C., 1905), pp. 30–31.

   B. H. Liddell Hart's introduction to the modern edition of Sherman's *Memoirs* draws the connection between the German *Blitzkrieg*, the Allies' strategic bombing policy in World War II, and Sherman's philosophy of war. Hart's works on Sherman were widely read in the German and American military academies in the 1930's.

20. Joseph Kirkland, *The Captain of Company K* (Chicago, 1891), p. 158. Frank Wilkeson, *Recollections of a Private Soldier* (New York & London, 1887), p. vi. Albion W. Tourgée, *The Story of an Earnest Man, Figs and Thistles* (New York, 1879), p. 259.

21. John William DeForest, *A Volunteer's Adventures* ed. James H. Croshore (New Haven, 1946), p. 117. These sketches were published in the mid 1860's and revised into this form over the following thirty years. DeForest paid great attention to the commonplace and routine in battle (e.g. pp. 14–15) before confronting the reader with gory scenes. No picture of carnage is complete in DeForest's fiction without some attractive detail of everyday life to set off the horror—e.g. *Miss Ravenel's Conversion from Secession to Loyalty* [1867], ed. Gordon S. Haight (New York, 1955), pp. 269–270. In that novel Lt. Col. Carter's swaggering, light-hearted response to battle prepared the way for Colburn's later discovery of the blood and confusion in the Union campaigns in the South.

22. Ambrose Bierce, *In the Midst of Life, Tales of Soldiers and Civilians* [1891] (New York, 1961), esp. "A Horseman in the Sky," "Chickamauga," "A Tough Tussle," "The Coup de Grâce."

23. Albion Tourgée, *The Story of a Thousand: A History of the 105th Volunteer Infantry: 1862–1865* (Buffalo, 1896), Preface, p. 232; see also Tourgée, *Figs and Thistles*, pp. 260–63, 276; DeForest, *Miss Ravenel's Conversion*, p. 110. Kirkland, *Captain of Company K*, p. 120. Stephen Crane, *The Red Badge of Courage* [1895] ed. R. W. Stallman (New York, 1960), p. 17; Fleming's self-concept also shrinks further in battle (pp. 41, 107).

24. "The Red Badge of Hysteria," *Dial*, XX (1896), 227–28. This was the response of an outraged veteran, but the *Dial*'s regular review of the book was also cold.

  Kirkland, *The Captain of Company K*, p. 347. Crane, *Red Badge*, p. 134. *Stephen Crane: Stories and Tales*, ed. R. W. Stallman (New York, 1955), "The Open Boat," p. 236.

25. Kirkland, *The Captain of Company K*, pp. 46, 280; DeForest, *Miss Ravenel's Conversion*, pp. 110, 319–20, and De Forest, *Volunteer's Adventures*, pp. 116, 111; Tourgée, *Figs and Thistles*, pp. 328–29; *The War Dispatches of Stephen Crane*, ed. R. W. Stallman and E. R. Hagemann (New York, 1964), p. 29.

26. DeForest, *A Volunteer's Adventures*, pp. 230, 93, also 61–65; Tourgée played off horror against the stoical endurance of his characters, e.g. *Figs and Thistles*, pp. 266–67. See also Wilkeson, *Recollections*, pp. 61–63. The hero of Kirkland's *Captain of Company K* (much like Henry Fleming in Crane's novel) has a dramatic initiation into the discipline necessary to survive on the battlefield (pp. 97, 120, 291). Bierce's stories are filled with soldiers torn between shock and the exhilaration of battle, e.g. *Tales of Soldiers*, p. 72.

27. DeForest, *Miss Ravenel's Conversion*, p. 461; Tourgée, *The Story of a Thousand*, p. 9, see also *Figs and Thistles*, pp. 216–17. (Tourgée dared to suggest—but did not develop—a jocular, cynical view of the war in *A Fool's Errand* [1879] (New York, 1966), pp. 19–20. At times the realists' stoicism turned to sadism and their respect for discipline led them to worship force. Wilkeson, in his *Recollections*, is gleeful about the mutilations inflicted on recalcitrant fellow soldiers and overcome with laughter when men behind his own lines are injured by enemy shells (pp. 150, 168).

2
## "THE SILENCE WITH HIM AND OF HIM"

1. DeForest to William Dean Howells, quoted in Wilson, *Patriotic Gore*, p. 684. Tourgée, *Figs and Thistles*, pp. 271–72.

2. *Speeches by Oliver Wendell Holmes* (Boston, 1896), p. 65. Holmes's realistic descriptions of battle were unknown to nineteenth-century readers; we have them in Holmes, *Touched With Fire*, ed. Mark De Wolfe Howe (New York, 1969).

3. Whitman's writing on the war is available in *Leaves of Grass and Selected Prose*, ed. John A. Kouwenhoven (New York, 1950), pp. 245, 635 (quoted). On early and late war poetry cf. "Not the Pilot" (1860) and "By the Bivouac's Fitful Flame" (1865).

4. *Harold Frederic's Stories of York State*, ed. Thomas F. O'Connell (Syracuse, N.Y., 1966), p. 276. These were written during 1892–93.

5. Francis Grierson, *The Valley of Shadows* [1909] (New York, 1966), pp. vii, 226, also 273–75.

6. Albion W. Tourgée, *The Veteran and His Pipe* (Chicago, 1888), pp. 71–72, 78; see also Preface.

7. Albion W. Tourgée, *An Appeal to Caesar* (New York, 1884), pp. 43–44 (Tourgée's emphasis), 48.

8. Grenville M. Dodge, *The Battle of Atlanta and Other Campaigns, Addresses, etc.* (Council Bluffs, Iowa, 1911), pp. 182–83. Nathaniel S. Shaler, *From Old Friends: Poems of the Civil War* (Boston & New York, 1906), p. 26.

9. Thomas Boyd, *Through the Wheat* [1922] (New York, 1927), p. 47. William Faulkner, *Sartoris* [1929] (New York, 1951), p. 227; see also 1. Discussion of the Civil War gets no further in Laurence Stallings's World War I novel, *Plumes* (New York, 1924), p. 82.

10. *The War Dispatches of Stephen Crane*, ed. R. W. Stallman and E. R. Hagemann (New York, 1964). Other reports make it clear there were many aspects of the Rough Riders' battles to support this view of "delirium." One man went into each fight shouting "Six slim, slick saplings" endlessly to boost his courage—see report to New York *Sun*, Sept. 16, 1898, reprinted in Edward Marshall, *The Story of the Rough Riders* (New York, 1899), pp. 243–44. Charles Herner, *The Arizona Rough Riders* (Tuscon, 1970), pp. 113–14, 134. Charles Johnson Post, *The Little War of Private Post* (Boston, 1960), pp. 120–21, 197. Theodore Roosevelt, *The Rough Riders* [1899] (New York, 1961), pp. 73, 62–63.

11. Elting E. Morison and John M. Blum, eds., *The Letters of Theodore Roosevelt*, 8 vols. (Cambridge, Mass., 1951–54), II (July 19, 1898), 853, to Henry Cabot Lodge; II, (June 15, 1898), 844, to Corrine Roosevelt Robinson. Donald Smythe, *Guerrilla Warrior: The Early Life of John J. Pershing* (New York, 1973), p. 56.

12. Herner, *The Arizona Rough Riders*, chap. 1 and p. 208; see also the remarks of the governor of Arizona quoted in Gerald F. Linderman, *The Mirror of War: American Society and the Spanish-American War* (Ann Arbor, 1974), p. 126. Post, *The Little War of Private Post*, pp. 257–58. The volunteers' songs are in Clifford P. Westermeier, *Who Rush to Glory: The Cowboy Volunteers of 1898* (Caldwell, Idaho, 1958), pp. 146–68; also 24–25. Roosevelt, *Rough Riders*, pp. 49–50.

13. John Fox, *Personal and Family Letters and Papers*, ed. E. Fox Moore, (Lexington, Ky., 1955), pp. 51–53; see 68 on the publishing success of the *Shepherd* book.

14. John J. Pershing, *My Experiences in the World War*, 2 vols. (New York, 1931), I, 50, 244–45; II, 51, 85, 257, 287–88. See also George C. Marshall, *Memoirs of My Service in the World War, 1917–1918*, ed. James L. Collins, Jr. (Boston, 1976).

15. On the sensational treatment of war in the antebellum tracts see *The*

*Book of Peace: A Collection of Essays on War and Peace* (Boston, 1845), Nos. 2, 3, 8, 10, 20. In contrast, see "War's Work on the Soul," *Peacemaker*, IV (1885–86), 25 (quoted); "Are We All at War?" *Peacemaker*, XXIII (Sept. 1904); *Lake Mohonk Conference on International Arbitration, Report of the Annual Meeting* (1895), p. 5; *Lake Mohonk . . . Report* (1898), p. 6. Jane Addams advised against vivid depictions of the battlefield: *Official Report of the Thirteenth Universal Peace Congress* (Boston, 1904), p. 120; Addams, *Newer Ideals of Peace* (New York, 1907), pp. 3–4. "The Peace Forum" began in *Out West* in 1912 with a notice that "nothing of a controversial nature will be admitted" (III, 227ff.).

16. "Roosevelt on the Strenuous Life," *Advocate of Peace*, LXI (May 1899), 100.

17. The vagaries of licentiousness in uniform throughout the 1890's can be studied in such anti-war literature as *Advocate of Peace*: LVI (Jan. 1894), 10; LVI (Apr. 1894), 83–84; LVI (Jan. 1899), 9–10; LXI (Oct. 1899), 204; LXII (May 1900), 128; see esp. Philip S. Moxom, "The Social and Moral Aspects of War," LV (Nov. 1893), 244–48; M. L. Holbrook, "War and Parentage," LXI (Jan. 1899), 16 (quoted). *Peacemaker* made the same charges: "Social Purity," XVII (1888), 67; "The Blight of Pure Manhood," X (1891), 37; "Depravity of War," XIX (1900), 128. These criticisms continued into the new century—see comments of Joseph J. Beale in *Lake Mohonk . . . Report* (1907), pp. 85–86; Lucia Ames Mead, *Outline of Lessons on War and Peace* (Boston, 1913), Lesson XII; David Starr Jordan, *Imperial Democracy* (New York, 1899), p. 202; Thomas E. Green, *The Forces that Failed: The Burden of the Nations* (Washington, D.C., 1914), p. 31. I have quoted Edward A. Atkinson, *The Anti-Imperialist*, No. 6 (Oct. 1, 1900), p. 37; George Ross Kirkpatrick, *War—What For?* (West Lafayette, Ohio, 1910), p. 221; "Untold Tales of the Navy," *International Socialist Review*, XIII (Nov. 1912), 401.

18. William E. Channing raised an early cautionary voice against realism; see his tract of 1816 in *The Book of Peace*, No. 38. Williams James, quoted from "The Moral Equivalent of War" (1910), in Staughton Lynd, ed., *Nonviolence in America* (Indianapolis, 1966), p. 143. John Bigelow, *World Peace* (New York, 1916), pp. 15–16.

19. Holmes, *Speeches*, p. 59. In 1909 young George Patton confessed to the same sentiment while visiting Gettysburg—a battle he found "bloody," "foolish," and "wonderful." *The Patton Papers, 1885–1940*, ed. Martin Blumenson, 2 vols. (Boston, 1972), I, 173. For a wider sampling of this sensibility see David Axeen, "Romantics and Civilizers: American Attitudes Toward War, 1898–1902" (Ph.D. diss., Yale Univ., 1969), pp. 40–43; Linderman, *The Mirror of War*, p. 97.

20. Albert J. Beveridge, "The Voice of the North to the Soul of the South" (1903), in *The Meaning of the Times* (New York, 1968), p. 218. Ray

Stannard Baker and William E. Dodd, eds., *The Public Papers of Woodrow Wilson*, 8 vols. (New York, 1925–27), V, 52.

21. [H. H. Thomas], *Toasts and Responses at Banquets Given Lt.-Gen. Sheridan* [1882–1883] (Chicago, n.d.), p. 60. Warren Lee Goss, *Recollections of a Private* (New York, 1890), pp. 225, 263; also 245, 250–54. Henry B. Carrington, *Beacon Lights of Patriotism* (Boston, 1894), pp. 311, 301 (I have quoted from two orators, one Northern and one Southern, given in this popular school text). Stanley Hirshson, *Farewell to the Bloody Shirt: Northern Republicans and the Southern Negro* (Bloomington, Ind., 1962), p. 60. See also John Gibbon, *Personal Recollections of the Civil War* [1885] (New York & London, 1928), p. 379; *Minutes of the United Confederate Veterans: 11th Meeting* (1901), p. 41; *UCV . . . 15th Meeting* (1905), p. 13; Buck has noted that lessons in patriotism in the postwar period tended to be drawn from the efforts of the enemy in the Civil War in *Road to Reunion*, p. 214.

22. "Wild Over a War Play," New York *World*, May 22, 1899, p. 5.

23. Baker and Dodd, eds., *Public Papers of Woodrow Wilson*, I, 370 (Sept. 28, 1915). President Taft expressed the same sentiment in a letter which became the frontispiece of Francis Trevelyan Miller, *The Photographic History of the Civil War*, 10 vols. (New York, 1911), I. It is also the theme of a best seller during the Spanish-American War—see Ira Seymour Dodd, *The Song of the Rappahannock* (New York, 1898), pp. vii, 156.

## 3
## RED, WHITE, AND THE ARMY BLUE

1. Roy Harvey Pearce, *Savagism and Civilization*, new ed., (Baltimore, 1965), studied American ambivalence toward primitive opponents up to the Civil War. See also Brian W. Dippie, "The Vanishing American: Popular Attitudes and American Army Policy in the Nineteenth Century" (Ph.D. diss., Univ. of Texas, Austin, 1970). Francis A. Walker, *The Indian Question* (Boston, 1874), pp. 15–16, 46–47. Edward A. Lawrence, *A Confession of Faith in Peace Principles* (n.p., 1876). This was an American Peace Society pamphlet. Francis Lieber, *Journal of the Military Service Institution of the United States*, IV (1883), 300. The arrogance of Quakers is brought out in Joseph E. Illick, " 'Some of Our Best Indians Are Friends . . . ,' " *Western Historical Quarterly*, II (July 1971), 289–94. For reformers' suspicions of the Army see Robert Winston Mardock, *The Reformers and the American Indian* (Columbia, Mo., 1971). Robert M. Utley, *Frontier Regulars: The United States Army and the Indian, 1866–1890* (New York, 1973), p. 190.

2. Sheridan to Sherman, Feb. 28, Mar. 5, 18, 1870, letter book, Sheridan Papers, Library of Congress, Manuscript Division, Box 91. Robert Debs

Heinl, ed., *The Dictionary of Military and Naval Quotations* (Annapolis, Md., 1966), p. 155.

3. Sherman to William F. Cody, Jan. 29, 1887, Sherman Papers, Library of Congress, Vol. 98. Sheridan made a similar accounting in *Report of the Secretary of War*, I (1878), 34–39. Sherman's rage against native Americans is clear in the standard published sources: see Rachel Sherman Thorndike, *The Sherman Letters* (New York, 1894), p. 287; Lloyd Lewis, *Sherman, Fighting Prophet* (New York, 1958), pp. 596ff.; R. H. Pratt, *Battlefield and Classroom*, ed. Robert M. Utley (New Haven, 1964). See also Sherman's widely reprinted reaction to the Custer debacle in *Boston Evening Transcript*, July 6, 1876, p. 1.

4. The Army reported only 2571 white casualties in winning the West and claimed that 5519 of the enemy had been put out of action. Oliver Knight, *Following the Indian Wars: The Story of the Newspaper Correspondents Among the Indian Campaigners* (Norman, Okla., 1960), pp. 9–12. Indian fighting was judged more difficult than combat in the Civil War: Sheridan, *Report of the Secretary of War*, I (1877), 35. See also George Crook, *Report of the Secretary of War*, I (1880), 80; Grenville M. Dodge, *The Battle of Atlanta*, p. 138. Even Sherman's memories of Georgia faded: he declared that Indian campaigns were the "hardest kind of war." "Difficulties with Indian Tribes," U.S., Congress, House, *House Executive Document*, 41st Cong., 2nd sess. (1870), Ser. 1425, No. 240, p. 177. Sherman, *Report of the Secretary of War*, I (1876), 36. Robert G. Athearn, *William Tecumseh Sherman and the Settlement of the West* (Norman, Okla., 1956), gives the most balanced picture of Sherman's anger (pp. 99–101, 223, 301) set against his moments of pity for the enemy (pp. 64, 67, 82–83, 321). Sheridan's compassion for the defeated Indian is clear in *Report of the Secretary of War*, I (1878), 35, 38 (quoted). See also Henry E. Fritz, *The Movement for Indian Assimilation* (Philadelphia, 1963), pp. 127–28. Sheridan's private papers show the same attitude: see e.g. draft of letter to General Townsent(?) Dec. 1878, Sheridan Papers, Library of Congress, Manuscript Division, Box 92. Sheridan also approved of the views of his regiment's war correspondent, De Benneville Randolph Keim, *Sheridan's Troopers on the Borders* (New York, 1885). An endorsement from Sheridan served as an introduction to those reports. Keim wrote that whites were generally at fault in the Indian conflicts and that the white civilization of the time was "selfish and aggressive." Neither judgment, however, destroyed the journalist's joy in the campaigns (pp. 294, 283). Sheridan's ambivalence is clear in his *Personal Memoirs*, 2 vols. (New York, 1888), I, 88–89, 111.

5. Charles King *Campaigning with Crook* [1890], 2nd ed. (Norman, Okla., 1964), p. 33. King, great-grandson of Rufus King, can be compared with another connoisseur of Indian lore, General Hugh Lenox Scott, grandson of Charles Hodge. Scott paused in his campaigns to

rejoice in becoming part of "primitive America," studied Indian culture closely, and feared for native Americans faced with the "blighting power" of civilization: *Some Memoirs of a Soldier* (New York, 1928), pp. 30–32, 156–57. It is perhaps appropriate that the descendants of those antebellum conservatives should have appreciated some alternative to the culture of modern America while at the same time they fought to defend the nation.

6. George A. Custer, *My Life on the Plains* [1874] (Norman, Okla., 1962), pp. 19–20, 22. Custer also confessed he enjoyed the heroic escape of Indians he pursued, and predicted that as the Indians yielded to civilization they would grow weak and die (pp. 201, 21).

7. Nelson A. Miles, *Serving the Republic* (New York, 1911), pp. 117–18; *Personal Recollections and Observations* (Chicago, 1896), pp. 88, 211. Earlier Miles had expressed his doubt about the justice of the Nez Percé war in his report from the field: *Report of the Secretary of War*, I (1877), 529. Miles said in private what he said in public—see Miles to Mrs. Miles, Virginia W. Johnson, *The Unregimented General* (Boston, 1962), p. 294.

8. John Gibbon, "Hunting Sitting Bull," *American Catholic Quarterly Review*, II (Oct. 1877), 667, 672. "Our Indian Question," *JMSIUS*, II (1881), 102, 109. Major Eugene A. Carr left a manuscript record of this expedition to avenge Custer ("Campaign of 1876 Against Sitting Bull"); it is marked by the same lack of vindictiveness and shows the same respect for the native Americans' point of view, Carr MS, Nebraska State Historical Society, Lincoln, Neb.

9. John G. Bourke, "General Crook in the Indian Country," *Century*, XLI (Mar. 1891), 653. *General George Crook, His Autobiography*, ed. Martin F. Schmitt (Norman, Okla., 1960), p. xvi. Crook to Herbert Welsh, *Harper's Weekly*, XXVIII (Aug. 30, 1884), 565; Crook, *Report of the Secretary of War*, I (1883), 167; John Pope, *ibid.* I (1875), 76. See also Colonel James B. Fry, *Army Sacrifices* (New York, 1879), p. 4.

10. Richard I. Dodge, *A Living Issue* (Washington, D.C., 1882), pp. 5, 18, 20, 22; Dodge, *Our Wild Indians: Thirty-Three Years Personal Experience Among the Red Men of the Great West*, Introduction by Sherman (Hartford, Conn., 1882), pp. 499, 533. Dodge's sympathy for native Americans is less prominent but still clear in his earliest book, *The Plains of the Great West and Their Inhabitants* (New York, 1877), pp. 306, 431.

11. Margaret I. Carrington, *Ab-sa-ra-ka* (Philadelphia, 1868), pp. 182, 186, 211. Colonel Carrington's official report (Jan. 3, 1867) is reprinted as a supplement: [*Some Phases of*] *the Indian Question* (Boston, 1884). Margaret I. and Henry B. Carrington, *Ab-sa-ra-ka*, 3rd ed. (Philadelphia, 1878), pp. vi, vii, 262–63, 353–55, 357–58, gives a picture of Col. Carrington's disillusionment. He claimed that he identified with the red warrior even (or especially) when his own life was in danger on

the battlefield (*Indian Question*, pp. 7–8). Henry B. Carrington, "The Decotah Tribes: Their Beliefs, and Our Duty to Them Outlined," *Proceedings*, A.A.A.S., XXIX (1880), 690, 692.

12. John G. Bourke, *On the Border with Crook* (New York, 1892), p. 115. The most convenient guide to Bourke's ethnological work is the memorial essay by F. W. Hodge, *Journal of American Folk-Lore*, IX (1896), 139. Most of Bourke's notebooks have been published: see Lansing S. Bloom, "Bourke on the Southwest," *New Mexico Historical Review*, VIII–XIII, XIX (1933–38, 1944).

Bourke's attitude is particularly evident in Bourke, *The Snake-Dance of the Moquis of Arizona* (New York, 1884), p. 162; Bourke, *Scatalogic [sic] Rites of All Nations* (Washington, D.C., 1891), pp. iv, 467. He was not alone in combining serious anthropological work with the military life. Washington Matthews's major research on the Sioux and Navaho was done when he served as a doctor with the Army in the West. What is most significant, however, is the respect and attention ordinary officers paid to the culture of the enemy. An example is "Notes on Indians," MS, c. 1876, Walter Scribner Schuyler Papers, sect. B, Huntington Library, San Marino, Calif.

13. Peter Farb has a vivid sketch of the Plains "make-believe Indians" and their "ritualized" warfare in *Man's Rise to Civilization . . .* (New York, 1968), pp. 112–26. W. W. Newcomb emphasizes how the introduction of white goods and the red migrations accentuated conflicts within the Plains culture in "A Re-examination of Plains Warfare," *American Anthropologist*, LII (1950), 317–29. See also Bernard Mishkin, *Rank and Warfare Among the Plains Indians* (New York, 1940), pp. 57–63.

14. John M. Schofield, *Forty-Six Years in the Army* (New York, 1907), p. 428. Col. J. E. Tourtellotte to Gen. Sherman, Feb. 1, 1891, Sherman Papers, Library of Congress, Manuscript Division, Box 82.

15. A classic statement of the interrelations of anger and bereavement is Sigmund Freud, "Mourning and Melancholia," *The Standard Edition . . .*, ed. James Strachey, 24 vols. (London, 1953–74), XIV, 243–58, esp. 248. A modern text is Otto Fenichel, *The Psychoanalytic Theory of Neurosis* (New York, 1945), pp. 394–95. Detailed formulations of the dynamics of guilt are offered in the literature, and it is tempting to apply such models to these Army officers. Since I am interested in the public response of these men to their enemy, and because personal data is insufficient, I have not pursued this analysis. Here, I think, psychological theory is most useful and accurate when left stated in general terms.

16. Sherman, *Report of the Secretary of War*, I (1883), 45–46; Custer, "Battling with the Sioux on the Yellowstone," *Galaxy*, XXII (July 1876), 91. Miles, *Personal Recollections*, pp. 481, 317, 329. Miles, "A Glance at a Generation of Progress in Military Appliances," *Cosmopolitan*, XXVIII (1900), 627–29. Miles became a prominent promoter of aviation in World War I.

17. Bourke, *An Apache Campaign in the Sierra Madre* (New York, 1886), p. 49. Bourke, "General Crook in the Indian Country," *Century*, XLI (Mar. 1891), 652. See also Bourke, *On the Border with Crook*, p. 112. Carrington and Carrington, *Ab-sa-ra-ka*, 3rd ed., p. 186. Crook, *Report of the Secretary of War*, I (1883), 167. Crook stressed this in a later analysis, "The Apache Problem," *JMSIUS*, VII (1886), 262–63.

18. Wood, "Our Indian Question," *JMSIUS*, II (1881), 123–81. The main points in Wood's analysis are given on pp. 126, 133, 135–36, 157, 173. Wood, "Famous Indians: Portraits of Some Indian Chiefs," *Century*, XLVI (July 1893), 436. Wood offered many laudatory views of native culture to national audiences. See e.g. "Chief Joseph, the Nez Percé," *Century*, XXVIII (May 1884), 135–42; "An Indian Horse Race," *Century*, XXXIII (Jan. 1887), 447–50; A *Book of Tales* (Portland, Ore., 1901). Col. George Bliss Sanford, the senior cavalry officer with Wood in the Northwest, was also an appreciative student of Indians, and he, in time, shared some of Wood's guilty feelings. See E. R. Hagemann, ed., *Fighting Rebels and Redskins: Experiences in Army Life of Colonel George B. Sanford* (Norman, Okla., 1969), pp. 17, 58, 100–101.

19. Wood, *The Poet in the Desert* (Portland, Ore., 1915), develops the case against technology; see esp. pp. 77, 107. In the 1918 revision a detailed recollection of the Indian campaigns is given; see pp. 90–95 (90, 92 quoted). The longer 1915 version of the poem uses the last line of this passage (p. 103), but avoids the detailed references to Indians that Wood put in the briefer 1918 revision. It seems that Wood's memory and guilt sharpened as his disillusionment with World War I deepened.

## 4
## IN SEARCH OF A WORTHY ENEMY

1. *The Indian Bulletin*, II (Apr. 1891), printed letters from 8 officers in support of enlisting Indians; the officers included Miles, Schofield, and King. See also Eric Feaver, "Indian Soldiers, 1891–95: An Experiment on the Closing Frontier," *Prologue* VII (Summer 1975), 109–18.

2. Friedrich Nietzsche, *On the Genealogy of Morals . . .* , ed. Walter Kaufman (New York, 1967), p. 39 (First Essay, section 11). Also suggestive of this relationship are "War Memories," *The War Dispatches of Stephen Crane*, ed. R. W. Stallman and E. R. Hagemann (New York, 1964), pp. 271–72; Lincoln Colcord, *Vision of War* (New York, 1916), p. 40.

3. Tourgée, *The Veteran and His Pipe*, p. 84; A *Fool's Errand* [1879] (New York, 1966), pp. 326, 323, see also 253–55.

4. On the qualms over the word "battle" see Frederick Funston, *Memories of Two Wars: Cuban and Phillipine Experiences* (London, 1912), p. viii; Albert G. Robinson, *The Philippines: The War and the People* (New York, 1901), p. 336; *Mark Twain On the Damned Human Race*, ed.

Janet Smith (New York, 1962), p. 120. Finley Peter Dunne, *Mr. Dooley's Opinions* (New York, 1901), pp. 101–2.

5. Donald Smythe, *Guerrilla Warrior: The Early Life of John J. Pershing* (New York, 1973), chap. 8. Smythe thinks the rumors were wrong as to particulars, but that Pershing "may well have fathered some native children" (p. 141). New York *World* (Nov. 30, 1899), p. 6 (editorial). Later the paper concluded that there were no heroes "in this whole wretched Filipino business." (Mar. 30, 1901), p. 6 (editorial).

6. Edwin A. Falk, *Fighting Bob Evans* (New York, 1931), pp. 308, 339, 341–42, 344. *Official Souvenir Programme of the Grand Reception to the Nation's Hero: Admiral George Dewey* (New York, 1899), no p.—see opening remarks. *Official Dewey Souvenir Programme*, p. 5. Linderman, *The Mirror of War*, pp. 145–47. W. A. M. Goode, *With Sampson Through the War* (New York, 1899), pp. 14, 220. For other tributes to the Spanish soldiers see Frederick Funston, *Memories of Two Wars*, p. 145; Joseph Wheeler, *The Santiago Campaign, 1898* (Philadelphia, 1899), pp. 103–5, 128–31; Bradley A. Fiske, *War-Time in Manila* (Boston, 1913) p. 55; John J. Pershing, "Address on the Camp of Santiago" (typescript), delivered at Hyde Park M. E. Church, Chicago, Nov. 20, 1898, Pershing Papers, Library of Congress, Manuscript Division, Box 369.

7. T. Bentley Mott, "The Fall of Manilla," *Scribner's Magazine*, XXIV (1898), 687. John Bigelow, Jr., a scholarly officer, was candid about the Spaniards' weaknesses: *Reminiscences of the Santiago Campaign* (New York, 1899) pp. vi–vii. Roosevelt, *Rough Riders*, p. 297.

8. See e.g. Moorfield Storey and Julian Codman, *Marked Severities* (Boston, 1902). Twain's tracts are available in Smith, ed., *Mark Twain on the Damned Human Race*. See esp. "Comments on the Killing of 600 Moros."

9. Quoted by Ralph Barton Perry, *The Thought and Character of William James* 2 vols. (Boston, 1935), II, 311. See also Edward Ward Carmack, *Speech of Hon. E. W. Carmack in the United States Senate on Courts-Martial in the Philippines . . .* , (Philadelphia, 1903), pp. 12–13.

10. *Addresses and Presidential Messages of Theodore Roosevelt, 1902–1904* (New York, 1904), pp. 97, 156. *The Letters of Theodore Roosevelt*, III, (Mar. 19, 1902), 245, to Elihu Root; III, (July 19, 1902) 298, to H. S. Von Sternberg. Henry F. Pringle, *Theodore Roosevelt* (New York, 1931), p. 297. Roosevelt, *Rough Riders*, p. 102.

11. MacArthur quoted in Peter W. Stanley, *A Nation in the Making: The Philippines and the United States, 1899–1921* (Cambridge, Mass., 1974), p. 78.

12. Smythe, *Guerrilla Warrior*, p. 92. Fiske, *War-Time in Manila*, pp. 64–65.

13. John R. White, *Bullets and Bolos* (New York, 1928), p. 13; see also 342–43. Robert L. Bullard, "Autobiography," pp. 50, 58–59, Bullard

Papers, Library of Congress, Manuscript Division, Box 1. See also file on Moros, Box 10. I have quoted from Bullard's "Among the Savage Moros," *The Metropolitan Magazine*, XXIV (June 1906), 263. Scott, *Some Memoirs of a Soldier*, p. 313.

14. Dean C. Worcester, "General Lawton's Work in the Philippines," *McClure's*, XV (May 1900), 21.

15. Funston, *Memories of Two Wars*, pp. 340, 356, 421, see also 432.

16. Fiske, *War-Time in Manila*, p. 193. James Parker, *The Old Army: Memoirs, 1872–1918* (Philadelphia, 1929), p. 222. Peter W. Stanley, *A Nation in the Making: The Philippines and the United States, 1899–1921* (Cambridge, Mass., 1974), pp. 64–65.

17. John M. Gates, *Schoolbooks and Krags: The United States Army in the Philippines, 1898–1902* (Westport, Conn., 1973), Chaps. 2, 5, and p. 216. Smythe, *Guerrilla Warrior*, p. 80. Nelson A. Miles, quoted in San Francisco *Examiner* (Mar. 30, 1902), p. 1.

18. Edward John McClernand, "Our Philippine Problem," *JMSIUS*, XXIX (1901), 332 (quoted).

19. *History of the American Field Service in France, 'Friends of France,' 1914–1917*, 3 vols. (Boston & New York, 1920), II, 24–25 (Apr. 22, 1917).

20. James N. Hall and C. B. Nordhoff eds., *The Lafayette Flying Corps*, 2 vols. (Boston & New York, 1920), II, 98, 207–8, 210. James N. Hall, *New Republic*, XIII (Jan. 26, 1918), 380 (letter). Eddie V. Rickenbacker, *Fighting the Flying Circus* [1919] (Garden City, N.Y., 1965), pp. 252, 268. Edwin C. Parsons, *I Flew with the Lafayette Escadrille* (Indianapolis, 1963), p. 102. Curtis Kinney, *I Flew a Camel* (Philadelphia, 1972), p. 81. "The American Spirit, Letters of Briggs Adams," *Atlantic Monthly*, CXXII (Oct. 1918), 436. William B. Yeats, "An Irish Airman Foresees His Death," is the most perfect expression of the sense of disengagement from the passions of war that American aviators felt.

21. Francis P. Duffy, *Father Duffy's Story* (New York, 1919), p. 312. War correspondents often reported that the opposing forces were sportsmanlike and paid compliments to each other: see Irvin S. Cobb, *Speaking of Prussians* (New York, 1917), pp. 54–55; Ralph Pulitzer, *Over the Front in an Aeroplane* (New York, 1915), p. 148; Arthur Ruhl, *Antwerp to Gallipoli* (New York, 1916), p. 37; Albert J. Beveridge, *What Is Back of the War?* (Indianapolis, 1915), pp. 26–27, 261–63. Edith O. Shaughnessy, *My Lorraine Journal* (New York, 1918), p. 31; Elizabeth Frazer, *Old Glory and Verdun* (New York, 1918), pp. 21–22.

22. Robert W. Service, *Rhymes of a Red Cross Man* (New York, 1916), "A Song of the Sandbags," pp. 70–73; see also "Only a Boche," "My Prisoner," "My Foe," and "The Song of the Pacifist."

23. *The Patton Papers*, I, 616, 420, 368, 629. Frederick Trevenen Edwards, *Fort Sheridan to Montfaucon; the War Letters* . . . (De Land, Fla., 1954), pp. 60–61 (July 4, 1917).

24. E. I. Bosworth and the *Advocate of Peace*, cited by Ray H. Abrams, *Preachers Present Arms* (Scottsdale, Ariz., 1969), pp. 67, 160. See also Horace Bridges's argument that hatred could yield "the spiritual redemption of Germany" in "The Duty of Hatred," *Atlantic Monthly*, CXXII (Oct. 1918), 464–66.

25. Hector MacQuerrie, *How To Live at the Front, Tips for American Soldiers* (Philadelphia & London, 1917), p. 242. Alan Seeger, *Letters and Diary* (New York, 1917), pp. 141, 67. Captain Charles W. Whittlesey, quoted by *The Nation*, CVII (Dec. 12, 1918), 803. See also doughboy quoted by Harry Emerson Fosdick, letter, Oct. 9, 1918, "Contributors' Column," *Atlantic Monthly*, CXXII (Dec. 1918). Also sharing this view of the enemy were Russell A. Kelly, *Kelly of the Foreign Legion* (New York, 1917), p. 89; Arthur Guy Empey, '*Over the Top*' (New York & London, 1917), chap. 20; Edwin Austin Abbey, *An American Soldier* (Boston, 1918), pp. 58–59; Coningsby Dawson, *Carry On* (New York, 1917), pp. 17–18. E. E. Cummings paid dearly for his refusal to say he hated Germans: see *The Enormous Room* (New York, 1922). William Slater Brown's cordiality to the Germans at the front set the authorities on Cummings; Brown to Prof. Lower, Columbia Univ. (Aug. 29, 1917), in Charles Norman, *The Magic Maker: E. E. Cummings* (New York, 1958), p. 95. There was a good deal of testimony from combatants of all nations that soldiers in the trenches did not hate each other; Harold Stearns, "Pro-Allies" (review), *New Republic*, IX (Nov. 18, 1916), 26. Fritz Kreisler, the best known volunteer for the Central Powers, was articulate on this point: *Four Weeks in the Trenches* (Boston, 1915), p. 69.

26. Robert L. Bullard, *Personalities and Reminiscences of the War* (Garden City, N.Y., 1925), pp. 33, 118. James G. Harbord expressed the high professional regard for Germans present in so many memoirs: see *Leaves from a War Diary* (New York, 1925), pp. 68–69. On the occupation, see Willian B. Mitchell, *Memoirs of World War I* (New York, 1960), p. 307; Frederick A. Pottle, *Stretchers: The Story of a Hospital Unit on the Western Front* (New Haven, 1929), p. 314. Douglas MacArthur, whose father showed a prejudice against Germans in the U.S. Army ten years before Sarajevo, confessed the same admiration for the surrendered enemy: see *Reminiscences* (New York, 1964), pp. 72–73. Whitman (quoted), anonymous war letters, *An American Poilu*, ed. Sara Ware Bassett (Boston, 1919), pp. 243–44.

5
## KEEPERS OF THE PEACE

1. *The Complete Works of Benjamin Franklin*, ed. John Bigelow, 10 vols. (New York, 1887–88), VIII, B. F. to John Ingenhousz, Jan. 16, 1784, 433–34. This 18th-century material is pointed out in Hugo A. Meier's

essay, "American Technology and the Nineteenth-Century World," *American Quarterly*, X (Summer 1958), 118–19.

2. Fulton quoted by William Jameson, *The Most Formidable Thing* (London, 1965), p. 31. Fulton's optimism is also studied by Hugo A. Meier, "The Technological Concept in American Social History, 1750–1860" (Ph.D. diss., Univ. Wisconsin, Madison, 1950), pp. 280–94. Fulton published his plans, *Torpedo War, and Submarine Explosives* (New York, 1810). George Washington aided Bushnell's work. Fulton received the help of Thomas Jefferson in America and Joel Barlow in France.

3. Francis Wayland, *The Elements of Political Economy* [1837], 4th ed., rev. 1841 (Boston, 1864), pp. 64–65. See also Henry W. Halleck, *Elements of Military Art and Science* [1859] (New York, 1862), p. 408.

To give Wayland his due, the relationship between improved weapons and battle casualties in the 19th century cannot be exactly defined. Clearly, tactics, social attitudes, and political goals are as important as technology in determining the sacrifices an army will endure in war. We have no difficulty seeing that the modern machine gun is more deadly than the smooth bore musket (which took a minute to load between each shot and was accurate to about 50 yards). Yet some 18th-century musket battles produced moments of greater slaughter than most modern machine gun skirmishes between more protected (and more democratically recruited) soldiers. There was *some* rationality to the 19th-century faith that such new weapons mitigated war. Here I only wish to examine the fact that contrary, pessimistic evidence was ignored or distorted by supporters of the new weapons.

4. Robert V. Bruce, *Lincoln and the Tools of War* (Indianapolis & New York, 1956), has analyzed this approach to ordnance. See esp. p. 219.

5. Horace Edwin Hayden, "Explosive or Poisoned Musket Balls," *Southern Historial Society Papers*, VIII (Jan. 1880), 18–28. Milton F. Perry, *Infernal Machines, the story of Confederate Submarine and Mine Warfare* [Louisiana Univ. Press], 1965, pp. 5, 8, 42, 192.

6. Richard J. Gatling to Laura Wachschlager, June 27, 1888, U.S. Army Military Research Collection, Carlisle, Pa. See also interview, "Peace Arguments Made by Gatling Guns," New York *World*, Sunday Magazine, Oct. 15, 1899, p. 8.

7. *Proceedings of A Convention in Favor of International Arbitration* (Philadelphia, 1884), p. 47; Rev. Philip S. Moxom, *Lake Mohonk . . . Report* (1899), p. 77; Alfred H. Love, "The Conditions Essential to Peace," *Official Report of the Fifth Universal Peace Congress* (Chicago, 1893), p. 214. W. H. P. Faunce, *Lake Mohonk . . . Report* (1903), p. 32. For other appeals to the pacific force of modern inventions see Levie K. Joslin, "Some Historical, Economical, and Social Results of War . . . ," *Proceedings of the Universal Peace Congress* (London, 1890), p. 101. Josiah Strong, *Lake Mohonk . . . Report* (1901), pp. 68–72; Sam-

uel B. Capan, *ibid*. (1904), p. 90; Marcus M. Marks, *ibid*. (1908), p. 97. J. McKeen Cattell made a concise and eloquent statement of this view in 1912; see "Science and International Good Will," *Popular Science Monthly*, LXXXV (Sept. 1914), 306–7.

8. Plans for the plow can be followed in the peace journals: *Peacemaker*, XI (1893), 201–2; XII (1894), 82–90. *Advocate of Peace*, LV (1893), 253–4. See also David S. Patterson, "The Travail of the American Peace Movement, 1887–1914" (Ph.D. diss., Univ. California at Berkeley, 1968), p. 5.

   Functional design allowed some ambiguity. The peace plow was forged with metal that had rendered a variety of services—e.g. John Whittier's pen, an early Edison light bulb, a Revolutionary war bayonet, a pike used in John Brown's raid, a medal commemorating the Wyoming massacre. The symbolism must have been difficult for the fair-goers to sort out.

9. Longfellow, *The Voice of Peace*, I (1874), 42. Celebrations of this poem continued for thirty years in the peace journals.

10. Frederick P. Stanton, *The Peacemaker*, I (1882), 30–31. The Universal Peace Union played up the address and this view found other supporters in the movement; see Edward A. Lawrence, "The Progress of Peace Principles," (Boston, 1875), p. 4; *American Advocate of Peace*, LVI (1894), 113.

11. William N. Ashman, *Lake Mohonk . . . Report* (1899), p. 60. Bella Lockwood, *The Peacemaker*, VII (1889), 102. Joshua L. Baily, *Lake Mohonk . . . Report* (1895), pp. 29ff. See also A. C. Barnes, *Lake Mohonk . . . Report* (1896), p. 67. There were exceptions to the general optimism, but it seems significant that no peace leader argued for this darker view in any sustained way—certainly not with the energy of those at ease with armed peace. *The Peacemaker*, XII (1894), 118, e.g. made an oblique attack on the optimists, but its editorial shared the page with a report that "Science, [creating] a frightful force . . . is ready to annihilate war."

12. Josiah Quincy, *The Coming Peace* (American Peace Society pamphlet, Boston, 1891), pp. 16–17. For another example of the resurrection of the hopeful talk of the antebellum peace meetings see E. E. Hale's appeal to "the great pacifying power of steam" made after the Spanish-American War, *Lake Mohonk . . . Report* (1901), p. 14. On the *Maine* see *The Peacemaker*, XVI (1898), 157.

13. "Remarks on Modern Warfare," *Littell's Living Age*, XV (1876), p. 114. This British officer found some support from John Ruskin; *ibid*. p. 434. Similar English views were reprinted in *Popular Science Monthly*, XIV (1878–79), 817; and *Scientific American*, LIII (1885), 117. The English faith in destructiveness as a deterrent is also presented in the American edition of Archibald Williams, *The Romance of Modern Invention* (Philadelphia, 1904), p. 142. A French prediction of less horror

in modern war is given in *The Engineering Magazine*, III (1892), 234.

14. E. D. Mead, *Jean de Bloch and the Future of War* (Boston, 1903). Jack London was a somewhat more pessimistic popularizer of Bloch: "The Impossibility of War," *Overland Monthly*, XXXV, (Mar. 1900), 278–82; see also London to C. Johns (Mar. 15, 1900), *Letters from Jack London*, ed. King Hendricks and Irving Shepard (New York, 1965), p. 102.

15. The most concise summary of Thurston's optimism is his three presidential addresses to the American Society of Mechanical Engineers, 1880–83, quoted, *Transactions*, ASME, IV (New York, 1882), 93–4; *Transactions*, ASME [1881], II 2nd ed. (New York, 1892), 442. A more accessible source is Thurston, "The Border-land of Science," *North American Review*, CL (1890), 67–79, esp. 76. His influence extended well past his years of leadership in the engineering profession in the 1880's and 1890's. As late as 1918, his faith seems to have guided one of the most important engineers at work on national defense. See Thomas Parke Hughes, *Elmer Sperry; Inventor and Engineer* (Baltimore, 1971), p. 274.

16. This optimism was particularly strong in the hagiography of modern inventors: see esp. W. Sanford Ramey, *Triumphs of Genius* (Philadelphia, 1893), p. 227; Charles Henry Cochrane, *The Wonders of Modern Mechanism* (Philadelphia, 1896), p. 119; William H. Doolittle, *Inventions in the Century* (Toronto & Philadelphia, 1903), pp. 252, 271. For much more thoughtful but nevertheless optimistic speculation on war technology at the time see Frederic A. C. Perrine, "Testing Guns at Sandy Hook," *The Engineering Magazine*, III (1892), 357–71; W. D. Forbes, "War and its Value Again," *American Machinist*, XVII (1894), 5; Edward W. Bryn, *The Progress of Invention in the Nineteenth Century* (New York, 1900), pp. 394–95.

   Fulton's faith in the decisiveness and deterrence of underwater weapons is restated by John Philip Holland, "The Submarine Boat and Its Future," *North American Review*, CLXXI (1900), 894–903. Holland, an important naval inventor, felt uneasy with such "Utopian" conclusions but could not conceive of an alternative.

17. These points are made in Ericsson's correspondence between 1879–84: to C. H. Delamater & Co. (Aug. 7, 1880); to R. B. Forbes (Nov. 26, 1880), John Ericsson Papers, Library of Congress, Manuscript Division, Box 3. An important presentation of Ericsson's views to a wider audience is William C. Church, "John Ericsson," *Scribner's Monthly*, XVII (1897), 835–58, esp. 855. Bruce, *Lincoln*, p. 209, shows that Ericsson's assumption that greater destruction could lead to peace extended to land war as well. Admiral David D. Porter had a similar millennial view of monitors in the early 1870s: Kenneth J. Hagan, *American Gunboat Diplomacy and the Old Navy: 1877–1889* (Westport, Conn., 1973), p. 22.

18. Tesla's thinking on war can be followed in *Nikola Tesla: Lectures, Patents, Articles* (Beograd, Yugoslavia, 1956). The World War I judgment is on p. A-164. The most interesting of these articles is "The Problem of Increasing Human Energy," *Century*, LX (1900), p. 182 (quoted). See also interview with Tesla in San Francisco *Examiner*, Feb. 13, 1904, p. 3. Tesla's hatred of the traditional waging of war and his interest in a super-weapon to end it can also be seen in his correspondence with Robert U. Johnson, editor of the *Century*, Tesla Papers, Library of Congress, Manuscript Division, Oct. 1, 1899, June 22, 1900. Tesla's speculation on a death ray seems to have aided the work of British scientists during World War II: see E. H. G. Barwell, *The Death Ray Man: The Biography of Grindell Matthews* (London & New York, n.d.), p. 108.

19. The autobiographical writings of both Hudson and Hiram Maxim ignore or insult the achievements of the other: Clifton Johnson, *Hudson Maxim: Reminiscences and Comments* (New York, 1924); Hiram Maxim, *My Life* (London, 1915). Hiram claimed he was often further misrepresented by impostors who traveled through the United States giving bogus stories to the press.

20. Hudson Maxim, *Defenseless America* (New York, 1915), sums up the view he had given repeatedly in the Hearst newspapers since the turn of the century. The film inspired by this lurid book is "The Battle Cry of Peace," produced by J. Stuart Blackton. Maxim also patented a parlor game, "War."

21. Maxim, *Defenseless America*, has the machine-gun quote as a motto; pp. 110–11; 233; 297–98; quoted, p. 95. See also Maxim's introduction to Baron Horlf von Dewitz, *War's New Weapons* (New York, 1915).

22. Quoted, *The New York Times* (Oct. 26, 1914), p. 1 : 4. "A Talk With Edison," *Scientific American*, LXVI (Apr. 2, 1892), 216.

23. Quoted, Francis Trevelyan Miller, *Thomas A. Edison, Benefactor of Mankind* (Philadelphia, 1931), p. 252; *The New York Times* (Oct. 16, 1915), p. 4.

24. Henry Harrison Suplee, "The Great Transformation," *Cassirer's*, XXXX (1911), 60, 219–25; "The Peace Makers," *Cassirer's*, VIL (1913), 96–103. G. F. Cambell Wood, "Aeronautics in War," *Aero Club of America Bulletin (Flying)*, I (Feb.–Mar. 1912), 13. *Flying* reprinted comments that supported the view of airplanes as life-savers in war and harbingers of peace, e.g. I (Oct. 1912), 40; III (1914), 9.

Prophesies of air ships as peace-keepers long preceded practical flights. See e.g. Edmund C. Stedman, "Aërial Navigation (A Priori)," *Scribner's Monthly*, XVII (1879), 580–81; "Aerial Warfare," *Scientific American*, LIII (1885), 72; Daniel Caulkins, *Aerial Navigation* (Toledo, Ohio, 1895), pp. 11, 70; John K. Cree, "The Influence of the Air-Ship on War," *North American Review*, CLXII (1896), 69–83. George O. Squier, "The Present Status of Military Aëronautics," *Transactions*,

*ASME*, XXX (1908), 682–85. The financial crisis of American aviation can be followed in the editorial and feature stories of the leading journals: *Flying*, I (Sept. 1912), 18, 29 (quoted); *Flying*, II (1913), 19, 29–32.

25. Hudson Maxim's view on bombing is given in "Aeronautical Warfare," address, n.d., delivered c. 1915–16, copy, Wright Papers, Library of Congress, Manuscript Division. Woodhouse's analysis can be followed in *Flying*, II (1913), 5–9; *Flying*, III (1914), 10–11, 29. Woodhouse was particularly impressed by the communiqué the Italians dropped demanding surrender: "O Arabs, before the aeroplanes begin to throw their bombs which descend from on high . . . annihilating you and your domestic animals, burning your homes and your crops, destroying your wells . . . (surrender)." "These expressions of friendship," Woodhouse concluded, "weakened the antagonism." *Flying*, III (1914), 11.

26. On World War I see *Flying*, III (1914), 293 (quoted), 318. The view that aerial warfare would be like carnival stunt exhibitions is particularly evident in T. L. Brant, "Our War with Germany," *Flying*, II (1913), 5ff.

27. *Flying*, III (1914), 306–7.

28. Suplee's presentation of the airplane as peacemaker is given in the articles cited earlier (note 24, p. 225); "Policing the Pacific," *Cassirer's*, XXXXIV (1913), 11–12 (quoted). Both Suplee and his rival, J. Bernard Walker, editor of *Scientific American*, had a taste for technological war. Walker conjured up scenes of a crumbling battleship—"The greatest game—the grandest death"—when reviewing American naval progress before World War I. In 1915 he depicted the destruction of New York—the proper punishment for an unprepared America. He proclaimed the need to safeguard such ships and cities, but, again, it is clear that he took some satisfaction in contemplating the destruction he warned against. See "A Landsman's Log Aboard the Battleship 'North Dakota' . . . The Greatest Game in the World," *Scientific American*, CV (1911), 528; *America Fallen!* (New York, 1915).

29. C. Wendell Lansing, "The Foe Invincible," *Cassirer's*, XXXXIV (1913), 105–6. A similar prediction of the dramatic doom of the Army and Navy through air power is *Cassirer's*, XXXXII (1912), 352–54 (editorial). See also W. McDougall, "The Last Conflict, The Horror that Awoke the Nation," *American Magazine*, LXXVIII (1914), 33ff. Another fantasy, most flattering to science, was offered by an associate of F. W. Taylor: Hollis Godfrey, *The Man Who Ended War* (Boston, 1908).

30. H. R. Stiles, "The Surgical Significance of the New Small Calibre Rifle," *Journal of the Military Service Institution of the United States*, XV (1894), 1143–56. V. L. Mason, "New Weapons of the U.S. Army," *Century*, IL (1895), 572. A. C. Girard reached a different conclusion, "The Effects of the Modern Small-Calibre Rifles . . .," *JMSIUS*, XX

(1897), 55–70. But Girard acknowledged that so many experts in America and Europe were convinced war injuries would be mitigated in future action that he presented his dissent reluctantly—and quite defensively.

31. Nelson A. Miles, "Vital Factors of the South African War," *New York World*, Jan. 7, 1900, p. 5E. See also Miles's address, *Official Report of the Thirteenth Universal Peace Congress* (Chicago, 1904), p. 187.

H. H. Sargent, "Limitation of Armaments," *JMSIUS*, XXXXI (1907), 2–3. See also Valery Havard, "The Modern Field Sanitary Service . . .," *JMSIUS*, VIII (1888), 71–72; H. L. Abbot, "War Under New Conditions," *Forum*, IX (1890), 23; "Testing the New Maxim Gun," *JMSIUS*, XVIII (1896), 201–3; Charles Miller, "Independent Patrols" *JMSIUS*, XXIII (1898), 197. The similarity between the conclusions of the technical community and the military is evident in R. L. Bullard, "A Moral Preparation of the Soldier . . . ," *JMSIUS*, XXXI (1902), 788. The Army's attempts to "soothe and encourage" soldiers by claiming that modern weapons were humane while at the same time trying to raise fighting men to a "pitch of imaginary terror" about this ordnance was ridiculed by a critic of Bullard's essay: J. J. O'Connell, *JMSIUS*, XXXII (1903), 119. In the face of the Army's stubborn denial of greater bloodshed in modern war, O'Connell thought it necessary to comment: "N.B. Even under our improved conditions of warfare, one bullet continues to kill one man if it hits him the right place."

*The Patton Papers*, I, 222. *The Holmes-Einstein Letters* ed. J. B. Peabody (New York, 1964), p. 101. The imperviousness of military experts to the increase in violence in modern war is well illustrated by R. M. Johnson, *Arms and the Race* (New York, 1915), p. 26; Alfred J. Lotka, "War the Destroyer," *Scientific American*, CXI (Nov. 7, 1914), 375; John Bigelow, *World Peace* (New York, 1916), p. 16.

32. Edward B. Williston, "Machine Guns and the Supply of Small-Arm Ammunition on the Battlefield," *JMSIUS*, VII (1886), 121–22, emphasis in original.

E. L. Zalinski, "The Future of Warfare," *North American Review*, CLI (1890), 688, emphasis added.

33. Samuel S. Cox, U.S., Congress, House, *Congressional Record*, 48th Cong., 1st sess., 1884, 5813.

34. Rep. Charles Allen Sumner, U.S., Congress, House, *Congressional Record*, 48th Cong. 1st sess., 1884, 1636–37 (quoted), and John F. Follett, speech, ibid. 5819–20, are revealing aspects of this extended debate. A sense of the vulnerability of the massive steel ships was very strong in debates on the new Navy in the 1880s and 1890s. Some Congressmen seemed unsure whether the ships they voted would float, and many of the champions of military readiness despaired at the precarious condition of the modern Navy. Secretary of the Navy Long, on the eve of the war with Spain, fretted that "our great battleships are ex-

periments which have never yet been tried and in the friction of fight have almost as much to fear from some disarrangement of their own delicate machinery or some explosion of their own tremendous ammunition as from the foe." *America of Yesterday as Reflected in the Journal of John Davis Long*, ed. L. S. Mayo (Boston, 1923), p. 168. Government support for a new Navy rested much more on an untested faith that such modern technology was a peace-keeper than on proof of the effectiveness of the new weapons.

Recognition of the precariousness of naval technology (esp. in battleships) was widespread before 1898: "Our Navy," *Scientific American*, XXVIII (Jan. 4, 1873), 7; "A Militia for the Sea," ibid. XLV (Aug. 27, 1881), 128; J. R. Soley, "Our Naval Policy—," *Scribner's*, I (1887), 223–35; G. W. Van Deusen, "Which Are the More Needed for Our Future Protection . . . ," *JMSIUS*, XV (1884), 986–93; Philip St. George Cooke, "Our Army and Navy," *JMSIUS*, VIII (1888), 430; *American Machinist*, XVI (1893), 8; T. A. Dodge, "Van Moltke and Future Warfare," *Forum*, XI (1891), 353–66; Dodge, "The Death of the Czar and the Peace of Europe," *Forum*, XVIII (1894–95), 396–405.

35. James Brown Scott, ed., *The Proceedings of the Hague Peace Conferences: The Conference of 1899* (New York, 1920), pp. 83–84, 278–84, 353–55, 365–67. The Peace delegation's position on exploding bullets pushed the logic of deterrence further than ever before in peacetime. The U.S. commission to an international arms show in 1867, for example, observed that any invention that could destroy an entire fleet or "sweep away whole battalions at once, would be hailed as a welcome means of shortening the horror of war"—but they drew the line at exploding bullets and suggested they be prohibited. Charles B. Norton and W. J. Valentine, *Paris Universal Exposition, 1867—Reports of U.S. Commissioners . . . on the Munitions of War* (Washington, D.C., 1868), p. 133.

36. Crozier and Andrew D. White, also a delegate, worried about the fate of noncombatants, which seemed to get lost in the debate, "but what can a layman do," White complained, "when he has against him the foremost contemporary military and naval experts?" In fact, he went along with the military. See *Autobiography*, 2 vols. (New York, 1906), II, 319–20. White's optimism over the "constant and terrible additions to means of destruction" was reaffirmed in the *Lake Mohonk . . . Report* (1907), p. 37. For John Hay's instructions see James Brown Scott, ed., *Instructions to the American Delegates to the Hague . . .* (New York, 1916), p. 7.

37. See "Robbing War of Its Terrors by Narcotic Bullets," San Francisco *Examiner*, July 21, 1912 (American Magazine), p. 2; "A Bullet That Heals Every Wound it Makes," Apr. 11, 1915 (American Magazine), p. 2.

38. "How They Are Going To Move the Greatest Gun that Was Ever Built

. . ." San Francisco *Examiner*, July 20, 1902 (American Magazine), n.p.; "Training the 'Man Behind the Gun,' " Feb. 6, 1910 (American Magazine), p. 5. "Biggest Gun Built To Defend New York," New York *World*, May 19, 1901 (Sunday Magazine), p. 11; "Greatest Gun in the World Shoots Well," Jan. 18, 1903, p. 1W; "Here's the Gun that Will Fight Air Ships," Mar. 28, 1909 (World Magazine), p. 2; "Salvo of the 12-Inch Guns," Mar. 30, 1913 (World Magazine), p. 9; "The Greatest Gun on Earth," June 29, 1913 (World Magazine), p. 24.

39. Ambrose Bierce, San Francisco *Examiner*, Feb. 3, 1900, p. 3. Bierce, "Modern Warfare" [1899], in *Collected Works*, 12 vols. (New York, 1909–12), IX, 217; see also "Turko-Grecian War" [1897], p. 293.

40. *Jack London Reports: War Correspondence, Sports Articles, and Miscellaneous Writings*, ed. King Hendricks and Irving Shepard (Garden City, N.Y., 1970), pp. 98, 106. London's dispatches appeared in the Hearst press during the first two weeks of June 1904. Similar denials of increased bloodshed on the modern battlefield: "Bullets To Make Modern Warfare Even More Horrible," San Francisco *Examiner*, Mar. 13, 1898 (Sunday Magazine), p. 4; Richard J. Gatling, "Peace Arguments . . . ," New York *World*, Oct. 15, 1899 (Sunday Magazine), p. 8; "With this Little Machine War Is To Be Made Bloodless," Oct. 4, 1903 (Sunday Magazine), p. 10.

41. "President at the Bottom of the Sea in the Risky Trip of Submarine Boat," San Francisco *Examiner*, Aug. 26, 1905, p. 1. See also "The Great Wizard . . . ," New York *World*, Apr. 10, 1898 (Sunday Magazine), p. 1; "Submarines in the Storm," Dec. 5, 1903, p. 6. "The Treacherous Submarine Boat," San Francisco *Examiner*, Aug. 20, 1905 (American Magazine), pp. 6–7; "Is the Submarine Worthwhile?" June 26, 1910 (American Magazine), p. 4.

42. "Tesla Thinks His Invention Is in Use," San Francisco *Examiner*, Feb. 13, 1904, p. 3 (quoted). Absolute confidence in underseas weapons is shown: "Submarine Fleets—Useless Ironclads," San Francisco *Examiner*, May 1, 1898, p. 10; "Our New Submarine Wonder," Jan. 17, 1904 (American Magazine), p. 5; "Wickedest of All Engines of War," Jan. 31, 1904 (American Magazine), p. 9. "400 Miles Under Water . . . ," New York *World*, Aug. 4, 1901 (Sunday Magazine), p. 4; "The Next Great Naval Battle . . . ," Jan. 25, 1903 (Sunday Magazine), pp. 6–7; "This Wonderful Torpedo Really Seems To Think," May 16, 1909 (World Magazine), p. 2; "The Mother of Submarines," Nov. 14, 1909 (World Magazine), p. 1.

43. The sense of impotence is clear in "Is Flying a Failure?" New York *World*, Aug. 10, 1913, p. 2E; "Training Great Eagles To Destroy the Air Fleet," San Francisco *Examiner*, July 21, 1912 (American Magazine), p. 1. Mastery is suggested in "Men Are Really Flying at Last!" New York *World*, Apr. 18, 1909 (World Magazine), p. 1; "Look Out for Airships When the Next War Begins," San Francisco *Examiner*, Sept.

17, 1910, p. 18; "The War in the Air at Last!" May 26, 1912 (American Magazine), n.p.

44. "Airships Effect on War and Commerce," San Francisco *Examiner*, Dec. 3, 1910, p. 20. "Discovered! How to Blow Up Battleships," New York *World*, Sept. 7, 1913 (World Magazine), pp. 14, 21.

45. Holt's judgment is given in *Lake Mohonk . . . Report* (1909), p. 122. The blindness of the peace movement to the arms race before 1914 is pointed out in Patterson, "The Travail of the American Peace Movement," p. 376.

46. Michael A. Lutzker, "The Pacifist as Militarist: A Critique of the American Peace Movement, 1898–1914," unpubl. paper, pp. 11, 17.

47. *Peacemaker*, XXIV (1905), p. 40. Ashman, presidential address, Pennsylvania Peace Society. Similar gruesome specifications for a super-weapon to ensure peace were given by the Right Rev. Monsignor M. J. Lavelle, *Proceedings of the National Arbitration and Peace Congress* (New York, 1907), pp. 21–22. It is interesting that America's first detailed vision of germ warfare was given (though not advocated) in an anti-preparedness book: Allan L. Benson, *Inviting War to America* (New York, 1916), pp. 33–36.

48. Atkinson, "The Influence of Mechanical Science on the Social Conditions of Humanity," *The Anti-Imperialist*, No. 6 (1900), pp. 47–48. Atkinson's advice was widely reprinted by peace groups. He later reaffirmed his praise of the new arms makers: *Official Report of the Thirteenth Universal Peace Conference*, p. 109. A fellow anti-imperialist took a similar view: see George S. Boutwell, *The Crisis of the Republic* (Boston, 1900), pp. 57–62.

49. Mead's early optimism about technology as a peace-keeper can be found in pamphlets such as *A Primer of the Peace Movement* (Boston, 1904), p. 4; *Teaching Patriotism and Justice* (Boston, 1907), p. 5. The material cited during World War I is "America's Danger and Opportunity" (speech read at the International Peace Congress at San Francisco), *The Survey*, XXXV (1915), 90–91; "The Submarine a Negation of Sea Power," *Unity* (Sept. 30, 1915), 73. Mead drew some of her enthusiasm for submarines from another peace publicist, Herbert Quick, "The Submarine as a Peacemaker," *American Magazine*, LXXX (Aug. 1915), 62–63.

## 6
## "CUNNING CONTRIVANCES"

1. *The Complete Writings of Nathaniel Hawthorne*, 22 vols. (Boston & New York, 1900), XVII, 413.

2. Leo Marx, *The Machine in the Garden: Technology and the Pastoral Ideal in America* (New York, 1964), pp. 162ff. *The Marx-Engels Reader*, ed. Robert C. Tucker (New York, 1972), p. 300.

3. *The Complete Poems of Herman Melville*, ed. H. P. Vincent (Chicago,

1947), "A Utilitarian View of the Monitor's Fight," p. 40. See also "The Stone Fleet," pp. 16–17; "The Temeraire," pp. 37–39.

4. Ambrose Bierce, "Appliances for Making Cowards," (from San Francisco *Examiner*) in Bierce Scrapbook, Stanford Univ.

5. New York *World*, May 8, 1898, p. 29; New York *World*, May 15, 1898, p. 6 (quoted); see also New York *World*, Sept. 25, 1899, p. 6; Sept. 26, 1899, p. 6; Sept. 27, 1899, p. 6. Other military leaders were treated in the same way. See the sketches of Gen. Funston, New York *World*, May 21, 1899 (Sunday Magazine), p. 8; Apr. 7, 1901, p. 3; Gen. Miles, New York *World*, Feb. 3, 1901, p. 1E; Gen. Otis, New York *World*, Feb. 12, 1899, p. 11; Gen. Ballance, San Francisco *Examiner*, Jan. 26, 1902 (Sunday Magazine), n.p. David Axeen has found that the Hearst press in New York bemoaned planning and efficiency because it reduced the glory of the victory over Spain: "Romantics and Civilizers: American Attitudes Toward War, 1898–1902," (Ph.D. diss., Yale Univ., 1969), p. 55.

6. [Edward M. House], *Philip Dru: Administrator, A Story of Tomorrow, 1920–1935* [1912] (New York, 1919), pp. 134–35.

7. Cited in Donald N. Bigelow, *William Conant Church and the Army and Navy Journal* (New York, 1952), pp. 216–17. A related argument about Army ordnance was that the complexity of the new guns made them unsure (and unbecoming) tools. The soldier would, quite rightly, refuse to become the "passionless automaton" required by modern war: Gen. Henry L. Abbot, "War Under New Conditions," *Forum*, IX (1890), 23; John Bigelow, Jr., "The Sabre and Bayonet Question," *JMSIUS*, III (1882), 65–96.

8. Alfred T. Mahan, *From Sail to Steam* (London & New York, 1907), pp. 10–11, 136; see also 106–7.

9. Edward Berwick, "American Militarism," *Century*, XLVII (Dec. 1893), 316. See e.g. the analysis of the president of the American Red Cross during the Spanish-American War, New York *World*, June 19, 1898, p. 34 (quoted). Another example is *Proceedings of the National Arbitration and Peace Congress* (New York, 1907), esp. Gov. Charles E. Hughes and Samuel Gompers, p. 250 (quoted). David Starr Jordan also used this argument: *Imperial Democracy* (New York, 1901), pp. 4, 91. On Mahan's distaste for technical aspects of the new Navy see his *From Sail to Steam*, p. 45. Elting E. Morison, *Men, Machines, and Modern Times* (Cambridge, Mass., 1966), p. 35. Morison (pp. 114–16) points out that discomfort with the ethical implications of naval improvements sometimes weighed heavily on Congressmen.

10. F. M. Bennett, "Engine Room Experience in War Times," *Cassierer's*, XV (1898–99), 217–24. See also *American Machinist*, XXI (1898), 263, 319–20, 344, 586, 637, 643. "The Arms and the Man," *Scientific American*, LXXXI (1899), 210. Strictures on proper usage of "machine" are in *American Machinist*, XVII (1894), 8–9.

11. Walter Millis, *Arms and Men: A Study in American Military History*

(New York, 1956), p. 21, shows that Alexander Hamilton used this metaphor.

12. Freedom from the "machine" through the mastery of technical skills was a recurrent theme in professional discussion: W. Merritt, "Important Improvements in the Art of War . . . ," *JMSIUS*, IV (1883), 182; R. I. Dodge, "The Enlisted Soldier," *JMSIUS*, VIII (1887), 280–81, 315; W. C. Sanger, "Organization and Training of a National Reserve for Military Service," *JMSIUS*, X (1889), 71–72; J. P. Jervey, "Esprit de Corps . . . ," *JMSIUS*, XXXIV (1904), 394.

13. T. L. Brant, "Our War with Germany," *Flying*, II (1913), 5ff. quoted, 7. Simon Lake, *The Submarine in War and Peace* (Philadelphia, 1918), p. 196; see also John A. McSparan, House Committee on Military Affairs, Hearings on H. R. 12766, *To Increase the Efficiency of the Military Establishment of the United States*, 2 vols., U.S., 64th Cong., 1st sess. (1916), II, 1243.

14. J. H. Parker, *JMSIUS*, XXXII (1903), 126; *Tactical Organization and Uses of Machine Guns in the Field* (Kansas City, Mo., 1899), pp. 60–61.

15. Charles W. Eliot, "Destructive and Constructive Energies of Our Government Compared," *Proceedings of the American Association for the Advancement of Science*, IIIL (1898), 594.

16. J. W. Powell, "Presidential Address . . . ," *Proceedings AAAS*, XXXVIII (1889), 4.

17. Bradley A. Fiske, "Naval Power," *United States Naval Institute Proceedings*, CLXIII (1911), 714–16.

18. Edison, quoted in *The New York Times* (Oct. 16, 1915), p. 4.

19. Tesla, "The Problem of Increasing Human Energy," *Century*, LX (1900), 183–84; *Lectures*, pp. A-166, A-172.

20. Frederick Remington, *Men with the Bark On* (New York, 1900), pp. 16–18. The Hearst press much preferred to report heroism unaided by such technology. But the few reporters who studied the modern soldier's dependence on machinery were just as amazed and uneasy as Remington—see e.g. James Creelman, "Big Guns at Sandy Hook," San Francisco *Examiner*, May 29, 1898 (Sunday Magazine), n.p.

21. Twain, *A Connecticut Yankee in King Arthur's Court* [1889] (New York, 1963), pp. 316, 309.

22. Twain, *Connecticut Yankee*, p. 112. Justin Kaplan, *Mr. Clemens and Mark Twain: A Biography* (New York, 1966), "The Yankee and the Machine" chap. 14. Mark Twain Papers, Univ. of California at Berkeley. Notebook, No. 18 (1884), p. 17, illustrates Twain's fascination with new weapons (especially the machine gun) as he worked on early versions of *A Connecticut Yankee*. This material is discussed in Henry Nash Smith, *Mark Twain's Fable of Progress* (New Brunswick, N.J., 1964). Twain to Tesla (Nov. 17, 1898), copy in Twain Papers. See also Twain to W. T. Stead (Jan. 9, 1899), Albert Bigelow Paine, ed.,

*Mark Twain's Letters*, 2 vols. (New York & London, 1917), II, 673–74.

23. James Chester, "Outline of Modern Tactics," *JMSIUS*, XVII (1895), 668; "Military Discipline . . . ," *JMSIUS*, XXIII (1898), 268–79; "The Organization of Artillery Defense," *JMSIUS*, XII (1891), 990; "Musketry," *JMSIUS*, XII (1891), 233, 235; "The Great Lesson of the Boer War," *JMSIUS*, XXXII (1903), 1–6.

24. The most important articles that develop Chester's analysis are "Modern Bobadilism . . . ," *JMSIUS*, XII (1891), 30–41; "Artillery Difficulties . . . ," *JMSIUS*, XII (1891), 558; "War," *JMSIUS*, XII (1891), 1310–15; "Military Misconceptions and Absurdities," *JMSIUS*, XIV (1893), 502–18; "The Invisible Factor . . . ," *JMSIUS*, XXVIII (1901), 352–64; "Musings of a Superannuated Soldier," *JMSIUS*, XLVII (1910), 387–97. "The furor of war," Admiral Mahan wrote to Theordore Roosevelt, "needs all the chastening it can receive in the human heart, to still the mad impulses toward conflict." Robert Seager II and Doris Maguire, eds., *Letters and Papers of Alfred Thayer Mahan*, 3 vols. (Annapolis, Md., 1975), II, 113 (Dec. 27, 1904).

25. Homer Lea's response to technology can be seen in *The Valor of Ignorance* (New York, 1909), pp. 7, 9, 11, 43, 49–50, 52–53, 56, 88, 213, 289; and *The Day of the Saxon* (New York, 1912), p. 178.

26. Jack London, "On the Great War," *Overland Monthly*, LXIX (1917), 434.

7
## THEODORE ROOSEVELT: ROUGH RIDER AND GADFLY

1. John H. Finley, "Soldiers of Peace," *Proceedings of the National Arbitration and Peace Congress* (New York, 1907), p. 208. Edward Bellamy, *Looking Backward: 2000–1887* (1888), and "How I Came to Write Looking Backward," *The Nationalist*, I (1889), 2–3. Herbert Croly, *The Promise of American Life* (1909), chap. VIII, part VI. Walter Camp and Lorin F. Deland, *Football* (Boston & New York, 1896), pp. 278–83.

2. Various threats from the Orient are analyzed in Lord Chester [Cyrus Reed Teed], *The Great Red Dragon* (Estero, Fla., 1909); M. J. Phillips, *In Our Country's Service* (Columbus, Ohio, 1909); Marsden Manson, *The Yellow Peril in Action* (San Francisco, 1907); Robert Woltor, A *Short and Truthful History of the Taking of California and Oregon by the Chinese in the Year* A.D. *1899* (San Francisco, 1882). The British threat is chronicled (and forgiven) in Samuel Barton, *The Battle of the Swash and the Capture of Canada* (New York, 1888), p. 115.

3. Richard Hofstader's judgment that Americans only rarely celebrated war for its own sake in this period seems to me correct. See Hofstader, *Social Darwinism in American Thought* (Boston, 1955), p. 184. In addition to

Homer Lea, war was extolled by S. B. Luce, "The Benefits of War," *North American Review*, CLIII (Dec. 1891), 672–83; H. C. Taylor, "The Study of War," *North American Review*, CLXII (Feb. 1896), 181–89.

On the fascination of *fin de siècle* writers for armed cataclysm see *M'lle New York*, II (Nov. 1, Dec. 1, 1898). *The Great Battles of All Nations*, 2 vols. (New York, 1898), ed. Archibald Wilberforce [Edgar Saltus]. In Saltus's columns for *Collier's* between May and August of 1898 he gave his blessings to the war with Spain. Like other aesthetes of the 1890s, Saltus lived to celebrate American intervention in 1917; see also Gelett Burgess, *War: The Creator* (New York, 1916); Francis Grierson, *Illusions and Realities of the War* (New York, 1918).

4. Brooks Adams to Roosevelt, Feb. 25, 1896, Roosevelt Papers, microfilm, series 1, reel 1.

5. Hermann Hagedorn, *Roosevelt in the Bad Lands* (Boston, 1921), p. 236.

6. Henry Cabot Lodge, *Selections from the Correspondence of Theodore Roosevelt and Henry Cabot Lodge, 1884–1918*, 2 vols. (New York, 1925), I, Aug. 20, 1886, 45 (hereafter cited as *Lodge*). Also interesting on Roosevelt's identification is Roosevelt, *Ranch Life and the Hunting Trail* [1888] (New York, 1899), p. 56, and his most formal statement, "The Northwest in the Nation," *Proceedings of the State Historical Society of Wisconsin*, XI (1893).

7. Cited in Hagedorn, *Bad Lands*, p. 355. The extent of this "Western view" was evident earlier that year (1886) when he defended the Sand Creek massacre in Colorado. He called that mob action against a surrendered band of Indian children and women "on the whole as righteous and beneficial a deed as ever took place on the frontier." Roosevelt, *Thomas H. Benton* [1886] (Boston & New York, 1899), p. 187. Roosevelt's judgment may have been the last serious defense of the incident in American historical writing. *Benton* is the most important source for Roosevelt's feelings about the West. The portrait was written largely without access to source material, "mainly evolving him from my inner consciousness," as Roosevelt explained. See *Lodge*, I (June 7, 1886), p. 41.

8. *Lodge*, II (Aug. 18, 1908), 313. See also Roosevelt, *Ranch Life*, pp. 85, 96.

9. *The Winning of the West* [1889–1896], 4 vols. (New York, 1904), I, 118; III, 265 (hereafter cited as *West*). *Benton*, p. 162.

10. *Benton*, p. 15. *West*, III, 131. Roosevelt's verbal assaults on native Americans hid considerable respect for their culture and some shame at white lawlessness. See Roosevelt, "Red and White on the Border," in *Lend a Hand*, I (1886), 68–70; *The Rough Riders* [1899] (New York, 1961), p. 22. Edward S. Curtis ed., *The North American Indian*, 20 vols. (New York, 1907–30), Roosevelt, I, foreword [1907]. Roosevelt, *A Book-Lover's Holidays in the Open* (New York, 1916), pp. 77–78.

11. *Benton*, pp. 15, 36, 158. Roosevelt's view of Wounded Knee was caustic and at variance with the whitewash in the official Army reports that had been accepted by most historians at the turn of the century. See Elting E. Morison and John M. Blum, eds., *The Letters of Theodore Roosevelt*, 8 vols. (Cambridge, 1951–54), III, (Mar. 19, 1902), 245, to Elihu Root (hereafter cited as *Letters*).

12. Roosevelt, *The Naval War of 1812* [1882], 2 vols. (New York, 1904), II, 211, 102.

13. Roosevelt, *Benton*, p. 14. *Lodge*, I (Aug. 10, 1886), 45. *Letters*, III (June 28, 1901), 103, to Eleonora Kissel Kinnicutt. *Ranch Life*, p. 109.

14. *Letters*, I (Apr. 14, 1889), 157, to Cecil Arthur Spring Rice; *Lodge*, I (Dec. 20, 1895), 200.

15. *Lodge*, I (July 31, 1897), 333. Henry F. Pringle, *Theodore Roosevelt* (New York, 1931), p. 181.

16. Roosevelt, *Rough Riders*, p. 149.

17. *Ibid.* p. 207.

18. *Ibid.* pp. 130, 145.

19. *Ibid.* pp. 73, 64, 71. Crane's report appeared in New York *World*, June 26, 1898, p. 2.

20. George Ross Kirkpatrick, *War—What For?* (West Lafayette, Ohio, 1910), pp. 140–41. See also Allan L. Benson, *Inviting War to America* (New York, 1916), pp. 139–40. *Four Lights*, I (Mar. 24, 1917), 1.

21. Roosevelt, *Rough Riders*, p. 38. See also Roosevelt, *Autobiography*, [1913] (New York, 1920), p. 232. The remarks on disfigurement are cited by Irving C. Norwood, "Exit Roosevelt the Dominant," *Outing*, LIII (1909), 718.

22. Roosevelt, "Military Preparedness and Unpreparedness" in *The Strenuous Life* [1900] (New York, 1904), p. 139. See further his anger at an Assistant Secretary of the Navy who used the arguments of "industrial efficiency" to restrict uneconomical maneuvers—*Letters*, IV (June 25, 1904), 847, to P. Morton. Roosevelt's cautious endorsement of military efficiency is given in "Military Preparedness," cited above. A good example of his growing caution with the term is his *California Addresses* (San Francisco, 1903), esp. May 12, 1903, pp. 63–73.

23. David Axeen, "Romantics and Civilizers: American Attitudes Toward War, 1898–1902," (Ph.D. diss. Yale Univ., 1969), pp. 123–25. Root, quoted by Walter Millis, *Arms and Men* (New York, 1956), pp. 157–58.

24. Roosevelt, "Army Reforms," *Outlook*, LXIII (Dec. 16, 1899), 915–16.

25. *Addresses and Presidential Messages of Theodore Roosevelt, 1902–4* (New York, 1904), p. 329; (hereafter cited as *Addresses and Messages*). Roosevelt, *Outdoor Pastimes of An American Hunter* [1905] (New York, 1908), p. 255. The same lesson had been drawn earlier in *Letters*, II (Dec. 2, 1899), 1103–4, to C. A. Spring Rice. See *Letters*, III (May 4, 1901), 70, to Gerald Charles Kitson, on the advantage of Cuban disorganization. For examples of imaginary calls to the colors after Cuba see *Letters*, II (Sept. 18, 1899); 1075, to Samuel Baldwin Marks Young; *Letters*, III (Mar. 30,

1901), 35, to Frederick Funston; *Letters*, VII (Jan. 5, 1911), 203, to Ian Standish Monteith Hamilton; *Letters*, VII (Mar. 14, 1911), 243, to William Howard Taft.

26. Roosevelt, *Strenuous Life*, pp. 29, 33. David H. Burton, *Theodore Roosevelt: Confident Imperialist* (Philadelphia, 1968), p. 106 on Cuba. *Letters*, V (Aug. 27, 1907), p. 776, to Silas McBee. See Burton, *Confident Imperialist*, pp. 176–77. Roosevelt's allies (and personal friends) in the preparedness movement testified that the possession of the Philippines was a source of American weakness: M. V. Z. Woodhull, *West Point in our Next War* (New York, 1915), p. 14; R. M. Johnson, *Arms and the Race* (New York, 1915), pp. 177–78; Leonard Wood, House Committee on Military Affairs, *Hearings on H.R. 12766, To Increase the Efficiency of the Military Establishment of the United States*, 2 vols., U.S. Congress, House, 64th Cong., 1st sess. (Washington, D.C., 1916), II, 742.

27. *Letters*, I (Aug. 13, 1897) 645, to C. A. Spring Rice; to W. Reid, April 4, 1906, TR Papers, microfilm, series 3B, reel 413; *ibid.* to Carl Schurz, Sept. 8, 1905.

28. Roosevelt, *African Game Trails* (New York, 1910), pp. 19, 327–28, 414. Roosevelt, *Through the Brazilian Wilderness* (New York, 1914), pp. 177–78. *Letters*, VII, 258, to Endicott Peabody, May 5, 1911, is a confession of the exhaustion Roosevelt felt after encountering the wilderness.

29. Roosevelt, *America and the World War* (New York, 1915), pp. 16, 44, 67; pp. 2, 277 (quoted); this work collects Roosevelt's published commentary on the war through the last four months of 1914. *Letters*, VIII (Feb. 2, 1915), 890, to Cecil Arthur Spring Rice.

30. Roosevelt, *World War*, pp. 61, 55.

31. Roosevelt, *World War*, pp. 67, 17, 72. As originally published in *Outlook*, these remarks were even more unguarded. Arthur Bullard, *Outlook*, CVIII (Oct. 7, 1914), p. 289, also held up the German model for Americans. Russell Buchanan, "Theodore Roosevelt and American Neutrality, 1914–1917, *AHR*, XLIII (1938), 775–90, accepts Roosevelt's argument that his public praise of Germany was a pose.

32. *Letters*, VIII (Oct. 3, 1914), 824, to H. Münsterberg. Roosevelt, *Fear God and Take Your Own Part* (New York, 1916), p. 41, 283.

33. Roosevelt, *World War*, pp. 12, 123. See also his *Outlook* piece, "The World War: Its Tragedies and Its Lessons," CVIII (Sept. 23, 1914), and Roosevelt material cited in *Foreign Affairs*, IV (1925), 151. George Sylvester Viereck, *Roosevelt* (New York, 1919), p. 113.

34. Wilson (Dec. 8, 1915), cited in George E. Mowry, *Theodore Roosevelt and the Progressive Movement* (New York, 1960), p. 318. *The Cabinet Diaries of Josephus Daniels*, ed. E. P. Cronin (Lincoln, Neb., 1963), p. 216. Joseph L. Gardner, *Departing Glory: Theodore Roosevelt as Ex-President* (New York, 1973), pp. 379, 382. George Creel also brought public discussion of preparedness to a very personal level at this time: he

suggested that Roosevelt's announced enjoyment of bloodletting in his published writings made him a doubtful guardian of American men. Creel, "Red Blood," *Harper's Weekly*, LXI (July 3, 1915), 9–10.

35. Roosevelt, *Roosevelt in the Kansas City Star* (Cambridge, Mass., 1921), pp. 13–15 (Oct. 17, 1917). *Letters*, VIII (Feb. 7, 1917), 1154, to H. Johnson; see also pp. 1089, 1125.

36. This correspondence is at the end of Roosevelt, *The Foes of Our Household* (New York, 1917). American planners were more hostile to Roosevelt's proposal than Europeans were. Georges Clemenceau, for example, supported his plans. David R. Beaver, *Newton D. Baker and the American War Effort* (Lincoln, Neb., 1966), pp. 28–30. Ray Stannard Baker and William E. Dodd, eds., *The Public Papers of Woodrow Wilson*, 8 vols. (New York, 1925–27), V, 40.

37. Robert H. Davis and Perley Poore Sheehan, *Efficiency, A Play in One Act* (New York, 1917). A letter of endorsement by Roosevelt serves as the Preface (Nov. 8, 1917). He supported another Allied propaganda effort that cast "the fight of the living spirit against the war-machine," in Arthur and Helen Hayes Gleason, *Golden Lads* (New York, 1916), Introduction, p. ix.

38. Roosevelt, *National Strength and International Duty* (Princeton Univ., 1917), p. 54. Roosevelt, *Kansas City Star*, p. 120 (Mar. 26, 1918), p. 141 (Apr. 20, 1918). See also his Introduction to Mrs. Humphry Ward, *Towards the Goal* (New York, 1918).

39. *Letters*, VIII (Sept. 1, 1917), p. 1234, to Q. Roosevelt.

## 8.
## THE AMERICAN VANGUARD ON THE WESTERN FRONT

1. Roosevelt at an AFS meeting, Sept. 1916, quoted in *History of the American Field Service in France, 'Friends of France,' 1914–1917*, 3 vols. (Boston and New York, 1920), I, 8.

2. Edmond C. Genêt, *War Letters* (New York, 1918). E. A. Abbey, *An American Soldier: Letters of Edwin Austin Abbey* (Boston & New York, 1918).

3. Edwin C. Parsons, *I Flew With the Lafayette Escadrille* [1937] (Indianapolis, 1963), p. 104. Frederick C. Hild, "War Experiences of an Air Scout-I," *Scientific American*, CXI (Dec. 26, 1914), 520. See also " 'Big Bang'—Story of an American Adventurer," in Francis Trevelyan Miller, ed., *True Stories of the Great War*, 6 vols. (New York, 1917), VI, 158.

4. William J. Robinson, *My Fourteen Months at the Front* (Boston, 1916), p. 2. A similar spirit behind enlistment is confessed to in James Norman Hall, *Kitchener's Mob* (Boston & New York, 1916); James R. McConnell, *Flying for France* (Garden City, N.Y., 1917), pp. xi–xii; Edward

R. Coyle, *Ambulancing on the French Front* (New York, 1918), pp. 17–20. Derby R. Holmes, *A Yankee in the Trenches* (Boston, 1918), pp. 2–3; "How I Helped Take the Turkish Trenches . . . ," in Miller, ed., *True Stories of the Great War*, VI, 145. *Selected Letters of E. E. Cummings*, ed. F. W. Dupee and George Stade (New York, 1969), pp. 15, 19 (April 7, and May 4, 1917). Cf. Frederick Trevenen Edwards, *Fort Sheridan to Montfaucon; the War Letters . . .* (De Land, Fla., 1954), p. 90.

5. General James A. Drain to Frank A. Scott, July 30, 1917, Scott Papers, Box 4, Princeton Univ. I have corrected mistakes in the letter that are not significant.

6. John Iden Kautz, *Trucking to the Trenches* (Boston & New York, 1918), pp. 44–45 (July 3, 1917). See also Coningsby Dawson, *Carry On: Letters in War-Time* (New York, 1917), p. 98 (Dec. 20, 1916). For the same sentiment in the professional military literature, see Louis C. Duncan, "The Evolution of a Military Arm," *JMSIUS*, (1916), p. 73.

7. Dos Passos to Arthur K. McComb, Aug. 10, 1917, quoted in Melvin Landsberg, *Dos Passos' Path to USA* (Boulder, Col., 1972), p. 56.

8. This genre of war reports is represented by New York *World*, May 1, 1915, p. 1, May 3, 1915, p. 2; also San Francisco *Examiner*, Aug. 15, 1915, p. 3E; Sept. 26, 1915, p. 12; Jan. 12, 1916, p. 2. Arthur and Helen Hayes Gleason, *Golden Lads* (New York, 1916), pp. 80, 86, 111. Laura S. Portor, "The Bright Side of War," *North American Review*, CCIII (June 1916), 883–894.

9. C. de Florenz, 'No. 6' *A Few Pages from the Diary of an Ambulance Driver* (New York, 1918), quote from Foreword by Frederic R. Coudert, p. viii; Hall, *Kitchener's Mob*, p. 101. See also John J. Chapman's memoir in J. J. Chapman, *Victor Chapman's Letters from France* (New York, 1917), p. 26; and Dawson, *Carry On*, p. 75 (Nov. 1, 1916).

10. Edwards, *Fort Sheridan to Montfaucon*, pp. 60–62.

11. '*Friends of France*,' *The Field Service of the American Ambulance Described by its Members* (Boston, 1916), p. 120 (J. G. B. Cambell); see also pp. 84–85 (J. R. McConnell). For similar reports see *Diary of Section VIII, American Ambulance Field Service* (n.p., 1917), p. 10; Arthur Gleason and Helen H. Gleason, *With the First War Ambulances in Belgium* (New York, 1915), p. 18; Coleman Tileston Clark and Alter Storrs Clark, Jr., *Soldier Letters* (n.p., 1919), p. 29 (June 28, 1916). A. Piatt Andrew, *Letters Written Home from France* (Cambridge, Mass., 1916), p. 37.

12. Richard Harding Davis quoted in William G. Shepherd, *Confessions of a War Correspondent*, (New York & London, 1917), p. 75; Edwards, *Fort Sheridan to Montfaucon*, p. 280. Malcolm Cowley, *Exile's Return* (New York, 1934), pp. 47, 79.

13. Henry A. Butters, *Harry Butters, R.F.A.—'An American Citizen*,' ed. D. O'Sullivan (New York, 1918), pp. 231, 258, 261 (Mar. 22 to June 9, 1916).

14. James Parker, *The Old Army: Memories, 1872–1918* (Philadelphia, 1929), p. 449.
15. Leslie Buswell, *Ambulance No. 10* (Boston & New York, 1916), pp. 56–60, quoted p. 60 (this volume includes a recruiting poster). Arthur Gleason, *With the First War Ambulances in Belgium* (New York, 1915), pp. 141–2. Florenz, 'No. 6.' Hall, *Kitchener's Mob*, pp. 98–9, 68, 101, 197. See also *Victor Chapman's Letters*, p. 121 (June 4, 1915); Julian H. Bryan, *Ambulance 464: Encore des Blessés* (New York, 1918), pp. 50–51.
16. Edwin C. Parsons, *I Flew With the Lafayette Escadrille* [1937] (Indianapolis, 1963), p. 249.
17. Cited in Donald Smythe, *Guerrilla Warrior: The Early Life of John J. Pershing* (New York, 1973), pp. 277, 329n.; see p. 278 for his political views. Cf. John Dos Passos's "The Body of An American" at the conclusion of *Nineteen Nineteen* (New York, 1932).
18. W. Reginald Wheeler, *A Book of Verse of the Great War* (New Haven, 1917), published Nov. The Preface is dated Mar. 1917; pp. xv, 2, 42 (quoted). See also poems by William Rose Benét, Gilbert Frankau, W. N. Eyer, Joseph Lee, Robert W. Service, and Percy Mackaye.
19. Ellen N. LaMotte, *The Backwash of War* (New York & London, 1916), p. 111 (quoted), p. vi, p. 105. For a similar acid treatment of male behavior see Charlotte Perkins Gilman, *The Man Made World* (London, 1911), p. 219; Anna Garlin Spencer, "Women and War," *Independent*, LXXXI (Jan. 25, 1915), 121–24; Mary Austin, "Sex Emancipation Through War," *Forum*, LIX (May 1918), 610.
20. Arthur Sweetser, *Roadside Glimpses of the War* (New York, 1916), pp. 196–97. Other prominent correspondents expressed shock in the same terms: Shepherd, *Confessions of a War Correspondent*, p. 59; Will Irvin, *Men, Women, and War* (London, 1915), pp. 78–79. Hearst and Pulitzer continually relied on metaphors taken from machinery to describe fighting men—see e.g., San Francisco *Examiner*, Aug. 30, 1914, p. 1, Sept. 17, 1914, p. 19; New York *World*, Dec. 26, 1915, p. 10, Aug. 27, 1916, p. 12. The shock of battle expressed in mechanical images was also common among soldiers—e.g., Genêt, *War Letters*, p. 137 (Jan. 19, 1916).
21. *'Friends of France,'* pp. 17–18. Harrison, *When I Come Back* (Boston & New York, 1919), p. 58.
22. Celebrations of the freedom and honor of war work with these machines is evident e.g. in Jack Wright, *A Poet of the Air* (Boston & New York, 1918), p. 14; *Victor Chapman's Letters*, pp. 25, 182–83; Granville Fortescue, *France Bears the Burden* (New York, 1917), p. 123. For the hidden heroes see Eric Fisher Wood, *The Note-Book of an Intelligence Officer* (New York, 1917), p. 214; and the Council of National Defense, release, Aug. 20, 1916, p. 14, in Frank A. Scott Papers, Princeton Univ., Box 1.
23. Edwin C. Parsons, *I Flew with the Lafayette Escadrille* [1937] (Indian-

apolis, 1963), pp. 102, 249–50. James N. Hall, *High Adventure* (Boston & New York, 1918), p. 44. Bert Hall, *"En l'Air!"* (*In the Air*) (New York, 1918), pp. 78–79. Charles A. Fenton, "Ambulance Drivers in France and Italy: 1914–1918," *American Quarterly*, III (1951), 332.

24. "The Red Country," in Wheeler (ed.), *Book of Verse of the Great War*, p. 3.

25. *Harry Butters*, p. 99 (Mar. 21, 1915); Wood, *The Note-Book of an Intelligence Officer*, pp. 237–38; Philip Dana Orcutt, *The White Road of Mystery, the Note-Book of an American Ambulancier* (New York, 1918), pp. 20, 97–8, 159. James Scott Brown, *Robert Bacon: Life and Letters*, (Garden City, N.Y., 1923), p. 241 (from *The New York Times*, Oct. 3, 1915).

26. Alan Seeger, *Letters and Diary* (New York, 1917), pp. 95–96, 117; see also 38. Kautz, *Trucking to the Trenches*, adopted Seeger's metaphor. Abbey, *An American Soldier*, p. 106, quoted (Jan. 12, 1917); see also 59. An American surgeon in charge of a volunteer ambulance group during the first year of the war gave the most detailed picture of how military organization and technology made soldiers pieces of "mechanism": George W. Crile, *A Mechanistic View of War and Peace* (New York, 1916), pp. 95–96. See also Coningsby Dawson, *Living Bayonets* (New York, 1919), esp. p. 147.

27. Beveridge, *What is Back of the War*, pp. 30–31; Dawson, *Carry On*, pp. 130–31 (Feb. 6, 1917). Francis Trevelyan Miller collected six volumes of war memoirs; he concluded that fighting men "lost all fear of death . . . and stood before Calvary." Miller, comp., *True Stories of the Great War*, I, iv.

9
MANAGERS, MUCKRAKERS, MARTYRS

1. Daniels interview, *The New York Times*, Aug. 8, 1915, Part IV, pp. 14–15; see also Daniels quoted in *The New York Times*, July 16, 1915, p. 1; New York *World*, Oct. 3, 1915, p. 6N; San Francisco *Examiner* Aug. 22, 1915, p. 78. At that time, the Under-Secretary of the Navy was not always so impressed by inventors: *FDR: His Personal Letters, 1905–1928*, Elliot Roosevelt, ed., 4 vols. (New York, 1947–50), II, 296 (Oct. 10, 1915). On the well-advertised (and self-advertised) efficacy and prestige of science see Samuel Haber, *Efficiency and Uplift; Scientific Management in the Progressive Era, 1890–1920* (Chicago, 1965).

2. American parsimony and the resultant decay in the armed forces is perhaps the most constant theme in military writing in this period—see e.g. A. L. Wagner, "The Military and Naval Policy of the United States," *Journal of the Military Service Institution of the United States*, VII (1886), 371–403; W. D. McAnaney, "Desertion in the United States Army," *JMSIUS*, X (1889), 450–65; "Mob Law at Camps," *Army*

*and Navy Journal* XXXVI (1898), 26; A. S. Bacon, "Is Our Army Degenerate?" *Forum*, XXXII (1889), 11–23; R. L. Bullard, "Cardinal Vices of the American Soldier," *JMSIUS*, XXXVI (1905), 104–14.

3. Croly, "The Effect on American Institutions of a Powerful Military and Naval Establishment," *Annals of the American Academy of Political and Social Science*, LXVI (July 1916), 157–172. Still the best account of the Progressives' commitment to the use of armed force is William E. Leuchtenburg, "Progressivism and Imperialism: The Progressive Movement and American Foreign Policy, 1898–1916," *Mississippi Valley Historical Review*, XXXIX (Dec. 1952), 483–504, esp. 494. J. A. Thompson has reviewed the controversy over this article and studied a group of intellectuals that supports Leuchtenburg's thesis: "American Progressive Publicists and the First World War, 1914–1917," *Journal of American History*, LVIII (Sept. 1971), 364–83. Jane Addams, *Official Report of the Thirteenth Universal Peace Congress* (Boston, 1904), pp. 145–46.

4. The use of Army reform to educate and discipline civilians was widely advocated in the professional literature: see E. L. Zalinski, "The Army Organization Best Adapted to a Republican Form of Government. . . ." (Prize Essay), *JMSIUS*, XIV (1893), 926–77; G. W. Wingate, "Military Training in Secondry Schools," *JMSIUS*, XXXIX (1902), 295–99; J. Frazier, "The Military Education of the Youth of the Country," *JMSIUS*, L (1912), 329–50; J. J. Mayes, "The Right to Condemn," *JMSIUS*, LIII (1913), 7–18.

5. For example, Elmer Sperry in 1909 negotiated with Krupp as eagerly as with the U.S. Navy: Thomas Parke Hughes, *Elmer Sperry; Inventor and Engineer* (Baltimore, 1971), p. 122. Elihu Thomson carried on similar international business with the British and American navies around the turn of the century—David O. Woodbury, *Elihu Thomson, Beloved Scientist* (Boston, 1960), pp. 238–39. Both John Philip Holland and Simon Lake sold submarines to the belligerents in the Russo-Japanese War. Lake refused foreign work during the first years of the European conflict—not, apparently, in the interests of national security, but only because he wanted his fame recognized by Americans. See Lake, *The Submarine in War and Peace* (Philadelphia, 1918), p. 142.

6. "Scientific Men and Conscription," *Scientific American*, CXI (Oct. 10, 1914), 298.

Wilbur Wright, quoted in *The New York Times*, July 15, 1915, p. 2; War Records Committee of Alumni Association of M.I.T., *Technology's War Record* (Cambridge, Mass., 1920), pp. 2, 4, 58. Other examples of this peace sentiment are "Editor's Table," *The Popular Science Monthly*, XIV (1879), 817–19; "The Mechanical View of War," *American Machinist*, XVII (1894), p. 3; "Random Reflections," *Scientific American*, CXI (Sept. 12, 1914), p. 214.

[Luis Philip Senarens], *Frank Reade, Jr., and His New Steam Man,*

or the Young Inventor's Trip to the Far West by 'noname,' Frank Reade
Library, vol. I, no. 1 (1892), p. 13; Reade makes a similar refusal in
another episode in this series; see *Exploring a Submarine Mountain
. . .* , vol. III, no. 77 (1894), p. 3. The inventor's co-optation by government and enjoyment of destruction are clear in Senarens's stories in
the later Pluck and Luck series (also published by Frank Tousey): *Jack
Wright's Submarine . . .* , no. 197 (1902); *Jack Wright's Flying Torpedo . . .* , no. 278 (1903); *Jack Wright's Air and Water Cutter . . .* ,
no. 1011 (1917), esp. p. 3.

7. Modeling preparedness after German programs was advised in "Science
and National Welfare," *Popular Science Monthly*, LXXXVII (1915),
310–12; "True Preparedness," *Century*, XCI (Mar. 1916), 195–97. See
also testimony of a representative of the American Institute of Consulting Engineers, House Committee on Military Affairs, Hearings on H.R.
12766, *To Increase the Efficiency of the Military Establishment of the
United States*, 2 vols., U.S., Congress, House, 64th Cong., 1st sess.
(1916), II, 1206. Perry Belmont, "International Relations and Home
Politics," *Sea Power*, I (Sept. 1916), 39–41. John Patrick Finnegan,
*Against the Specter of a Dragon: The Campaign for American Military
Preparedness, 1914–1917* (Westport, Conn., 1974), p. 107.

8. Examples of the focus of the preparedness advocates on disciplining and
controlling peacetime America: "Student Military Camps," *Outlook*,
CVIII (Dec. 9, 1914), 813; C. F. Talman, "The Industrial Army," *Scientific American*, CXV (July 22, 1916), 80–81; House Hearings, *To
Increase the Efficiency* (1916), I, p. 412, II, 743, 1202–3; L. R. Gig-
nilliat, *Arms and the Boy*, Introduction by N. D. Baker (Indianapolis,
1916). Roosevelt quoted by Finnegan, *Specter of a Dragon*, p. 110.

9. "Scientific Men and Conscription," *Scientific American*, CXI (Oct. 10,
1914), 298; "The Warrior at the Lathe," *Scientific American*, CXV
(July 15, 1916), 56. For a similar proposal see Howard E. Coffin of the
Naval Consulting Board in *The New York Times*, July 30, 1916, p. 13.

10. "Minutes of Meeting of Munitions Standards Board" (typescript), Mar.
21, 1917, pp. 1, 5, Frank A. Scott Papers, Princeton Univ., Box 1.

11. Croly, "The Effect on American Institutions," p. 162.

12. House Hearings, *To Increase the Efficiency* (1916), I, 99–101 (Gen.
Scott). The bugaboo of an invasion after the European war was raised by
other creditable military experts in these hearings: see II, 773, 863–64,
and esp. 870–83. Popularizations of these forecasts were very common
at the time; see e.g. "The United States; an Undefended Treasure
Land," *Scientific American*, CXII (Feb. 6–20, 1915), 118–20, 158–59,
178–79, 198–99, 204. Cleveland Moffett, "The Conquest of America in
1921," *McClure's*, VL (1915), and his "Saving the Nation" series in the
next volume (1916). J. Bernard Walker, *America Fallen! The Sequel to
the European War* (New York, 1915); Eric Fisher Wood, *The Writing*

on the Wall (New York, 1916), esp. pp. 38–39, 78. J. W. Muller, The Invasion of America (New York, 1916).

13. Finnegan, Against the Specter of a Dragon, p. 4, see also 47–49, 56, 155.

14. The preparedness movement's usable past was almost completely the product of one book: Emory Upton, The Military Policy of the United States, written about 1880 and published (and energetically promoted) by Secretary of War Root in 1904. I have quoted from the government's 1916 edition, p. xi. Frederic L. Huidekoper, The Military Unpreparedness of the United States (New York, 1916), p. 535.

15. Leonard Wood, America's Duty [1917] (Chicago, 1921), p. 156. Wood's diary of the campaign in Cuba strikes the same note of anger and shame about the "sickening" American inefficiency: Leonard Wood Papers, Library of Congress, Manuscript Division, Box 2 (July 9, 1898). M. F. Stelle, "Democracy and Our Armies, JMSIUS, XXXVIII (1906), 358–61. Jennings C. Wise, The Call of the Republic (New York, 1917), p. 76. Moffett, "Saving the Nation," McClure's, XXXXVI (1916), 74–76. Huidekoper, Military Unpreparedness of the United States, was the most acid and exhaustive book in the Upton tradition of military history; see e.g. pp. 40, 59, 101–2, 145, 205–6, 209, 282.

16. Wise, Empire and Armament, quoted p. 207. Another preparedness advocate who stressed the belligerence and self-interest of American foreign policy was Wood, The Writing on the Wall, p. 16.

17. Oswald Garrison Villard, 'Preparedness' (New York, 1915), p. 4. A similar attempt to turn cries of weakness against the preparedness movement is Allan L. Benson's pamphlet for the American Union Against Militarism (c. 1916), Common Sense About the Navy.

18. Robert R. McCormick, "Ripe for Conquest," Century, XCI (Apr. 1916), 833–39, quote on 834. Muller, The Invasion of America, quote on p. 95. See also J. Bernard Walker, America Fallen!; Cleveland Moffett, "The Conquest of America" and Moffett, "Saving the Nation," McClure's, VL–IVL. "Memorandum of Moving Picture Censorship Port of New York," Clifford N. Carver Papers, Princeton Univ., Box 18.

19. The Outlook is a particularly good source on the treatment of atrocities as unprecedented, purposeless violations of the rules of civilized warfare; see "Aerial Warfare," CVIII (Oct. 28, 1914), 450–53; "The Lusitania Massacre," CX (May 19, 15), 103; (Aug. 25, 1915), 931.

20. Irvin S. Cobb, 'Speaking of Prussians' (New York, 1917), pp. 43–44. James M. Beck, The War and Humanity, 2nd ed. (New York, 1917), p. 323. The Hearst press, similarly, viewed Verdun as a credit to the planners—and dead soldiers—of both sides: San Francisco Examiner Mar. 18, 1916, p. 22; Dec. 8, 1916, p. 20. Arthur Gleason, "Chantons, Belges! Chantons!" Century, XCI (Apr. 1916), 874–75. The psy-

chological dangers of nonintervention are discussed in "The Present Danger to Americans," *Outlook*, CX (July 14, 1915), 599; and Henry Osborn Taylor, "The Pathos of America," *Atlantic*, CXVII (Feb. 1916), 250–51. Owen Wister, *The Pentacost of Calamity* (New York, 1915), 139–41.

21. Samuel McComb, "Christianity and the Sword," *North American Review*, CCIV (Aug. 1916), 199. Rev. Charles A. Eaton, quoted in *The New York Times*, Sept. 20, 1915, p. 9. President Shankin of Wesleyan made Christianity into a warrior's faith for the class of 1917: "Christianity and Democracy," *The Wesleyan Alumnus*, I (July 1917), 10–11.

22. James Scott Brown, *Robert Bacon: Life and Letters* (Garden City, N.Y., 1923), p. 225 (Dec. 1916); see also 287. J. A. Thompson has found quite similar language in Ray Stannard Baker's private reflections on intervention; see "American Progressive Publicists," p. 381. Another strong statement flagellating prosperity and predicting doom is an editorial from *The Manufacturer's Record* in *America's Relation to the World War* (Baltimore, 1917), pp. 41–42.

23. Lincoln Colcord, *Vision of War* [1915] (New York, 1916), quoted, pp. 21, 23, 51, 104. In Clifford Carver Papers, Princeton Univ., Box 9, there are letters and drafts of articles by Colcord written during the summer of 1915 which give further testimony to his pleasure in watching the war. For a comparable view of Colcord, drawing on different sources, see Christopher Lasch, *The New Radicalism in America, 1889–1963: The Intellectual as a Social Type* (New York, 1965), chap. 7.

24. Ray Stannard Baker and William E. Dodd, eds. *The Public Papers of Woodrow Wilson*, 8 vols. (New York & London, 1925–27), IV, 23 (Jan. 29, 1916); see also III, 225 (Dec. 8, 1914); IV, 30, 36 (Jan. 29, 1916); IV, 346 (Oct. 5, 1916); IV, 390 (Nov. 4, 1916). The inferno metaphor is continued in his image of the war as "maelstrom" IV, 7 (Jan. 27, 1916). The lack of clear goals in the ongoing war is stressed in IV, III (Feb. 3, 1916) and 346 (Oct. 5, 1916).

25. Wilson, *Public Papers*, IV, 12–13 (Jan. 27, 1916), pp. 19–21 (Jan. 29, 1917); see also Wilson's discussion with members of the American Union Against Militarism in *The New York Times*, pp. 1–2, May 9, 1916.

26. Wilson, *Public Papers*, III, 129 (June 5, 1914); IV, 34 (Jan. 29, 1916); V, 14 (Apr. 2, 1917).

27. In Wilson, *Public Papers*, V, 56–57.

## 10
## WARTIME PEACE OF MIND

1. The extreme reluctance of Americans to do what the Allied authorities thought was prudent and essential is documented in Charles Seymour,

ed., *The Intimate Papers of Colonel House*, 4 vols. (Boston & New York, 1926–28), III, 301; John J. Pershing, *My Experiences in the World War*, 2 vols. (New York, 1931), I, 152–53. Edward M. Coffman, *The War to End All Wars: The American Military Experience in World War I* (New York, 1968), is an excellent study of this idiosyncratic American strategy; see esp. pp. 173–4, 213, 271. Harvey A. DeWeerd, *President Wilson Fights his War; World War I and the American Intervention*, (New York, 1968), p. 209.

2. On Creel's "treasonable moderation" see Walton Bean, "George Creel and his Critics: A Study of the Attacks on the Committee on Public Information, 1917–1919" (Ph.D. diss., Univ. of California at Berkeley, 1941), chap. VI. Also George T. Blakey, *Historians on the Homefront; American Propagandists for the Great War* (Lexington, Ky., 1970). On the primacy of local interests in explaining the war and repressing dissent see Bruce Frazer, "Yankees at War: Cohesion and Cooperation on the Connecticut Homefront 1917–1918." (Ph.D. diss., Columbia Univ., 1975). James Morgan Read, *Atrocity Propaganda, 1914–1919* (New Haven, 1941), p. 32, on Pershing.

3. Ray Stannard Baker and William E. Dodd, eds. *The Public Papers of Woodrow Wilson*, 8 vols. (New York & London, 1925–27), V, 436 (Feb. 24, 1919); see also V, 450 (Mar. 4, 1919) and V, 332 (Dec. 25, 1918) on the soldier's "spiritual force" and gallantry. On Wilson's earlier suggestions of vengeance see V, 202 (Apr. 6, 1918). Following close behind the President were those who denied aggressive feelings toward the enemy and pleaded for fair play; such thoughts occupied a good part of planners' attention: see *Home Reading Course of Citizen Soldiers*, "War Information Series," Committee on Public Information, no. 9 (Oct. 1917), pp. 5, 60. Josephus Daniels, *The Navy and the Nation* (New York, 1919), pp. 84–85. The German theory of war was proven unprecedented through a selective use of historical examples in *The War Message and the Facts Behind It*, "WIS," CPI, no. 1 (June, 1917); George W. Scott and James W. Garner, *The German War Code*, "WIS," CPI, no. 11 (Feb. 1918).

4. Laurence Stallings, *The Doughboys, the Story of the AEF, 1917–1919* (New York, 1963), p. 1.

5. Raymond B. Fosdick, "Letters From the First World War" (bound typescript) in Fosdick Papers, Princeton Univ., Box 1, pp. 2–3 (May 30, 1918); pp. 9–10 (June 9, 1918). The correspondence is addressed "to the family." For another example of this split response to combat see R. Derby Holmes, *A Yankee in the Trenches* (Boston, 1918), pp. 123–24, 199. Will Judy, *A Soldier's Diary* (Chicago, 1930), p. 172, suggests the sacrilegious tone of the doughboys' humor.

6. Stewart Hughes to his father (July 23, 1918), William Phillips Collection, U.S. Army Military History Research Collection, Carlisle Barracks, Pa. William Howard Taft shared this vocabulary: see "The Health

and Morale of America's Citizen Army," *National Geographic*, XXXIII (Mar. 1918), 223. Coningsby Dawson, *Living Bayonets* (New York, 1919). See also Sara Ware Bassett's introduction to *An American Poilu* (Boston, 1919). *Letters of Warwick Greene*, ed. R. W. Hale (Boston & New York, 1931), p. 109 (June 29, 1919). On the doughboys' love of poetry see "Mlle. Soixante-Quinze" and "The Tank" in *The Stars and Stripes* (Apr. 26, 1918), p. 8; (June 21, 1918), p. 4.

7. A good example of the self-congratulations of the units is *History of the 1st Division During the World War, 1917–1919* (Philadelphia, 1922), p. xvii. The pride in units torn by dissension and official condemnation is clear in Charles B. Hoyt, *Heroes of the Argonne* (Kansas City, Mo., 1919), and Clair Kenamore, *From Vauquois Hill to Exermont, A History of the 35th Division of the United States Army* (St. Louis, Mo., 1919). *A History of the 63rd Infantry* (n.p., 1920) is the proud record of a unit that never sailed.

8. Examples of the journalists' work are Floyd Gibbon, *'And They Thought We Wouldn't Fight'* (New York, 1918); Arthur S. Riggs, *With Three Armies* (Indianapolis, 1918), esp. pp. 296–303; Irvin S. Cobb, *The Glory of the Coming* (New York, 1918), p. 170. The YMCA presentation of the war is given by William L. Stidger, *Soldier Silhouettes on Our Front* (New York, 1918), p. 187 (quoted); William B. West, *The Fight for the Argonne, Personal Experiences of a Y Man* (New York & Cincinnati, 1919); Charles W. Whitehair, *Out There* (New York, 1918), esp. pp. 90–91, 107. Other examples of the saccharine view of the Front are Elizabeth H. Ashe, *Intimate Letters from France* (San Francisco, 1918), esp. p. 79; Gelett Burgess, *War—the Creator* (New York, 1916); Carol K. Corey, "Plain Tales from the Trenches," *National Geographic*, XXXIII (Mar. 3, 1918), 300–12; Curtis Wheeler, *Letters from an American Soldier to his Father* (Indianapolis, 1918); Chester Walton Jenks, *Our First Ten Thousand* (Boston, 1919), pp. 93–94.

9. William L. Langer, *Gas and Flame in World War I* [1918–1919] (New York, 1965), p. xviii; MacQuarrie, *How To Live at the Front*, p. 251; Arthur Gleason, "The Red Triangle in France," *Survey*, XL (July 6, 1918), 389; Franklin H. Martin, *Digest of the Proceedings of the Council of National Defense during the World War* (Washington, D.C., 1934), p. 348.

Some of the most interesting expressions of this mood by individuals are Carroll J. Swan, *My Company* (Boston & New York, 1918); Chester W. Jenks, *Our First Ten Thousand* (Boston, 1919), esp. pp. 93–94; *Letters of Warwick Greene, 1915–1928*, ed. R. W. Hale (Boston & New York, 1931), p. 11; Elizabeth S. Sergeant, *Shadow Shapes* (Boston & New York, 1920).

10. Mark Sullivan, *Wake Up America!* (New York, 1918), p. 11.

11. Newell Dwight Hillis, *Studies of the Great War* (New York, 1915), pp. 18, 33, 114–15.

12. Hillis, *German Atrocities* (New York, 1918), p. 19 (quoted), see also 21,

23. *The Blot on the Kaiser's 'Scutcheon* (New York, 1918), quoted pp. 56, 59; see also 51, 57, 63. Hillis had sterilization of Germans in mind, not death camps. William T. Hornaday's book for the American Defense Society, *Awake! America* (New York, 1918), was another attempt to incite soldiers (and the Administration) to greater violence against Germans.

13. Samuel Cranston Benson, *Back from Hell* (Chicago, 1918), pp. 35, 55.

14. Arthur Guy Empey, *First Call* (New York, 1918), p. 241 (speaking of throwing himself on a grenade). Hillis's nerve went untested, but the War Loan Committee made his service comfortable: in four months of stump speeches in 1917 he was provided with traveling expenses, an assistant, and $5000. The agreement is in Clifford N. Carter Papers, Princeton Univ., Box 15.

15. Hough, *The Web*, pp. 64–65, 453–54.

16. E.g. see, *War Letters of Edmond Genêt* (New York, 1918), p. 314. [Lambert A. Wood], *His Job* (Portland, Ore., 1936), p. 9; several of the letters in this collection were published before 1920.

17. [Wood], *His Job*, pp. 72–73, 90–91. (Wood continually felt betrayed by girl friends at home.) Other extravagant letters to mothers are *War Letters of Edmond Genêt*, p. 314; *One Who Gave His Life, War Letters of Quincy Sharpe Mills*, ed. J. Luby (New York, 1923), p. 292; see also Dorothy Canfield, *The Day of Glory* (New York, 1919), p. 117. Library of Congress, Manuscript Division, World War I Collections, "Miscellaneous Letters from Soldiers Overseas," has similar letters from Ohio papers—these clippings are not identified. Willa Cather, *One of Ours* [1922] (New York, 1949), p. 332; Stanley Cooperman, *World War I and the American Novel*, (Baltimore, 1967), pp. 129–37, is a valuable discussion of Cather.

18. Contrast e.g. the multiple atrocities and counter-atrocities in Albert N. Depew, *Gunner Depew* (Chicago, 1918), with the medical evidence of the great rarity of any type of bayonet wounds: Fred D. Baldwin, "The American Enlisted Man in World War I" (Ph.D. diss., Princeton Univ., 1964), p. 98; Pottle, *Stretchers*, p. 134; W. Kerr Rainsford, *From Upton to the Meuse with the Three Hundred and Seventh* (New York, 1920), p. xix.

19. *The Patton Papers, 1885–1940*, ed. Martin Bluemenson (Boston, 1972), I, 408, see also 368, 420, 616, 629, 700, 723.

20. Robert A. Woods, "The Regimentation of the Free," *Survey*, XL (July 6, 1918), 398; Ben B. Lindsey and H. O'Higgins, *The Doughboy's Religion and Other Aspects of Our Day* (New York, 1919), is similarly sanguine. John Erskine, *Democracy and Ideals* (New York, 1920), chap. 5. William E. Leuchtenburg, "The New Deal and the Analogue of War," in John Braeman, Robert H. Bremner, and Everett Walters, eds., *Change and Continuity in Twentieth-Century America* (New York, Evanston, & London, 1966).

21. T. S. Ames, "The Trained Man of Science in the War," *Science*,

XLVIII (Oct. 25, 1918), 402–3. The scientists' campaign for power and prestige is studied in detail by Ronald C. Tobey, *The American Ideology of National Science, 1919–1930* (Pittsburgh, 1971). The optimism about the war took most extreme form in Aleš Hrdlička, "The Effects of the War on the American People," *Scientific Monthly*, VIII (May 1919), 544–45. For other expressions see George T. W. Patrick, "The Next Step in Applied Science," *Scientific Monthly*, VIII (Feb. 1919), 118–28; Robert A. Millikan, "The New Opportunity in Science," *Science*, L (Sept. 26, 1919), 285–97; A. Russell Bond, *Inventions of the Great War* (New York, 1919), p. viii. Robert M. Yerkes, ed., *The New World of Science* (New York, 1920); Morris F. Hall *et al.*, *The Next War* (Cambridge, Mass., 1925), p. 37.

22. William Crozier, "Remarks . . . at the Presentation of the John Fritz Medal . . . ." (Apr. 23, 1924); F. A. Scott to W. C. Crozier, (May 28, 1924); Scott, "On the Problem of Munitionment," *Army Ordnance*, VIII (May–June 1928), 349–53; Invitation to the Army Ordnance Association 8th Meeting (1926); all in Frank A. Scott Papers, Princeton Univ., Box 4.

23. William Townsend Porter, *Shock at the Front* (Boston, n.d.), p. 151. I wish to thank Nathan G. Hale for sharing with me a draft of a chapter on psychiatrists and the war destined for Volume II of *Freud and the Americans*. *The Medical Department of the United States Army in the World War: Neuropsychiatry* (Washington, D.C., 1929), p. 2.

24. Earl D. Bond, *Thomas W. Salmon: Psychiatrist* (New York, 1950), pp. 106, 104, 108, 101. Salmon Memo to Raymond B. Fosdick, "A Preventable Type of Mental Disease in the AEF," (Dec. 21, 1918), p. 4, Fosdick Papers, Princeton Univ., Box 1. For contrasting therapy that did encourage the doughboy to talk see *The Medical Department of the United States Army in the World War: Neuropsychiatry* (Washington, D.C., 1929), p. 402.

25. Simon Lake, *The Submarine in War and Peace* (Philadelphia, 1918), pp. 229, 294, see also 146–47; Simon Lake, "Submarines that Are Strictly Invisible," *Scientific American*, CXII (Jan. 16, 1915), 68.

26. Howard Coffin, *The New York Times*, July 8, 1917, p. 2, section 2; Arthur Sweetser, *The American Air Service* (New York & London, 1919), reprints aviation boosterism by Orville Wright and Gen. Squier during the war: pp. 80–81; U.S. Congress, House, *Congressional Record*, 65th Cong., special session. (James R. Mann quoted, p. 5108), pp. 5123, 5125, give other expressions of enthusiasm for airplanes on the House floor. For an ace's testimony on the humanity of bombing see "The American Spirit, Letters of Briggs Adams," *Atlantic Monthly*, CXXII (Oct. 1918), 438. Henry Woodhouse made extravagant claims for airplanes as keepers of the peace in *Flying*, IV (May 1915), 497–505; *Flying*, V (Jan. 1917), 492. On the promise of military aviation in the 1920s, see William B. Mitchell, *Memoirs of World War I* (New York,

1960), pp. 3–4 (quoted). Lawrence La Tourette Driggs, *Heroes of Aviation* (Boston, 1927), p. 346.

27. Amos A. Fries and Clarence J. West, *Chemical Warfare* (New York, 1921); Harry L. Gilchrist, *A Comparative Study of World War Casualties from Gas and Other Weapons* (Washington, D.C., 1928), p. 47 (quoted). Admiral Mahan's elaborate defense of gas warfare given at the First Hague Conference was publicized early in the war: *Literary Digest*, C (May 8, 1915), 1064.

28. Bradley A. Fiske, *Invention, The Master-Key to Progress* (New York, 1921), p. 315; see also 307. *The Diary and Sundry Observations of Thomas A. Edison*, ed. D. D. Runes [VIII, 1922] (New York, 1948), p. 97.

29. Edward M. House, "The Conquest of the Air," typescript (1928), House Papers, Yale Univ., Drawer 32, p. 304. *FDR: Columnist* (Chicago, 1947), pp. 63–65 (May 2, 1925); John Foster Dulles, untitled draft of speech (Nov. 1921), Section I.B, Dulles Papers, Princeton Univ.

## 11
## THE WAR OF THE DÉGAGÉ

1. Ernest Hemingway, *In Our Time* [1925] (New York, 1970), pp. 69–70.

2. Keith L. Nelson observes the narrow audience for revisionists in his foreword to C. Hartley Grattan, *Why We Fought* (Indianpolis & New York, 1969). Beecher Stowe to Frank A. Scott (Sept. 26, 1927), on Frothingham, Scott Papers, Princeton Univ. Townsend Ludington, ed., *The Fourteenth Chronicle: Letters and Diaries of John Dos Passos* (Boston, 1973), p. 205. I have quoted from Edward Streeter in his foreword to Thomas H. Barber, *Along the Road* (New York, 1924), p. x; see also Robert Herrick, "In General," *The Nation*, CXIII (Dec. 7, 1921), 658–59; Will Judy, *A Soldier's Diary* (Chicago, 1930), pp. 211–12.

3. Laurence Stallings, *Plumes* (New York, 1924), p. 80. John Dos Passos, *One Man's Initiation—1917* [1920] (New York, 1922), pp. 13–15. Thomas Boyd, *Through the Wheat* [1922] (New York, 1927), pp. 92–95. Barber, *Along the Road*, p. 91. Elliot H. Paul, *Impromptu* (New York, 1923), p. 113. Charles MacArthur, *War Bugs* (Garden City, N.Y., 1929), p. 2 (quoted). James Stevens, *Mattock* (New York, 1927), p. 104. For another view of personal breakdown see Hervey Allen, *Toward the Flame* [1922] (Pittsburgh, 1968).

4. See Kenneth Lynn, "Violence in American Literature and Folklore," in *Visions of America* (Westport, Conn., 1973).

5. John Dos Passos, *One Man's Initiation—1917* [1920] (New York, 1922), p. 24; see also 102–3.

6. Dos Passos, *Three Soldiers* [1921] (Cambridge, Mass., 1964), pp. 210, 416.

7. Dos Passos, *Three Soldiers*, part VI; *One Man's Initiation*, p. 103; *Nineteen-Nineteen*, pp. 317, 373. F. Scott Fitzgerald had reported on the loud and incoherent verdict on the war which was handed down in a café at the beginning of the decade: " ' 'S a mental was'e,' he insisted, with owl-like wisdom. 'Two years my life spent inalleshucal vacuity. Los' idealism, got be physical animal . . . ,' " Fitzgerald, *This Side of Paradise* [1920] (Harmondsworth, Eng., 1965), p. 180.

8. *Fourteenth Chronicle*, pp. 9, 35. Melvin Landsberg, *Dos Passos' Path to USA A Political Biography, 1912–1936*. (Boulder, Colo., 1972), pp. 40–41.

9. *Fourteenth Chronicle*, p. 71, to Rumsey Marvin (Apr. 10, 1917), p. 72, to Marvin (May 5, 1917); see also p. 61 (Dec. 12, 1916).

10. *Fourteenth Chronicle*, p. 12. Quoted in Landsberg, *Dos Passos' Path*, p. 51, Dos Passos to Arthur K. McComb (c. Apr.–June 1917), see also pp. 49–50, Dos Passos to McComb (Jan. 4, 1917). The Ludington collection omits these letters.

11. *Fourteenth Chronicle*, p. 75, to Marvin (June 1917).

12. *Fourteenth Chronicle*, pp. 92–93, to Marvin (Aug. 23, 1917); p. 95 (Aug. 26, 1917); see also p. 98, to Marvin (Aug. 29, 1917); p. 271, to Stewart Mitchell (Dec. 8, 1919).

13. *Fourteenth Chronicle*, pp. 108, to Mrs. Cummings (Dec. 16, 1917) and to José Giner Pantoja (Feb.–Mar. 1918) 149–153 on his troubles with censors; Diary, p. 230 (Nov. 15, 1918).

14. Ernest Hemingway, *In Our Time* [1925] (New York, 1970), pp. 11–12, 67. The Quai sketch was not added until the 1930 edition, though it was based on his journalism of 1922.

15. Ernest Hemingway, *A Farewell to Arms* [1929] (New York, 1957), pp. 37, 184–85; cf. Hemingway, *The Sun Also Rises* [1926] (New York, 1954), p. 17. Earlier, Thomas Boyd had shown doughboys retching as the war was explained to them: Boyd, *Through the Wheat* [1922] (New York, 1927), pp. 35, 215–17.

16. Quoted in Carlos Baker, *Ernest Hemingway: A Life Story* (New York, 1969), pp. 40, 52, 57.

17. Edmund Wilson, *The Shores of Light: A Literary Chronicle of the Twenties and Thirties* (New York, 1952), p. 121. Hemingway, *In Our Time*, p. 29, 37.

18. Hemingway, *A Farewell to Arms*, p. 232.

19. Hemingway, *In Our Time*, p. 142. See also "Now I Lay Me," in *Men Without Women* (New York, 1927).

20. Henry Grew Crosby, ed., *Anthology* (Dijon, 1924). Geoffrey Wolff, *Black Sun: The Brief Transit and Violent Eclipse of Harry Crosby* (New York, 1976), p. 63. The classic memoir of the man is Malcolm Cowley,

*Exile's Return* (New York, 1934), pp. 244–81; see also Edward Weeks, *My Green Age* (Boston & Toronto, 1973), esp. pp. 53–55, 240–63.

21. Harry Crosby, *Shadows of the Sun*, 3 vols. (Paris, 1928–30), I, 16; II, 27, 47; III, 18. Caresse Crosby, *The Passionate Years* (New York, 1953), pp. 120–21. Henry Grew Crosby, *War Letters* (Paris, 1932), p. 157 (Nov. 18, 1917). Harry Crosby, *Sleeping Together* (Paris, 1929), pp. 9, 55. Harry Crosby, *Torchbearer* (Paris, 1931), pp. 8–11.

22. Cummings, *Poems, 1923–1954* (New York, 1954), p. 39, 195.

23. Cummings, *The Enormous Room* [1922] (New York, 1950), pp. 99, 117.

24. *Selected Letters of E. E. Cummings*, ed. F. W. Dupee and George Stade (New York, 1969), p. 51 (Aug. 19, 1918); see also 52 (Sept. 11, 1918).

25. Cummings, *The Enormous Room*, pp. 51–52, 65, 84, 58–59, 255, see also 264. On this excremental vision see the excellent discussion by David Smith, "The Enormous Room and The Pilgrim's Progress," in *E. E. Cummings: A Collection of Critical Essays*, ed. Norman Friedman (Englewood Cliffs, N.J., 1972), pp. 121–32.

26. William Faulkner, *Sartoris* (New York, 1929), p. 62.

27. *Collected Stories of William Faulkner* (New York, 1950), pp. 525, 446. See also the revenge in "Turnabout," p. 509. That story was first published in the *Saturday Evening Post* (Mar. 5, 1932). Unless noted, all of Faulkner's stories appeared in *These Thirteen* (New York, 1931).

28. *Collected Stories*, pp. 511, 562 ("Honor," 1930); see the other death certifications: pp. 421, 423, 428.

29. *Soldiers' Pay* [1926] (New York, 1968), pp. 130, 82.

30. *Collected Stories*, p. 562 ("Honor," 1930); *Sartoris*, pp. 320–21.

# INDEX